THE
ROYAL HOUSE
OF
WINDSOR

Also by Elizabeth Longford

JAMESON'S RAID
(writing as Elizabeth Pakenham)

VICTORIA R.I.

WELLINGTON: THE YEARS OF THE SWORD

WELLINGTON: PILLAR OF STATE

LONG LIVE THE HOUSE OF WINDSOR!

THE
ROYAL HOUSE
OF
WINDSOR

Elizabeth Longford

WEIDENFELD AND NICOLSON
LONDON

To Jack and Frank

ISBN 0 297 76829 8

Layout by Margaret Downing

Printed in Great Britain
by Butler & Tanner Ltd, Frome and London

Contents

Illustrations

ILLUSTRATIONS

The royal train in India. (Guildhall Library)

Prince George and Princess Mary with their children. (By gracious permission of H.M. the Queen)

The families of Edward VII and Tsar Nicholas II. (Popperfoto)

Prince Edward and Prince Albert with their tutor. (Popperfoto)

Nine kings at the funeral of Edward VII. (By gracious permission of H.M. the Queen)

Between pages 60 and 71

The investiture at Caernarvon, 1911. (Popperfoto)

A coronation invitation, 1911. (By gracious permission of H.M. the Queen)

King George on a tiger-shoot. (Popperfoto)

Prince Albert in a carriage. (Popperfoto)

Prince Albert below decks. (By gracious permission of H.M. the Queen)

Prince Albert as midshipman. (By gracious permission of H.M. the Queen)

The Battenberg family, *c.* 1912. (By gracious permission of H.M. the Queen)

George V with the Kaiser. (Popperfoto)

King George on naval poster. (Radio Times Hulton Picture Library)

Silhouette of Edward, Prince of Wales. (National Portrait Gallery)

King George and General Haig with French leaders. (Camera Press)

King George with Lord Stamfordham. (By gracious permission of H.M. the Queen)

The proclamation of the House of Windsor. (Imperial War Museum)

The Royal Family digging at Windsor, 1917. (By gracious permission of H.M. the Queen)

Between pages 96 and 105

King George riding with his four sons. (Popperfoto)

The Prince of Wales in cowboy dress. (Radio Times Hulton Picture Library)

The Prince of Wales steeple-chasing. (Radio Times Hulton Picture Library)

The Prince of Wales in Canada, 1919. (Keystone Press)

The Prince of Wales in New Zealand, 1920. (Popperfoto)

The Duke of York playing golf. (Radio Times Hulton Picture Library)

The Duke of York playing at Wimbledon. (Radio Times Hulton Picture Library)

The Duke of York at his boys' camp. (Radio Times Hulton Picture Library)

Lady Elizabeth Bowes-Lyon as a child. (Courtesy of Mrs O.M.Clear)

The Duke and Duchess of York in carriage. (Popperfoto)

Queen Mary with Princess Elizabeth. (By gracious permission of H.M. the Queen)

The Duke of York outside Parliament House, Canberra. (Courtesy of Australia House)

Family group on balcony of Buckingham Palace. (Popperfoto)

Princess Elizabeth, 1931. (Keystone Press)

Between pages 112 and 121

The Prince of Wales, 1932. (Radio Times Hulton Picture Library)

ILLUSTRATIONS

George V at the microphone. (Popperfoto)

Funeral procession of George V. (Popperfoto)

Edward VIII carrying umbrella. (Popperfoto)

Edward VIII in South Wales. (Radio Times Hulton Picture Library)

King Edward and Mrs Simpson at Trogir. (Popperfoto)

King Edward exercising. (Popperfoto)

The Duke and Duchess of Windsor on their wedding day. (Courtesy of Sir Cecil Beaton)

The Instrument of Abdication. (Radio Times Hulton Picture Library)

Cartoon on the Abdication. (Punch)

The Duke and Duchess of Windsor. (Camera Press)

Between pages 168 and 177

Queen Elizabeth with Princess Elizabeth and Princess Margaret. (By gracious permission of H.M. the Queen)

Royal Family on the balcony of Buckingham Palace, 1937. (Popperfoto)

King George and Queen Elizabeth in the gold state coach. (Popperfoto)

King George riding with his daughters. (Keystone Press)

King George with President Roosevelt. (Keystone Press)

King George and Queen Elizabeth talk to a bombed Londoner. (Radio Times Hulton Picture Library)

King George and Queen Elizabeth in the East End. (Popperfoto)

King George with General Alexander. (Imperial War Museum)

Princess Elizabeth in guide uniform. (Radio Times Hulton Picture Library)

Scene from a pantomime at Windsor. (Radio Times Hulton Picture Library)

Between pages 184 and 193

King George presents medal to 'She Elephant'. (Popperfoto)

King George at his desk with Princess Elizabeth. (Radio Times Hulton Picture Library)

The King and Queen with General Smuts. (Keystone Press)

Wedding picture of Princess Elizabeth. (Camera Press)

Prince Philip with Lord and Lady Mountbatten. (Keystone Press)

Princess Elizabeth with Prince Charles. (Radio Times Hulton Picture Library)

Family group at Sandringham, 1951. (By gracious permission of H.M. the Queen)

Cartoon on the death of George VI. (Keystone Press)

The coffin of King George arrives in London. (Popperfoto)

Between pages 218 and 229

The scene inside the Abbey at the coronation. (Popperfoto)

The Queen with her children at Balmoral. (Radio Times Hulton Picture Library)

The Queen and her children out driving. (Radio Times Hulton Picture Library)

The Queen with Sir Winston Churchill. (Radio Times Hulton Picture Library)

ILLUSTRATIONS

The Queen in Nigeria, 1956. (Radio Times Hulton Picture Library)

The Queen at Sandringham. (Keystone Press)

Princess Margaret with Antony Armstrong-Jones. (Keystone Press)

The Queen and Prince Philip in India, 1961. (Keystone Press)

The Queen and Prince Philip in Ghana, 1961. (Keystone Press)

A cartoon by Wally Fawkes. (*New Statesman*).

The Queen Mother in 1963. (Camera Press)

The Queen at the Trooping the Colour. (Bippa)

Between pages 244 and 257

The Queen with the Duke and Duchess of Windsor. (Keystone Press)

Prince Charles at Timbertop. (Keystone Press)

Prince Philip and Princess Anne at barbecue. (Camera Press)

The Queen at Stirling University. (*The Scotsman*)

Thanksgiving service for the Silver Wedding. (Syndication International)

Walkabout at the Barbican. (Associated Newspapers)

The Queen and Prince Philip. (Camera Press)

Family group on the occasion of the Silver Wedding. (Camera Press)

Portrait of Princess Margaret by Bryan Organ. (Courtesy of the Hon. Society of Lincoln's Inn)

The Queen with Commonwealth Ministers, 1973. (Associated Press)

Princess Anne on horseback. (*The Times*)

The marriage certificate of Princess Anne's wedding. (*Daily Express*)

Princess Anne curtsies to the Queen in Westminster Abbey. (Keystone Press)

Acknowledgments

The author and publishers gratefully acknowledge the gracious permission of The Queen to republish passages in *Queen Alexandra* by James Pope Hennessy, *George V* by Harold Nicolson and *George VI* by John Wheeler-Bennett, of which the copyright belongs to Her Majesty. They are grateful also to Macmillan, London and Basingstoke and St Martins Press for permission to quote from *George VI*, to Constable & Co Ltd for permission to quote from *George V* and to Cassell & Co Ltd for permission to quote from *A King's Story*.

Author's note

FIRST I must thank the Royal Librarian and his staff for answering certain questions on the period which I put to them, and for sending me some unpublished extracts from letters to King George V and Queen Mary on their Silver Jubilee.

It is impossible to mention all the friends whose kindness and help have meant much to me. I take this opportunity to thank them most warmly. I must, however, express special gratitude to those experts who have allowed me to tap their stores of knowledge on many points.

Sir John Wheeler-Bennett's generosity and expertise are incomparable, and his *King George VI* has been a sure guide throughout. *King George V* is an earlier landmark whose author Sir Harold Nicolson, alas, I can no longer thank. I am greatly indebted to Sir Martin Charteris, Viscount Gage, Lord Adeane, Sir Martin Gilliat, Miss Anne Hawkins, Mr John Marriott, Mr Jock Colville and Sir Edward Ford.

On particular aspects of the Royal House's history, I have received most valuable information from Mr Erskine Childers, President of Ireland, Professor P.N.S. Mansergh, Professor J.D.B.Miller, Sir James Butler, Sir Frank Twiss, Secretary to the Lord Great Chamberlain, Viscount Dilhorne, Mr Christopher Dobson, Librarian of the House of Lords, Earl Mountbatten of Burma, Mr Richard Hough, Lord and Lady Rupert Neville, Mrs J.M.Cowland of the Meteorological Office Library, Mrs Mollie Gillen, Miss Anna Collins, Mr Robert de Stacpoole and Mr Quintin J.Iwi.

I also wish to thank my agent Mr Graham Watson, and my publishers. Mr Christopher Falkus has given me active and energetic help at all stages. I owe much to Miss Gila Curtis, to Miss Celia Clear for her work on the manuscript and illustrations, and to Miss Susan Pinkus for picture-research.

It is a pleasure to thank Mrs Agnes Fenner once more for her typing, and also for the loan of the diary kept by her father on board HMS *Bacchante*. My family have spurred me on. Judith read the proofs, Antonia and Rachel showed unflagging interest, as did my sons. My grandchildren will be able to see the future development of the House of Windsor in ways which this book has at most been able to foreshadow. Above all, my profound gratitude to Frank for reading everything, step by step, including the sources.

PART

1

THE
ROYAL HOUSE

I

Changing the name at Buckingham Palace

'For the first time in its long history Windsor becomes the home of an eponymous House. The times are propitious to the innovation. Stet Domus!' The Times, 18 July 1917.

ABRIGHT hot sun concentrated upon London on 17 July 1917. It was the hottest place in the country, the temperature rising to seventy-six degrees Fahrenheit at Kew Observatory. Elsewhere there was cloud and rain. On this day, like an incandescent rock bursting from a volcano, the House of Windsor was proclaimed in the capital.

The simile of eruption following upon subterranean rumbles is not so far-fetched as might appear. The British and German Empires were locked in the agonising clinch of the First World War. Russia, Britain's hugest ally, was out of the War, her ruling dynasty toppled by revolution that spring. In Moscow on 17 July there was thunder and lightning; Petrograd was deeply overcast. The great offensive planned by France, most effective on land of all the Allies, had failed on the Western Front, while south of the Alps defeat was creeping up on a supine Italy. The British army floundered in the ooze of Passchendaele.

In their exasperation with the enemy, British civilians traced the cracks which war causes in every body politic to hidden German influence. A hue and cry broke out against the naturalised British subject, the long-established tradesman with a German name, or the elderly *fräulein* who had taught for years in English families. The family of Mr Asquith the Prime Minister, with a German governess, was a case in point. Even more so the Royal Family, whose own name was German, Coburg.

The King-Emperor George v of the House of Saxe-Coburg and Gotha (to give him his full title) had succeeded to the throne in 1910. Seven years later this seemed a shocking name for a king fighting against Kaiser William ii of the House of Hohenzollern. The royal combatants sounded more like compatriots. (They were first cousins, sharing Prince Albert of Saxe-Coburg as grandfather.) 'Coburg' must go.

The British people by 1917 had already had the satisfaction of expelling things and persons in various high places which bore a Germanic stigma.

The most ludicrous victims in 1915 had been certain Garter banners in St George's Chapel at Windsor. These picturesque flags, each about three feet square, hung above the richly carved stalls belonging to the Knights of the Garter. With their golden fringes, vivid backgrounds of scarlet, blue, black, green or orange and their family emblems of lions, eagles, doves, castles, shells or bulls, they shone like a many-coloured sunrise over the dark stalls beneath. Prominent in this double row of armorial splendour were eight banners of what *John Bull* and the *Daily Mail* called 'enemy Emperors, Kings and Princes', including the Kaiser and Crown Prince of Germany. Get them out, demanded the press. Even the King's Danish mother, Queen Alexandra, urged her son 'to have down those hateful German banners in our sacred Church'. As long as they remained, stormed *John Bull*, their owners would be prayed for in the Garter services! 'What *are* the King's advisers doing?'

Notwithstanding the agitation King George v clung to common sense. The offending flags were mere symbols of past history, he pointed out. He declined to begin obliterating the past while there were more important things to be done in the present. The banners could always be reorganised – 'after the war'.

But the Prime Minister of the day, Mr Asquith, was more sensitive than the King to the pressures of public hysteria. Not only did Asquith insist that the names of the eight enemy Knights should be struck off the Garter roll and their banners ejected – as was done – but he also set up a committee to consider the case of enemy princes who held British titles, among them the Dukes of Cumberland and Brunswick.

Again King George strongly objected. It was 'too petty and undignified', he wrote, for Parliament to waste time in fighting a paper battle against titles when all was far from well on the Western Front. His argument did not prevail; and in 1917 – the year when his own royal title came under fire – the Titles Deprivation Act was passed as a result of the committee's labours, by which the Dukes of Cumberland and Brunswick among others were eventually deprived of their British rank. Nevertheless, King George had earlier won two small victories for the cause of sanity. A demand that the name of the German Kaiser and his son should be publicly erased from the Army List in which they figured as holding honorary commands was flatly refused. The King would consent only to the unostentatious dropping of their names – no ridiculous drumming out. Nor would he allow 'enemy' names inscribed on the historic brass plates above the Garter stalls – incidentally all written in French in accordance with medieval custom – to be removed along with the flags. As the man responsible for the stalls in St George's Chapel, the Dean of Windsor was tersely informed: 'They are historical records and His Majesty does not intend to have any of them removed.' H.M. deplored 'dramatic action' in response to 'hysterical clamour'.

Striking cases of hounding occurred nearer home. Lord Haldane was dismissed in 1915 from the eminent post of Lord Chancellor. He had had the misfortune to describe Germany as his 'spiritual home', though all he meant was that he had spent an agreeable youth studying philosophy at the University of Heidelberg. His country felt no gratitude to him for having reorganised the British Army when War Minister, in the nick of time. But King George gave him the Order of Merit.

There had been an equally bad case the year before. The First Sea Lord of the British Navy in 1914 possessed a German name. He was Prince Louis of Battenberg.

The marriage of Prince George, Duke of York, and Princess Mary of Teck in the Chapel Royal, St James's Palace in 1893, painted by Tuxen. Queen Victoria (holding fan) sits opposite the bride's mother, the Duchess of Teck. Edward, Prince of Wales, and Princess Alexandra stand to the right of Prince George with the King of Denmark between them. The two kneeling bridesmaids are Princesses Victoria and Maud of Wales.

Queen Alexandra with her grandchildren, Prince Edward, Prince
Albert (left) and Princess Mary, painted by Frederick Morgan and
Thomas Blinks.

He came of an unusually attractive German family which had the gift – and still has it – of throwing up brilliant young men. Prince Louis' brother Alexander of Battenberg had been chosen by the Bulgarians as their king, and but for the jealousy of the Tsar, who expelled him, might have been their leader in 1914. Then there was Prince Louis' other brother Henry, married to Queen Victoria's youngest daughter Beatrice and source of life and light in a stifling court, until he died serving as a British officer in the Ashanti War. Prince Louis himself had married Princess Victoria of Hesse, granddaughter of Queen Victoria, and had made his whole life in the British Navy. One of his sons was to be Earl Mountbatten of Burma, a grandson was to be Prince Philip, and a great-grandson, Prince Charles – all in their turn naval officers.

There were many examples to be found in Prince Louis' illustrious career of the Battenberg spirit. Most dramatic had been his emergency decision to halt the dispersal of the Third Fleet on his own initiative in July 1914. (It was immediately confirmed by Churchill on his arrival in London.) The original plan had been to follow up a test mobilisation with a general return to base, when all reservists and most of the active service officers and men would immediately be dispersed to unknown addresses for their summer leave. But Austria and Serbia were on the brink of war. Prince Louis saw what was coming. Through his and Churchill's independent spirit, the test mobilisation changed smoothly into action stations.

Nevertheless in the climate of 1914 Battenberg was apparently as bad a name as Hindenburg or Heidelberg. Among the first to point this out officially in a discreditable letter was Lord Charles Beresford, a retired naval officer and tremendous die-hard.

It must be noted that Beresford had not been exactly Battenberg's best friend ever since 1912, when Churchill had removed Beresford's political ally, Sir Francis Bridgeman, from the exalted post of First Sea Lord on grounds of age and ill-health and replaced him by Prince Louis. Bridgeman himself had seen King George v that December in an effort to keep out Prince Louis and retain his own post. But his considerable influence did not extend to the court.

Accordingly in 1914 Beresford wrote to Battenberg's political master, the First Lord of the Admiralty, who at the onset of the First World War was still Winston Churchill, now forty years old. Battenberg might be 'an exceedingly able officer', conceded Beresford, but 'he is a German, and as such should not be occupying his present position'; not only was he German by birth but he even employed German servants and owned property in Germany.

Beresford might have added that Battenberg had also retained his German accent. Despite all these alleged blemishes, however, the patriotism of Prince Louis was singularly pure and known to be so.

At first Churchill reacted with the barbed indignation of a young Liberal statesman. 'The interests of the country,' he retorted, 'do not permit the spreading of such wicked allegations by an officer of your rank, even though retired.' But as August 1914 passed into September, Churchill's initial effort to stem a growing tide of slander was seen to have failed. Venomous letters, most of them anonymous, began to reach the Admiralty and press. There was even a rumour that Prince Louis had been imprisoned in the Tower. This though absurd was ominous, echoing as it did the similar rumour against Prince Albert during the Crimean War.

As the barrage grew, Churchill felt that Battenberg's nerve had cracked under the double strain of war and scandal. In fact, Battenberg was well able to deal with the War, but the attacks on his honour had hit him hard. On 29 October Churchill asked for an audience of King George v and broke the news that the First Sea Lord must go, because of his 'name and parentage'. There was nothing the King could do to save his cousin – he was King George's first cousin by marriage – and Battenberg became the focus of feelings of national nastiness. His letter of resignation was frank and manly:

I have lately been driven to the painful conclusion, that at this juncture my birth & parentage have the effect of impairing in some respect my usefulness at the Board of Admiralty.

The King was 'anguished' by the whole situation but particularly when he read this letter. Not only was Prince Louis a close relation and intimate friend, but if the 'birth & parentage' of this cousin by marriage was obnoxious, what about the King's own? The jingoes, chauvinists and bigots of Britain had tasted blood in 1914 and again in 1915. Battenberg and Haldane had then been their nobly antlered quarry, and they had made two spectacular kills. Now the hunt was up again. This time they were after a 'Royal'.

On a day in April 1917 King George v received a shattering report. There was a new campaign of grisly anonymous letters, addressed to No. 10 Downing Street. How could the Prime Minister, they demanded, expect to defeat Germany when the very Sovereign he served and most of that Sovereign's kith and kin were Germans? A king hailing from Brunswick in Hanover; a queen from Teck; naturalised cousins living in England but bearing such outlandish names as Gleichen, Hohenlohe-Langenburg, Schleswig-Holstein and, of course, Battenberg – what sort of royal line was this?

The sudden disclosure of these attacks on his House hit the King just where the earlier wound still throbbed. An eye-witness reported that he 'started' and his normally ruddy countenance 'grew pale'. There is no reason to think that his pallor was due to alarm, though Sir Harold Nicolson's account, always authoritative, gives that impression. More likely, King George v turned white with rage. He was a man with a boiling temper rather than a palpitating heart. But whatever he may have felt in 1917 of shock or anger, the result was the same. He faced the need for a drastic change.

An element of urgency was added to this decision by some excited responses to the Russian revolution. Socialists such as H.G.Wells and Ramsay Macdonald indulged in heady thoughts. The world was perhaps entering the Age of Dethronements. Many years later at the time of Queen Elizabeth II's coronation the British Communist paper, the *Daily Worker*, was to refer nostalgically to the glorious days of 1917 when the great 'Slump in Monarchs' started and the human race began 'shedding Kings'. The year 1917 was indeed a golden opportunity for British socialists to preach republicanism: the abolition of 'an alien and uninspiring Court' at Windsor and the setting up of Workers' and Soldiers' Councils, according to the accepted revolutionary formula. King George, who was happily not to be 'shed', reacted vehemently against that word alien. 'I may be uninspiring,' he exploded, 'but I'll be damned if I'm alien.'

This was the moment for the Prime Minister, David Lloyd George, to act, especially if he could wrest an advantage from national despondency. He knew just how much was in a name. What could be more popular, more life-enhancing at a deadly period of the War, than to re-create this 'Teutonic' British monarchy from the oldest of English grass roots?

Faced with the Prime Minister's proposal for a change of name, King George V turned at once for advice to his secretary Lord Stamfordham and his cousin Prince Louis. Lord Stamfordham proved to be his usual practical self. There was no beating about the bush. Yes, His Majesty's family could muster a good few German names between them, he admitted, including his Majesty's own. As to what that last might be, opinions differed. The College of Heralds thought it might not be Coburg but 'Wettin' or 'Wipper', Wipper being the district where the House of Wettin originated, to which the Saxe-Coburg family belonged. We can hazard a guess that Wettin and Wipper, if given an English pronunciation, sounded quite as unsuitably comic in the ears of this sailor King in 1917 as they do to us today. But though it was obviously no wrench to part from his family name or names, what was to be the substitute? He and his court and relatives racked their brains.

There were suggestions for a return to the past, with York, Lancaster or even Plantagenet. The oddest was that of Tudor-Stewart, proposed by the old Duke of Connaught. It was rejected by Mr Asquith as 'inauspicious'. Another curious suggestion was Fitzroy. This title, meaning 'King's son', had been chosen by Charles II to indicate illegitimate royal descent. Its advocates argued, fortunately without success, that the name would not necessarily in 1917 imply a bar sinister. Nicolson tells us that the old Guelph name of D'Este, last used in the Royal Family for the Duke of Sussex's illegitimate progeny, was also suggested, by Prince Adolphus of Teck. But in fact the name D'Este had been put forward by Prince Adolphus for his own family, not the King's, since, as we shall see, there was to be a holocaust of all German royal family names, and a mass re-christening.

At last a solution was found. To Stamfordham goes the credit of inventing the most appropriate, the most euphonious, the most economical, the altogether most delightful, dignified and appealing name for a British royal house that could possibly be conceived – Windsor. The 'House of Windsor' had a four-square quality which compared favourably with, say 'House of Cerdic' (first) or the 'House of Bruns-wick-Luneburg' (penultimate). Stamfordham had even unearthed an authentic fragment of precedent: 'Edward of Windsor' had once been the title of King Edward III.

Considering the fallibility of human planning, it is extraordinary that a purpose-designed name should actually achieve exactly what was intended.

Windsor was as English as the earth upon which the Castle stood, its smooth, solid stone walls encircling its wards, mound, towers and chapel. How many thousand cavalcades, each an epitome of royal history on horseback or on wheels, had not dashed through the Henry VIII Gate, swept round the quadrangle of the Upper Ward and jingled to a halt at the State Entrance? One might begin by conjuring up the ghost of twenty-year-old Prince Albert, sent over from Germany 'on approval' to be Queen Victoria's bridegroom and arriving after dark on an autumn evening of 1839. The torches picked out a face ashen with sea-sickness, but still beautiful enough to rouse in the young Queen, his cousin, a rush of first love. Five years later the artist Joseph Nash painted another royal cavalcade consisting of the Prince Consort, the Emperor of Russia and King of Saxony about to depart through the same royal gate, for a review of Household troops in Windsor Home Park: so many prancing white horses, such glistening white feathers and plumes on cocked hats and helmets, such a superb Royal Standard floating over the Round Tower. Another four years passed and Nash painted again the same sunlit Castle, but this time on a Sunday from the Lower Ward, with the glowing Standard, the bright clouds, the choristers' white gowns and the ladies' full skirts all streaming and billowing in a stiff west wind.

Many hundreds of thousands of citizens were alive in 1917 who could remember Windsor under the stress of two great funerals. There was the 'white funeral' of Queen Victoria on a snowy January day of 1901. A moment of drama had occurred on the slippery slope outside Windsor railway station, when the horses, chilled with waiting for the coffin, began plunging and snapped their traces. It was Prince Louis of Battenberg, no less, who saved the situation by ordering the naval Guard of Honour to pull the gun-carriage, using as ropes the knotted harness of the horses and the train's communication cord. Queen Victoria had been laid to rest in the Mausoleum down below the Castle in Frogmore gardens. Her son King Edward VII was not to be buried in the Mausoleum with his parents but alongside his Stuart and Hanoverian ancestors in St George's Chapel. The private drama of this Windsor funeral had centred round a Teutonic *contretemps*. The German Kaiser had been invited to walk immediately behind his cousin King George V in the solemn procession. Two of the kings, however, those of Spain and Greece, claimed seniority over the German Emperor by prior date of accession. Fierce hostility to the Germans was assuaged only by King George's tactful assurance that his cousin's eminence was due to nothing more than close consanguinity.

So Windsor Castle itself gave credibility to the new House. To be named after a castle was plumb in the royal tradition of Western dynasties, as Prince Louis pointed out enthusiastically to the King: Habsburg, Oldenburg, Hohenzollern . . . Moreover, King George III had chosen the name Windsor to describe the uniform of his court – that handsome and not expensive dark blue 'Windsor Uniform' with bright red collars and cuffs, copied from the court dress introduced as a money-saver by Frederick the Great. On the other hand, Windsor had never yet been the title of a royal dukedom, like Cornwall, Kent, Edinburgh or York. It was unique – until twenty years later, when a royal duke and his duchess were to find the new name well adapted to a pressing need.

The news of the coming change was every bit as popular in the Britain of 1917 as Lloyd George had hoped, though naturally the monarchy's troubles did not vanish in a flash. A story has recently been published showing that even by the end of 1917 a trivial event could touch off working-class criticism. On 6 December the Labour Leader, J.H.Thomas, told the Cabinet secretariat 'that on the recent Zepp night the King was hidden in a tunnel in a train, much to the disgust of the railwaymen, for he badly dislocated the traffic'. That the King was equally disgusted is a safe bet.

Perhaps the most convincing tribute to its success was provided by the sour German reaction. On hearing of his enemy's dynastic transmutation, the Kaiser remarked that he was going to the theatre to see a performance of *The Merry Wives of Saxe-Coburg-Gotha*.

The Proclamation opened with two 'determinations' by his Majesty the King, which he had been 'pleased' (at least according to the Court Circular) to announce to his Privy Council. First, that 'henceforth Our House and Family shall be styled and known as the House and Family of Windsor'; second, His Majesty's determination 'to relinquish and discontinue the use of all German Titles and Dignities'.

Two further 'determinations' followed, affecting His Majesty's descendants. The first declared 'that all the descendants in the male line of Our said Grandmother Queen Victoria who are subjects of these Realms, other than female descendants who may marry or who may have married, shall bear the name of Windsor'. Furthermore, on behalf of all such descendants, His Majesty relinquished and enjoined 'the discontinuance of the use of the Degrees, Styles, Dignities, Titles and Honours of Dukes and Duchesses of Saxony and Princes and Princesses of Saxe-Coburg and Gotha, and all other German Degrees, Styles, Dignities, Titles, Honours and Appellations to Us or to them heretofore belonging or appertaining'.

That was enough of 'henceforths' and 'heretofores' for one day. Several other decisions, however, had also been made which found no detailed mention in the Proclamation. What of those dukes and duchesses, princes and princesses who had lost their German degrees, styles, dignities, titles, honours and appellations, if not the last shred of meaning and identity that had once been theirs?

Louis of Battenberg, brightest star among the princes, had been an ardent advocate of the name Windsor. He had also bent his mind, in consultation with the King, to the problem of the lesser names. A document has been preserved among his papers, typed by himself, in which he expounds to his two sons (the late Marquess of Milford Haven and the present Earl Mountbatten of Burma) the final results of their deliberations with his customary pithiness and punch.

Under the general heading 'Change of Title', he began by explaining that there were two reasons for the 1917 drama, as it affected the lesser lights. The first he called the principle of 'limitation'.

In the English Royal Family it was generally understood that the title of 'Prince' did not extend beyond a Sovereign's Grandchild. Strange to say the case had never been put to the test by actual experience. No Great Grandson of a Sovereign had ever lived, that is descended in the male line, from father to son. Arthur of Connaught's boy was the first example known and when he was born no-one quite knew what to call him.

King George v then decided to have the matter investigated by lawyers.

After a long delay they reported that the surmise was correct and consequently Uncle Arthur's Grandson was *not* a prince; but what was he?

The answer seemed to be plain mister. But 'Arthur of Connaught's boy', at any rate, was in luck. His mother was a peeress in her own right (Duchess of Fife) and so could give her son her own second title, making him Earl of Macduff.

In principle, however, the anomaly remained. If royal princes reverted to plain mister in the third generation from the Sovereign, foreign princes (still quoting the document) went on 'ad infinitum'. In other words, the descendants of foreign princes would have a titular advantage over the descendants of the Sovereign. The first reason, therefore, why the Battenbergs, Tecks and others had to change their titles was in order that 'some limitation, similar to the one now definitely adopted for the English Family should be applied'.

The second reason will already be familiar. This is how Prince Louis put it:

There was the further consideration that we all came from the nation now at war with England. It was my German origin that caused me to resign my office at the Admiralty. A change of name naturally suggested itself, although in the nature of camouflage.

It had been suggested to King George that he should give the head of the Teck and Battenberg families a British peerage each. Prince Louis continued:

I was sent for by H.M. as the oldest member of the families concerned, and we at once set to work at the details.

24

It was not all plain sailing, though Prince Louis admitted he favoured the change – 'in fact I had long thought of it', but could not take the first step, 'as it would have been an act of cowardice'. This scruple no longer operated since H.M. had expressed a definite wish for changes. Nor did the new name for the Battenberg family present any difficulty: 'a pure translation of Battenberg into Mountbatten seemed self-evident', wrote Prince Louis.

It was the situation of the Tecks which provoked most argument. After all, the innocent little name 'Teck' might have originated in any country; it did not sound particularly German. Why change it? However, since everyone knew it *was* German, 'it must go'. The Tecks eventually agreed to take Cambridge, the title of their grandfather the Duke of Cambridge, son of King George III.

More shoals ahead: exactly who was to get a peerage, and what rank was it to be? Certain members of both Houses of Parliament, whom the King had consulted, at first came up with the suggestion that there should be only three peerages, and these three of merely moderate grandeur: Prince Louis and the two Teck princes, brothers of Queen Mary, should be created earls (instead of marquesses); but as a sop, their children should have the rank and title of the children of marquesses. In other words, their younger sons should be 'lords' instead of 'honourables', i.e. plain misters.

Prince Louis knew too much history to fall for this:

I strongly objected; this was precisely what William IV did for the crowd of illegitimate children he had had by Mrs Jordan, his mistress, directly he succeeded to the throne (Nobody had thought of that).

Prince Louis further demanded a fourth peerage, to be bestowed on his nephew, Prince Alexander of Battenberg ('Drino'), son of Princess Beatrice and grandson of Queen Victoria. There would thus be two exalted British peerages each for the de-princed Battenbergs and Tecks. In putting his case Prince Louis further pointed out:

Our precedence at Court was after the Royal Princes, but before the Dukes, and that therefore we could very well aspire to be created English Dukes. At the same time I recognised that a Duke without landed estates, Castles or Palaces (which some of their London residences are), and no adequate fortune to maintain their high position, would be an absurd and unpleasant position for us.

The compromise of marquessates, as being halfway between dukedoms and earldoms, was accepted, though Prince Louis needed all his tact to bring even one of the Teck brothers round. Prince Adolphus ('Dolly') would have preferred to support a dukedom, despite the risk of becoming bankrupt in the attempt. Nevertheless he took the marquessate, in Prince Louis' words, 'Dolly reluctantly'. His younger brother, Prince 'Alge' of Teck, on the contrary, declared that 'Marquess sounded French, and that he preferred Earl; as he had only one son, the rank of a second one did not arise.'

The two sons of Princess Beatrice and the late Prince Henry of Battenberg, 'Drino' and Leopold, were stoutly fought for by their Uncle Louis. He got 'Drino' a marquessate (Carisbrooke), but the case of Leopold he considered 'rather hard, as the most I could get for him was that of the son of a marquess (lord) . . .' However, Prince Louis urged both his nephews to go on wearing 'the Coronets of a Grandson of a Sovereign, that is the circlet adorned with alternate strawberry leaves and fleur-de-lys'. The College of Heralds, when appealed to, agreed that he was quite correct.

Despite all this correctitude and logic, there remained certain nuts apparently too hard to crack. Count Gleichen, for instance, son of Queen Victoria's step-nephew Prince Victor Hohenlohe, had to drop the 'count' and become 'lord', while retaining the distinctly un-English name of Gleichen – 'a very illogical proceeding', as Prince Louis observed. He was comparing the Gleichen case with that of the Princesses of Schleswig-Holstein, grandchildren of Queen Victoria through her daughter Princess Helena. These two princesses, Helena Victoria and Marie Louise, had not been allowed to keep their Teutonic name. But because they were both elderly spinsters with no descendants to be provided for, the College of Heralds were spared the duty of racking their brains yet again. King George cut the knot himself: 'They were to be known as "Helena Victoria" and "Marie Louise" of *Nothing* . . .'

As for Prince Louis himself, the King wished him to take a title connected with the Navy. Since all the naval ports like Portsmouth, Plymouth, Devonport, Portland and Chatham were already somebody else's title, he fell back once more on history. The hereditary Prince of Hanover, before his father became King George I, had been created among other titles Earl of Milford Haven. Here then was a historic title with the necessary smack of the sea. So His Serene Highness Prince Louis of Battenberg disappeared for ever, except from the pages of history, and Louis Mountbatten, first Marquess of Milford Haven, stepped into his naval boots.

The new titles produced their quota of amiable jokes. General Freyburg was expected to change his name to Mount Fry, while the distinguished Max Müller, it was said, had shown his patriotism by dropping the *umlaut*, and becoming plain Muller.

The demise of the name Battenberg was marked by the new Lord Milford Haven in characteristic fashion. He was staying with his elder son at the latter's house, 'Keavil', near Rosyth, when the change of title was officially approved. He wrote in his son's visitors' book: 'June 9th arrived Prince Hyde; June 19th departed Lord Jekyll.'

Four weeks later King George of Windsor, as it might be 'King Jekyll', was proclaimed.

PART

2

KING GEORGE V
AND
QUEEN MARY

2

A sailor worth his salt

Prince George on qualities required by a sailor, 1899: '(*1*) *Truthful-ness* . . . (*2*) *Obedience* . . . (*3*) *Zest, without which "no seaman is worth his salt".*'

PRINCE GEORGE of Wales was born on 3 June 1865 into the happiest royal nursery for close on half a century. Gone was the crippling tradition of father–son hostility, imported by the House of Hanover. Indeed, the uninhibited fun enjoyed by King Edward VII's children reads more like a 'free' childhood of the present permissive age than youth under the mid-Victorian heel. He and his brother Prince Eddy had inherited a lyrical background of pranks, practical jokes and romps from the Danish royal family to which their mother belonged. Constance de Rothschild, daughter of Wellington's young friend of Waterloo days, Lady Georgiana Lennox, wrote of the two Waleses: 'they are very nice little boys, rather wild, but not showing signs of becoming too much spoiled'. They were soon, particularly Prince Eddy, to show every sign of it. Fecklessly indulged, they spent their first decade in the shapeless cocoon of mother-infatuation.

Prince George, continued Mrs de Rothschild, 'has a jolly little face and looks the cleverest.' The 'jolly little face' was enhanced by well-set blue eyes and the appealingly parted lips of his grandmother when a small girl, while his nose was once called by his doting mother a 'dear little turn-up snout'; he was lucky to have the Hanoverian family's thick, shining hair and fine complexion.

As a child, much of Prince George's cheerfulness was due to the unassuming but spacious comfort of Sandringham House, perfected and balanced by the 'sweet little room' which he called his own. This was the nest in which he never felt a cuckoo. (After Prince Eddy's death he was anguished by a sense of usurping his brother's place.) At seven Prince George learnt to handle a gun. Soon every inch of the romantic Norfolk marshes and heaths on his parents' estate was familiar and dear to him.

For Prince George in boyhood we have the reports of his tutor, the Rev. J.N.Dalton. They picture a sensitive younger brother, by now acutely aware of his inferior position in the family and unable as yet to accept it. 'Fretful' is an adjective applied to him more than once, and there are references to his temper, nervous excitability, disposition to find fault with Eddy and – most clearly indicative of his gnawing inferiorities – his one strong motive power, namely, 'self-approbation'. In manhood all but one of these defects had been conquered. His fretful temper was to remain and later to become explosive. His modesty, however, was proverbial, while his irritation with the lethargic and unstable Prince Eddy changed into genuine protectiveness. At all times Prince George had personality, an out-going nature and energy.

As the second son, he was always destined for the Navy, though Queen Victoria distrusted a 'nautical education'. Did it not imbue boys with the 'prejudices' of their own country, making them consider it superior to any other? Fortunately Prince George was not prevented from entering a profession for which his ability in mathematics and his skill in handling small craft made him eminently suited. He joined the *Britannia* training ship as a naval cadet in September 1877, having easily passed the entry examination two days after his twelfth birthday. Prince Eddy came too. This was followed by three cruises in the *Bacchante* lasting altogether three years. Their longest voyage began on 14 September 1880, a round-the-world cruise for the training of young seamen. After many adventures they left Sydney, Australia, to the strains of *Home Sweet Home* sung by dense crowds of what one diarist called 'good natured Colonials'. Australia was still a 'colony' but the Empire was to change radically within Prince George's lifetime. Word was sent ashore off Hongkong that 'T.R.H. would not accept any invitations except as Naval Officers. . . .' This was the procedure which had been agreed in advance. It fixed early and for ever in Prince George's young mind what was to become for him the first principle of monarchy: that the august office counted more than the person who represented it. At Yokohama, however, Prince George and his party landed 'officially' and visited the Mikado in Tokyo. As Harold Nicolson puts it, Prince George then found it wholly natural that he, Queen Victoria's grandson, 'should in some way be gilded with the rays' of her magnificent aura.

Nicolson reached an extraordinary conclusion about the first five years in Prince George's sea-going life.

His temperament, his prejudices and affections, his habits of thought and conduct, his whole outlook on life, were formed and moulded during the years between 1877 and 1882.

Such stability must be a rare phenomenon, but Nicolson has his explanation: 'Not being an intellectual he was never variable: he remained uniform throughout his life.'

The formative five years in the future King's youth were crammed with almost superhuman psychological development. From a spoilt, pampered, over-vivacious child, inclined to discouragement, he had become an attractive man. Indulgence had been corrected by the disciplines of punishing conditions and of service regulations. His brilliant cousin, Prince Louis of Battenberg, serving on the flagship of the Flying Squadron, had been a frequent companion and strong influence. The sentimental love of home and family had been extended to include patriotism, with its inexorable sense of duty towards the whole. Vivacity had become 'zest', without which, as he later told the boys of the *Conway* training ship, 'no seaman is worth his salt'.

Prince George sighted England at last, after being away for almost two years, on 4 August. It was a date which would mean much to him.

The next two major landmarks in Prince George's life both concerned Prince Eddy. There was the brothers' first, temporary, separation when Prince George's career took him to the Mediterranean. Then there was their final separation, when Prince Eddy died in 1892.

Prince George sailed away in tears in 1883 and remained home-sick for months. In his baggage was at least one mawkish romance and also Hugo's *Les Miserables*; but whether he brought the latter along as a classic or for its congenial title is not known.

Fearful lest her grandson should get into a scrape through suddenly being on his own, Queen Victoria wrote encouragingly:

It is in *your* power to do immense good by setting an example & keeping your dear Grandpapa's name before you.

But it was not the Prince Consort's name so much as Miss Julie Stonor's which was to keep Prince George straight. He was love-sick as well as home-sick. Julie, daughter of a lady-in-waiting, was much cherished by all the Waleses. She was a commoner, however, and a Catholic. That effectively doomed the boy and girl romance.

Meanwhile Prince George was stationed at Malta, where he indulged his wild enthusiasm for polo. He also faced, according to his father, a bad climate for fevers, 'gossip and tittle-tattle and what I call "coffee-housing"!' Sure enough, gossip fastened upon the young naval lieutenant, saddling him in 1890 with a wife in the shape of an admiral's daughter, Miss Culme-Seymour. The gossip was to lurk in the corridors of the press and burst out again when he became king.

At Malta he grew a considerable beard when Prince Eddy was still not shaving every day; and he began his famous stamp collection, of which more, when we consider culture and the House of Windsor. The beard aroused some criticism at home, where it seemed to challenge Eddy's masculinity. Eddy himself advised his brother to take it off for his own sake – 'it makes you look so much older' – but their mother was more honest. 'What I do not understand', she wrote to Prince George only half in jest, 'is why you, you little mite, should have so much hair about you, whereas he the biggest has none yet.'

There was something faintly reminiscent of Jacob-and-Esau about the situation. But the hairy man was the younger in this case and it was he who would one day enjoy the smooth man's birthright.

Prince George was a diarist of the most meticulous but impersonal kind. Unlike his grandmama, he aimed at keeping mere lists of engagements and people he met. Nevertheless, a series of almost too-interesting personal events had taken place in 1891.

First, Prince Eddy had a star-crossed love affair with Hélène, daughter of the Catholic Count of Paris. Since the Pope declined to grant her a dispensation, this match was abandoned. Next, Prince George fell in love with his cousin Princess Marie ('Missy') of Edinburgh but received little encouragement. Finally, the Princess of Wales, tried beyond endurance by her husband's liaisons, departed to her sister the Tsaritza in the Crimea, to teach him a lesson, whence she raced home when Prince George contracted typhoid in November, lying for weeks at death's door. Death, however, had knocked at the wrong door.

On 3 December Prince Eddy became engaged to Princess Mary (May) of Teck. There followed a family Christmas. It seemed that the tide had turned for the Waleses at last. But hardly had Prince George begun to recover his strength before Princess Victoria, their sister, brought influenza to Sandringham. Prince Eddy caught it on 7 January 1892, it turned to pneumonia and a week later he was dead.

Prince George had just reached the rank of commander in the Royal Navy. Now bereft of his brother and physically ill again with grief, he had to mount a new ladder, and to do it fast.

There was much for Prince George to learn. Though rising twenty-seven, he knew less constitutional history than a public schoolboy.

He was intensely insular, without being jingoistic. His father could make an effective political speech in either French or German, but Prince George always spoke French with a virgin English accent and German scarcely at all. Considering his Danish mother's rampant anti-Germanism, this latter was not surprising. On a visit to Germany with his father he had been made honorary colonel of a Prussian regiment. This was his mother's opportunity to write scornfully: 'my Georgie boy has become a real, live, filthy, blue-coated, *Pickelhaube* German soldier!!!' It is unlikely that her Georgie boy knew that the dreadful word *Pickelhaube* simply meant a spiked helmet. When sent to Heidelberg after Prince Eddy's death, he reported on their 'rotten language which I find very difficult', not to mention their 'beastly dull' town.

On 24 May 1892 he became a royal duke, as his mother facetiously put it, 'a grand old Duke of York'. But his energies were only partly deflected from the sea, to which he returned for summer manoeuvres. His political education crawled forward. In listening to a 'lovely' speech by Mr Gladstone, it was not the subject-matter which impressed him but the endurance: a man of eighty-three speaking for $2\frac{1}{4}$ hours! Then at last, on 2 May 1893, came the break-through.

Since March 1892 embarrassing rumours had been forecasting a royal marriage for the bereaved Princess May of Teck after all, though the younger brother of her late betrothed was still yearning hopelessly for 'Missy'. The clever but opinionated 'Missy', however, decided to keep her first cousin Georgie as a 'chum' and to marry Crown Prince Ferdinand of Roumania. With the decks thus cleared, the Duke of York was persuaded by his family in 1893 to propose to Princess May. The exchanges were made in a low but not a minor key, beside a pond at Sheen Lodge, the pretty home of his sister Louise. It was a lovely May day.

Queen Victoria had longed for either Eddy or Georgie to marry their cousin Alix of Hesse, but when Alix chose the future Tsar, Nicholas II, the Queen transferred her passionate hopes to May. Enchanted by the engagement, she congratulated her favourite grandson on winning such a wife: 'I am sure she will be a good, devoted and useful wife to you.' In nineteenth-century parlance, the word 'useful' covered a multitude of virtues, especially moral ones. A 'useful' friend was essentially a good influence, a source of improvement, a companion along the upward path. In all these ways Princess May was to prove incomparably 'useful' to the shattered young Duke of York.

They were married in the Chapel Royal at St James's Palace on 6 July 1893 in what was described as tropical sunshine and heat. But there was to be no 'tropical' honey-moon, or even a visit to the Continent. They spent their first weeks of wedded life in the same insignificant villa on the Sandringham estate which, as 'Batchelors Cottage', had long been Prince George's solitary retreat and which now, as 'York Cottage', was to be his most beloved family home for the next thirty-three years. Its walls were smothered in ivy, its view was obscured by shrubberies, the angles of its main bow-window clashed with the zig-zag of its gables. Large oblong sun blinds kept out the light in summer. The beams, chimneys and main rooms were of suburban Victorian gothic. Among the couple's early visitors was Bishop Lang, who felt that they might have been a young curate and his wife, proudly showing him over their little house. If Prince George's study was not quite as small as his child-hood's 'sweet little room' at the Big House, it was the next best thing. His life-style was set. There were to be no deviations.

At first glance it seems as if the same could be said of Princess May. Her 'going-away' dress (if such an inappropriate word can be used) had a small double shoulder cape in cream poplin, a herald of the many shoulder capes for which she was later to be known and loved. By the time Queen Victoria died, Princess May was firmly into toques for the rest of her life. But whereas Prince George's conservatism was innate and monolithic, his wife's was partly due to her love and respect for him. Her natural bent was towards mild liberalism and unlike her husband she was not antipathetic to all change. Indeed a life-long maxim of hers was, 'One must move with the times.'

This must be remembered in assessing her contribution to the House of Windsor, the new generation of which she was about to produce at York Cottage, all but the eldest that is to say, who was born in her parents' home, White Lodge at Richmond. It has been said with truth that her shy aversion from childbearing, child-rearing and all the instinctive intimacies which a natural mother develops with the young, resulted in her children's deprivation. Particularly was this so when her two elder sons, David and Bertie, the future King Edward VIII and King George VI, were adolescent. On the other hand it is fair to assume that much of the boys' broad-mindedness and imagination was inherited from their mother. The truth is that Princess May was deeply reserved in all her human relations. 'I am very sorry that I am still so shy with you', she had written to her fiancé. He too suffered from the same need to be liberated. Though his own love was growing 'stronger and stronger', he replied, he could not help still appearing 'shy and cold'. No doubt they affected one another. How strange that in two generations the wild, unrestrained passions of the little Victoria should have vanished so completely in the marriage of this inhibited pair.

There must be no suggestion, however, that emotional inhibitions were to blight a marriage which, having been quite definitely 'arranged', became with every passing year more of a love-match. It was Princess May's 'in-laws' who condemned her to a suffocating existence on the small Sandringham estate, neither encouraging her to develop her own cultural interests nor to go in for social work. They recognised for her only two duties: to fill the cradles and follow the guns.

Prince George's trouble in the Nineties was not conscious frustration; in a sense he was too fond of his chains. He could not imagine a better life than that of Sandringham. Moreover, his lack of political opportunity was only a function of his grandmother's exclusion of his father. To the end, Queen Victoria did not trust the Prince of Wales in her counsels. The Prince entirely trusted his son – 'Papa & I are on good terms with each other', wrote Prince George proudly when his father, immediately on becoming king, invited him to place his desk next to his own at Windsor – but up to 1901 there was nothing to trust him with.

No biographer, therefore, has found more than a few occupations, apart from shooting, stamps and babies, which beguiled the Duke and Duchess of York during this period of transition. The Duke had plenty of leisure for bathing his babies, which he did with gusto: 'I make a very good lap.' There was also coaching in the Constitution by a Cambridge don, with excursions into the ever green thickets of Bagehot. A summary by the Duke of Bagehot's lore concluded with the optimistic reflection,

a monarchy of the English type . . . offers a splendid career to an able monarch . . . he is the only statesman in the country whose political experience is continuous.

The splendid career offered to the Duke of York might be long a-coming, and the Duke's preparatory experience scanty to a degree; but there were several excursions to be made to the Continent (until the Boer War made British subjects too

OPPOSITE: Part of the painting by John Bacon of the coronation of George V in 1911.

ABOVE: Alexandra, Princess of Wales, with Prince Albert Victor (left) and Prince George in 1866.

LEFT: Queen Victoria with four of her numerous grandchildren, *c.* 1871. From left to right: Prince Albert Victor of Wales, Princess Victoria of Hesse, Prince George of Wales and Princess Elizabeth of Hesse. Princess Victoria became the grandmother of Prince Philip, and Prince George the grandfather of Queen Elizabeth II.

OPPOSITE: The Royal Family at Buckingham Palace in 1913, painted by Sir John Lavery. With King George and Queen Mary are the Prince of Wales, later Edward VIII, and the Princess Royal.

LEFT: HMS *Bacchante*, the ship which carried Prince Albert Victor and Prince George on three world cruises between 1879 and 1882. Prince George served as a midshipman while his brother continued his studies with Mr Dalton.

RIGHT: Princess Mary of Teck with Prince Albert Victor at their engagement in 1891. Within a few months the Prince died of pneumonia and after a suitable interval his younger brother proposed to Princess Mary.

BELOW RIGHT: Prince George, Duke of York, in 1892. Though he married for duty he was soon able to write to his wife, 'I adore you sweet May.'

BELOW: Princess Mary's sitting room at York Cottage, 1897. This unpretentious villa in the grounds of Sandringham was the chief home of Prince George and Princess Mary, Duke and Duchess of York, until their accession in 1910.

ABOVE: Prince George and Princess Mary with their eldest son,
Edward, on his father's lap, 1895. Alexandra, Princess of Wales
(right), the child's grandmother, and his aunt, Princess Maud of
Wales, stand behind. Prince George boasted, 'I make a very good
lap'.

ABOVE: Queen Victoria with Prince Edward, her great-grandson, in 1896. Prince Edward became King Edward VIII but was known in the family as David. He called her Gangan.

ABOVE RIGHT: Prince Edward (right) and Prince Albert with their groom, outside York Cottage in 1902.

BELOW: The royal train carries Prince George and Princess Mary on a six-month tour of India in 1905.

ABOVE: The entire family of Prince George and Princess Mary photographed at Abergeldie in 1906. The baby, Prince John, later suffered from epilepsy and died in 1919. The other children, from left to right, are Princess Mary, Prince Henry, Prince George, Prince Edward and Prince Albert.

RIGHT: The families of Edward VII and Tsar Nicolas II at Cowes in 1909. They were related in two ways: Queen Alexandra's sister was the Tsar's mother and King Edward's sister was the Tsarina's mother. There was a striking resemblance between the Tsar (holding cane) and Prince George (far right), but Prince George had more forceful gestures and a less dreamy look. Standing (left to right) are Prince Edward, Queen Alexandra, Princess Mary, Princess Victoria and two daughters of the Tsar. Seated are Mary, Princess of Wales, the Tsar, King Edward, the Tsarina, and George, Prince of Wales with a third daughter of the Tsar. The Tsarevitch and another sister are seated on the ground. King George V was deeply grieved when he heard in 1918 that the whole Russian family had been murdered by the Bolsheviks.

LEFT: Prince Edward (left) and Prince Albert with their tutor, the conscientious Mr Hansell, 1911. He told their father they ought to go to school, but Prince George would have none of it.

BELOW: Nine sovereigns at Windsor for the funeral of Edward VII, May 1910. Standing, left to right: Haakon VII of Norway, Ferdinand of Bulgaria, Manoel of Portugal, William II of Germany, George I of Greece, Albert of Belgium, seated are Alfonso XIII of Spain, George V, Frederik VII of Denmark.

unpopular) and one seminal tour among the Queen's most afflicted subjects. The Duke and Duchess of York were so well received during a visit to Ireland for the Dublin Horse Show (though the Duchess, like her husband, was criticised 'for not smiling when she bows') that the Duke for ever afterwards felt there was a special relationship between the Irish people and the throne. This was to stand him in good stead when bitter troubles arose next century. The young Duke's success encouraged his grandmama to visit Ireland herself in 1900 – the last state occasion of her reign and century. Then on 22 January 1901 the little old Queen died in state, her small bedroom crowded to the doors and beyond with the panoply of doctors, nurses, maids, clergymen and the great weeping throng of her family.

The reign of King Edward VII marked a real half-way house between old and new.

For the last forty years of Victoria's life no one had spoken in a raised voice at Windsor – except occasionally the Widow herself, when in a rare passion. After her death it was more than a physical 'hush' which was broken. Lord Esher, a courtier, has described the effect upon himself:

> For years, so it appeared to me, the windows of the Castle had been shaded against the outer light. Mysterious silence, whispered talk in the long corridors, light foot-falls and softly closing doors, a sense of furtively escaping men and women at some awe-inspiring unheralded approach, were an integral part of the royal influence. . . .

Suddenly this was changed and Esher found it difficult at first to realise that 'Kingship may assume different forms without losing its hold upon men's inconstant minds'.

One of Queen Victoria's many granddaughters, little Princess Elizabeth of Hesse, was brought in according to the fashion of the times to see her grandmama's corpse laid out. Much puzzled, Elizabeth peered silently at the departed saint and finally whispered, 'But I don't see the wings.' The death of King Edward was to take place scarcely a decade afterwards, but times had changed. There is no record of children thinking *he* had wings. A London schoolgirl was surprised to hear that everyone was to wear mourning and all games were cancelled at St Paul's Girls and Boys schools for the day of the King's funeral. What would have seemed right and proper to one generation appeared unnatural to the next.

The reverential 'hush' had departed for ever with Queen Victoria. In future the bang-bang of sporting guns close at hand, which she had so much deprecated, was to burst forth more and more loudly at Balmoral and become the perpetual music of Sandringham. King Edward VII instituted what has been called a 'social monarchy'. That is to say, he exchanged desk-work for more gregarious duties. His widowed mother had never dined out. He continually dined with his subjects, and not only subjects; he greatly liked Americans 'of the right sort', a predilection which some thought was later transmitted to his grandson, Edward VIII, but without the necessary qualification.

No doubt this wining and dining was not democracy. All King Edward VII's friends were of one set. Wealth and benevolence were the passport to Buckingham Palace. Notwithstanding this limitation, Edward VII left the monarchy far more relaxed and free than had seemed remotely possible after his mother had done with it. His remarkable talent for pageantry and splendour made sure that the masses also had some share in the new age of fun.

Walter Bagehot, the renowned if austere nineteenth-century authority on constitutional affairs, would not have liked King Edward's reintroduction of lavish expenditure on show, but there was another social philosopher in the more remote past who would have strongly approved. Before the Civil War the Duke of Newcastle had enumerated the kinds of ceremony which were particularly effective in exalting a king: the heralds, drums, trumpeters and great officers of state to keep you at a distance; the rich coaches, horses and guards; the marshal's men to cry 'now the king comes'. Even the very wisest subject of the king would shake in his shoes the first time he experienced all this – 'for this is the mist cast before us'. King Edward enthusiastically 'cast the mist', beginning with the State Opening of Parliament, which his mother had long since refused to perform. His enchanted subjects saw that in the 'mist' there danced once again a million motes of gold-dust.

Besides renewing the 'mist' or mystique of monarchy in so far as ceremony supplied it, Edward VII's 'art of constitutional government', as his biographer Philip Magnus puts it, consisted in cutting down official audiences to a minimum and talking to his ministers individually only when he met them at parties. An extra buffer was developed between him and them by a 'magic circle' of seven intimate friends. Six of them were men, including Lord Esher, while the most magical seventh was his opulent, preternaturally discreet and politically liberal mistress, Mrs George Keppel. It worked perfectly in those far-off Edwardian days.

As a family man, King Edward VII set in motion many changes. He had intended to send his son and heir, Prince Eddy, to Wellington School if his character and intellect proved suitable for such an experiment. Unhappily they did not. After Prince Eddy's death, Prince George became the apple of his eye. He could not bear to be parted from this beloved remaining son, and on one occasion, after saying goodbye, wrote with vivid bathos, 'I had a lump in my throat, which I am sure you saw.' Unlike Queen Victoria, he kept no state secrets from the heir to the throne. His love was generously reciprocated. If the youngest generation were not entirely at ease with him it was not his fault. They were too much awed to make any comment when he showed himself to a group of them in his coronation robes before leaving for the Abbey. 'Good mor-r-ning, childr-r-en,' he gurgled benignly. 'Am I not a funny-looking old man?'

Perhaps it was the voice that overawed them, a voice rumbling in a bronchial chest and issuing with a guttural roll of dr-r-ums. This marked his German descent, though strangely enough he transmitted scarcely a decibel of his Germanic inheritance to King George V, a fact which can be proved by listening to the excellent recordings of King George's Christmas and other messages.

Passing from King Edward's voice to his character, it is difficult to decide which attributes King George V inherited from his father and which were the legacy of their times. Take for instance their sentimentality. The emotion poured out on his son by Edward VII would seem extraordinary did one not remember the even more senti-mental manner in which Prince George's tutor, the Rev. J.N.Dalton (father of the Labour Cabinet Minister Hugh Dalton), addressed his eighteen-year-old ex-pupil while at sea: 'my darling little Georgie'. In his ending to another letter Dalton sounded more like a nanny than a tutor: 'How is the nail (Finger nail). Alright, I hope. Tattah.'

Equally sentimental were Queen Alexandra's letters to her grown-up naval son, and his replies to her. Her biographer, Georgina Battiscombe, reveals that when he was twenty-five and bearded she ended a letter to him 'with a great big kiss for your lovely little face'. He would sign himself 'Your loving little George' or refer to him-self as 'your Georgie dear'.

Allowing as one must for the sugary idiom of that era, it still seems that a special glaze had somehow been applied to the Royal Family. In a sense none of them had ever become quite adult. Queen Alexandra, the 'darling Mother dear' of fact, was at heart a heroine of Edwardian fiction – Mrs Darling or even Wendy of Barrie's *Peter Pan*. When Mrs Gladstone came to stay with the Waleses at Abergeldie, Princess Alexandra would visit the Prime Minister's wife last thing at night and tuck her up in bed. Naturally she did her best to make her 'Georgie dear' into the boy who never grew up. Her greatest success, however, was in persuading her daughters, the Princesses of Wales, to cling tenaciously to childhood. Princess May, the future Queen Mary, described how she and her brother had gone to a party of the Waleses at Marlborough House, 'a *children's party* for Louise's *19th* birthday! Does that not seem too ridiculous?'

King Edward's character, replete with ripe masculinity, was not to be influenced by such aberrations. But unfortunately his habit of 'chaffing' was presented to his son Prince George as the alternative male behaviour. It was duly copied by the Prince in approaching his own children. These small sons of his, David and Bertie, did not like Papa's chaffing. Their maternal grandmother, Princess Mary Adelaide of Teck, had liked it no more when practised by Prince George's father, then Prince of Wales. 'Wales, who is in very good looks, was most dear and nice', she wrote on a February day in 1875, 'and not in that odious chaffing mood I so dislike.'

'Dear' and 'nice' are not the adjectives which first spring to mind in describing King Edward VII. All agree however that he was kindly at heart, showing his warmth by a quick return to good humour after an outburst of temper. He further possessed that most agreeable family trait, a photographic memory. His judgment was held to be exceptionally good, assuming that judgment means 'ability to go to the root of a 'problem', as defined by the constitutional writer, Sir Ivor Jennings. The King's right hand man, Lord Esher, summed up his gifts thus:

> He had an instinct for statecraft which carried him straight to the core of a great problem without deep or profound knowledge of the subject.

For the rest, he possessed the clockwork punctuality of the born king and was a stickler for correct dress. Queen Alexandra was pathologically unpunctual. This, however, may be regarded as a queen consort's prerogative, since it humanises the impossible punctuality of the monarch. King Edward never scolded his wife when late but enjoyed putting on the face of a martyr.

Perhaps his most appealing trait was courage – again a family characteristic. When his mother, Queen Victoria, had become pregnant for the first time she was told by her doctor that she must expect some pain in childbirth. 'I can bear pain as well as anybody else,' she said stoically and with truth. Her son used almost the same words after refusing gas for a tooth extraction: 'I can bear pain.'

At Edward's accession, the new heir to the throne was an unsophisticated thirty-five. Another seven years were to pass before he made a once-for-all conducted tour of the Paris night-clubs, having watched a show he described as 'the hottest thing I have ever seen on the stage'. He had indeed known nothing of the Naughty Nineties, wisely leaving all that sort of thing to his father.

Yet behind the Nineties' laughter and 'last high kicks' could be heard the sound of many other footsteps: of Trade Unionists walking purposefully to branch meetings, of workers marching four deep on strike, of socialist politicians preparing to invade Westminster, of the 'New Woman' climbing northern hills unchaperoned by a single maiden aunt. Cosmo Gordon Lang, who as Archbishop of Canterbury was to play a conspicuous part in the Windsor story, recalled typically contrasting scenes from the new and the old. There were the demure young ladies of the old school who had promised mama never to read a novel – 'but our maid reads them to us'; and the beautiful young lady of the new school, Miss Beatrice Potter (afterwards Mrs Sidney Webb), who went on a ramble to the Brontë moors with a mixed group from a Co-operative Society. When the exhausted wives 'in their long dresses and elastic-sided boots' decided to call it a day, Beatrice said, 'but I'm going on' – with the men. The female herd cast lowering glances at the outsider and one muttered to another, 'The impident huzzy!'

When Edward VII came to the throne motor cars were already in use, the Royal Family exercised on bicycles (Princess May on a tricycle), spoke on the telephone and read novels by electric light, Queen Alexandra and Princess May smoked, though usually in private, and the New Woman appeared in City offices, not merely as a cleaner. And the last high kicks of the Nineties were not only designed to exhibit a long black silk stocking, but also to kick poverty under the carpet. A gesture as futile as it was compassionless.

King Edward VII's excellent personal relations with his heir were shown in two ways. He appointed Queen Victoria's private secretary, Sir Arthur Bigge, to be the Duke's. Bagehot, writing in 1867 that 'an able monarch is the only statesman in the country whose political experience is continuous', naturally did not allow for the developing role of a Bigge or his successors – Lascelles, Adeane, Charteris and the whole dynasty of 'able' but invisible men who have served the House of Windsor as private secretaries. In some sense the monarch's private secretary shares the assets of continuity and experience. Curiously enough his unique place in the constitution is rarely discussed.

Sir Arthur Bigge's experience by 1901 was far greater than Prince George's, and was to be just as 'continuous'. Transparently honest, devoted and industrious but no more of an intellectual by nature than his master, Bigge was nonetheless determined to use the years of King Edward's reign to bring the Prince's education up to that of a public schoolboy of leaving age. In this he did not succeed. Nor did he always manage on public occasions to arouse his master's Hanoverian features from their natural state of rather heavy repose. Princes must not look bored. 'We sailors never smile when on duty,' expostulated Prince George; but his final judgment of Bigge was characteristically truthful: 'he taught me how to be a King.'

King Edward's next laudable act was to tell his son that all the red boxes of state would be available for him to read. 'You can show them to May,' added the King.

'But Mama doesn't see them,' replied the Prince.

'No, but that's a very different thing.'

Prince George and Princess May were received by the people of Australia and New Zealand, Natal and Cape Town, Canada and Newfoundland, during the first year of King Edward's reign. This long voyage in SS *Ophir* began with the usual heartbreak at parting – 'May & I came down to our cabins & had a good cry', wrote the Duke – but ended by affording the future monarch some memorable insights into the feelings of his distant peoples. He discovered it was often his grandmother's personal example which had forged such strong links of loyalty to the crown, not always the institution of monarchy. This he stored in his mind, amid all the pleasant distractions of collecting stamps and statistics of the number of hands shaken by him (24,855) and of tons of coal burnt by the *Ophir* (14,500). Prince George was a dedicated statistician, often wearing a pedometer while out shooting, not to mention keeping a meticulous count of 'heads'.

On returning home he made at the Guildhall the first important speech of his career. It was known as his 'Wake up England!' speech, since he had concluded by calling on the 'Old Country' to wake up if she intended to maintain her colonial trade against foreign competition. More accurately, the speech and the tour proved to be 'Wake up Prince'. For both the Prince and Princess had at last enjoyed the opportunity to stand on their own feet. Throughout his journals King George v's reactions to events were 'stable', writes John Gore, 'he took everything in his stride'. But whither, one may ask, was he striding in 1901? After *Ophir* he began to know.

Acute appendicitis had meant the postponement of King Edward vii's coronation from June to August 1901. Prince George, in tearing spirits at his father's recovery, stood in for him at reviews, shot better than ever at Sandringham and took his growing family for ever stricter 'march discipline' on their walks round the estate. 'I shall soon have a regiment, not a family,' he jested. He would have been more at ease with the former.

On the King's birthday, 9 November 1901, he was created Prince of Wales. As soon as Queen Alexandra could be persuaded to move from Marlborough House into Buckingham Palace, the Waleses moved into Marlborough House, the Princess painting out as many colours as possible and leaving it a clean, sensible white. But another three years were to pass before the Waleses were on the move again. No less important for the Prince's development than the earlier Australasian tour, were the 1905–6 visits to India and Burma. The colour question dawned on him and he felt for educated Indians who were not admitted to British clubs. After watching the myriad faces of huge crowds he claimed to 'understand the look in the eyes of the Indians'. His claim was based on his sudden awareness of that spark which flies between sovereign and people, according to the 'mystique' doctrine of monarchy. If this experience did not widen his intellectual grasp of the imperial problem, it did widen his paternalist sympathies. At his home-coming Guildhall speech the new watchword announced by him for the Government of India was 'Wider Sympathy'.

By 1906 the native British proletariat was no longer to be appeased by the sympathies available, however wide. Russian communism indeed, as personified by Lenin, had 'sympathies cold and wide as the Arctic Ocean', to quote Churchill. But Lenin was about to begin his ten-year exile; and in any case Marxism was not what the British workers wanted. At Westminster a Liberal landslide victory had swept away the Conservatives while the Waleses were abroad. This was the moderate British tip of the revolutionary European iceberg. Fifty-three of the new parliamentary members called themselves Labour. The Prince of Wales hoped they were 'not all Socialists'.

At Madrid, where he attended the marriage of his first cousin, Princess Ena of Battenberg, to King Alfonso xiii of Spain, revolution looked quite different. In the shape of an anarchist's bomb, it wrecked the wedding procession, killing spectators, footmen and horses, and giving the English bride herself a Continental baptism of blood. She had to change her satin dress before she could enter the Cathedral.

A few weeks later the Waleses learnt about a novel kind of hazard which Continental monarchies were heir to. The Prince's sister Maud and her Danish husband had been elected Queen and King of the new kingdom of Denmark, a break-away state from Sweden, and the Waleses represented King Edward VII at this democratic coronation. 'The whole thing seems curious', admitted Princess May to her German Aunt Augusta, 'but we live in *very* modern times.' To Aunt Augusta the times were not merely modern but '*revolutionary*'. How could a future king and queen of England witness a coronation conducted by grace of the People and of the Revolution? She emphasised the 'farce' of an elected monarchy with three indignant exclamation marks.

The elective versus the hereditary principle was now to be fought out in the British Parliament, thanks to the two general elections of King Edward's reign, the first in 1906 and the second in 1910. It was to take the form of an historic battle between the House of Commons and the House of Lords.

By April 1908 the Liberal Prime Minister, Sir Henry Campbell-Bannerman, had resigned through ill health. Two younger characters took over at Westminster, H.H.Asquith as Liberal Prime Minister and Lloyd George as his Chancellor of the Exchequer. It had fallen to the Liberal party, supported by socialists and Irish nationalists, to fulfil the hopes of the new century. The hereditary chamber had already killed an assortment of Campbell-Bannerman's liberal bills, ranging from education, land and plural voting right through to drink. Asquith now hoped to limit his naval programme to the building of only four new dreadnoughts, in order to save money for social reform. But the Admiralty insisted on six dreadnoughts, and the Cabinet, in Churchill's witty phrase (he was a member of it), 'finally compromised on eight'.

As a result Lloyd George had to raise money for the eight, as well as for long-awaited old-age pensions, by new taxation. In 1909 he successfully presented his 'People's Budget' to the Commons, to be paid for by income tax at one-twelfth of a pound, some land taxes and light duties on goods which today are enormously taxed as a matter of course: tobacco, drink, cars and petrol. The Budget was thrown out by the Lords, in defiance of the 250-year-old convention that money bills were the concern of the people's elected representatives. Asquith went to the country and the second general election of the reign was won by the Liberals – but this time with a majority over the Conservatives of only two. Asquith depended on Labour and the Irish.

In this inflammable situation the Government were committed to a major reform of the House of Lords, involving a burning debate with the King. They promised Parliament, first to break the Lords' veto on all future money bills, whether or not the peers again opposed the 'People's Budget'; second, to limit the peers' powers over all other bills to a veto in three successive sessions, after which the voice of the people in the Commons would prevail, such legislation being the only road to Home Rule for Ireland; and third, five-year instead of seven-year parliaments. This triple programme of reform would become law under a Parliament Act.

The issue with King Edward was as simple as it was explosive. What should a constitutional monarch do if the hereditary chamber vetoed the destruction of its veto?

Between autumn 1909 and spring 1910 there had been intricate and irritable negotiations on this topic between King and Cabinet, with Sir Francis Knollys and Lord Esher acting for the King. The word 'referendum' was heard for a time and then heard no longer; the phrase 'creation of Liberal peers' was launched, torpedoed and refloated. 'Dragging the monarchy into politics' and 'destruction of the House of Lords' were other ominous slogans.

How much of this did the Prince of Wales know? His father, who was ill, wrote to him from Biarritz on 12 April 1910 about the behaviour of the Liberal government: 'Their ways get worse and worse. . . .' Our great Empire, he explained, was now being ruled by Irish nationalists 'aided and abetted by Messrs Asquith, L.George and W.Churchill!'

Sixteen days after the King's angry letter to his son, on 28 April, the Lords passed the Budget without a division, realising that the election had at least given Asquith a mandate for this measure. But the Parliament Bill remained.

Already becoming something of an expert on naval and military problems, the Prince of Wales was still labouring to master the mysteries of an unwritten constitution. He did not doubt, however, that 'our great Empire' was in reality ruled by his father. As long as the Parliament Bill had to pass through those experienced hands for the Royal Assent, there could be no cataclysm.

Not a month later, on 6 May 1910, the issue slipped from King Edward's hands and he was dead. A splendid photograph was taken of the nine Kings who attended his funeral. Not a sign, not a shadow appears on those nobly moustached faces, each raised on its stiff gold collar above the shimmering sea of ribbons and medals which rolled over the royal uniforms – not a hint anywhere of the terrors that lay ahead. Alfonso XIII of Spain was certainly staring somewhat oddly and 'Foxy Ferdy' of Bulgaria looked suitably sly. But who would have expected the most handsome and relaxed pair of kings to have been William II of Germany and Albert I of Belgium, villain and victim respectively of the coming Armageddon? King George V sat in the front row centre, his square, bearded countenance radiating immutable goodness.

3

We don't reverse

'As you know, I've loved him since he was a little middy. . . .
He has come on immensely – au fond has always had goodwill,
simplicity and fine courage.' Mrs Asquith on King George V, 1918.

PRINCESS MARY, only daughter of King George V, once met Cynthia Asquith, daughter-in-law of the King's first Prime Minister, at a tea-dance. Somebody asked Princess Mary to waltz. She accepted, but with the proviso, 'We don't reverse'.

That could have been the motto for the new King and Queen. King George was universally agreed to be 'straight'. He never deviated from the right course, as he saw it; and he infinitely preferred the right course to be a plain, simple, familiar, straightforward one. The idea of himself, his family, his ministers or his country going into reverse was anathema. Yet from the very opening of his reign he was to be beset by problems which were anything but straightforward. Like an early motor-car tackling a steep gradient in reverse, King George drove month after month at the Parliament Bill.

The entry in his diary at his father's death poignantly expressed his sense of being suddenly rudderless. 'At 11.45 beloved Papa passed peacefully away & I have lost my best friend and the best of fathers.' By his 'best friend' the new King meant his guide and philosopher as well as friend. He not only mourned a loss, he was at a loss.

The Prime Minister had no wish to put undue pressure upon the new man. Fully aware of the difference between Edward VII and George V – the 'trained sagacity' of the former as against a successor 'without political experience' – Asquith felt almost as 'bewildered and indeed stunned' as King George himself. He had heard the news while holidaying at Gibraltar, and the first thing he saw on that early morning of 7 May 1910 was Halley's comet blazing in the darkness before dawn. Was it an omen? 'We were nearing the verge of a crisis almost without example in our constitutional history. What was the right thing to do?'

The right thing, Asquith decided, was to have a party political truce for a few months. King George in turn followed one of the few signposts his father had left him and initiated an inter-party conference for the settlement of the dispute. The conference failed, just as the Lambeth Palace Conference of April had failed. What King George did not know was that the Lambeth Palace Conference had left a thorny constitutional problem behind. Arthur Balfour, Conservative leader and representative, had made a rash statement. If the King (still Edward VII) refused to support the

Parliament Bill with his royal prerogative and Asquith in consequence resigned, he Balfour, would attempt to form a Conservative government.

What was this royal prerogative which the King, apparently, had it in his power to use or not as he thought fit? It was the monarch's ancient right to create peers. As early as January 1910 Asquith had consulted King Edward about creating three hundred new Liberal peers to swamp the Tories if they persisted, despite the Liberal election victory, in vetoing the Parliament Bill. But the victory had been desperately narrow. The King had wisely warned Asquith against using the weapon of the prerogative until a second general election had firmly established the will of the people. Asquith, with equal wisdom, had agreed.

So far so good. Nothing unconstitutional had been done or even contemplated. A monarch had warned a prime minister and the latter had accepted his advice. But now came the crux. Asquith's Cabinet demanded a guarantee of the new King; a guarantee that he would create the necessary hundreds of peers, *if* the Liberals won the second election and *if* the Lords threw out the Parliament Bill yet again. It was all very hypothetical. The guarantee was in fact called 'a contingent guarantee', and as such was unacceptable to Britain's present plain-speaking, straightforward monarch. Why a guarantee for a situation which might never arise? Why not trust him to do the right thing at the right time?

Besides, he had misunderstood Asquith. At an audience the Prime Minister had assured him he would not require guarantees 'for this Parliament'; now he was asking him to go into reverse and give them. The King did not realise that the guarantees were to be given *during* this Parliament *for* the next one – a kind of distinction which King George was not trained to appreciate.

Again, the guarantees were to be a secret between himself and the Cabinet. This was Asquith's way of protecting the monarchy. To the King, it did not sound aboveboard.

Lastly, the King's two secretaries, Arthur Bigge and Francis Knollys, were giving him contradictory advice. Bigge considered it offensive, 'un-English' and partisan of the Liberals to demand advance guarantees for a policy which the electorate might reject. He hotly advised King George to reject their demands.

Knollys could not agree. He could not visualise his new, untried master succeeding in such a bold manœuvre. By refusing the guarantees the King would force Asquith to resign. An election must follow. For Balfour, argued Knollys, would not be willing or able to form a government dependent on a minority of votes in the Commons. That seemed decisive. But either by accident or design Knollys forgot to tell King George that Balfour, as he had said at the Lambeth Palace Conference, *was* willing to form a minority government if the King called on him. To accept Balfour's offer, however, would have put the royal fat in the fire. It would suggest an alliance between monarch and peers which would quickly escalate into a 'Peers versus People' election, with the monarchy fatally embroiled in party politics.

Knollys got his way and King George gave Asquith the guarantee on 16 November, though 'most reluctantly'; but as the guarantee was secret, so was the reluctance. The King, however, did not blame Asquith, whom he regarded as being the victim of his own extremists; it was they whom he afterwards accused of having 'behaved disgracefully to me'. Nor did he blame Knollys. Three years passed before he discovered about Knollys's 'forgetfulness', and by that time Knollys was no longer his joint secretary with Bigge, but had been retired. The Liberals won their second general election in December 1910, the King's secret guarantee was dramatically revealed on 10 August 1911 and the Lords passed the Parliament Bill that day by seventeen votes. The temperature in the chamber was suffocating, and so were the emotions of the defeated minority.

The King had not misjudged Asquith's extremists. Among them had been Winston Churchill, cheerfully advocating the creation of *five hundred* peers right away, in order to increase the power and prestige of the Liberal party. Let the Liberals 'clink the coronets in their scabbards', Churchill advised, and if clinking were not enough, draw out and brandish the noble five hundred forthwith.

Asquith's own list had contained 249 names, including such Liberal worthies as Thomas Hardy, O.M., the novelist, and Joseph Chamberlain's brother Arthur, grandfather of the present writer. But rather than admit such impurities into their blue bloodstream, the Lords accepted the Parliament Bill. For the same reason, under the same threat, they had accepted the Reform Bill of 1832. They preferred to be diminished rather than diluted.

In these titanic constitutional struggles the reigning monarchs of the time, William IV, Edward VII and George V, had all taken a battering. William forfeited his popularity, while Edward was actually believed by some Tories to have succumbed to his ordeal. 'Traitor!' they howled at Asquith across the House in 1911. 'Who killed the King?'

King George V was miserable throughout. For a man who had found supreme happiness at sea, either obeying or issuing unequivocal commands, this complex, protracted, arguable method of carrying democracy forward seemed neither necessary nor ennobling.

Meanwhile the King had carried his reign forward on other fronts.

A journalist named Edward Mylius who had resurrected the old libel about Prince George's morganatic marriage at Malta in 1890 was punished. It was shown in detail that, of Admiral Culme-Seymour's two daughters, one had never met the Prince at all and the other had met him, first, when she was eight, second, after they were both married. Nor was the Prince in Malta between 1888 and 1901. Mylius was prosecuted, convicted and sentenced to twelve months' imprisonment for what the King rightly called 'a damnable lie'. Queen Mary hoped 'the story was doomed for ever', while Queen Alexandra wrote to her son, 'My poor Georgie – it really was too bad and must have worried you all the same. It is hard on the best people like you, who really have steered so straight. . . .'

Apart from Mylius, King George had had to live down another totally unjustified rumour. His blotchy complexion (due to the after-effects of typhoid and bouts of indigestion) together with his loud voice were interpreted as signs of addiction to the bottle. In fact he was abstemious.

His Queen also suffered from unfair gossip. Because of her reserve and height (she was only half-an-inch taller than her husband but her toques towered higher and it was he who insisted on her wearing them) she was said to keep the King in deadly fear of her. 'George and the dragon' was a phrase from across the Atlantic. In fact she was 'much in awe of him', Lord Cromer told Nicolson. Queen Mary's economies may have contributed to the criticism. She abolished maids-of-honour, perhaps a blow to aspiring families.

King George's habits were thought by some to be over-domestic. 'We had a lot of generals to dinner, but the evening was dull,' wrote Asquith, ' – no Bridge. . . .' Even the loyal Bigge, now Lord Stamfordham, tried to change King George's predilection for dining at home. Lord Esher also recognised the quiet character of the new court, though he welcomed it: 'His domesticity and simple life are charming . . . we have reverted to the ways of Queen Victoria . . . all very homelike and simple. . . .'

A 'homelike' April passed into a brilliant June, when a truce in the Parliament Bill allowed for the coronation. King George heralded the day, 22 June 1911, in his diary as if he were still afloat: '. . . some showers & a strongish cool breeze'. But he characteristically appreciated the breeze for the sake of the crowds. 'The Service in the Abbey was most beautiful but it was a terrible ordeal.' As the ancient ceremony reached its climax he almost broke down, the homage of 'dear David', his eldest son, reminding him so poignantly of his own homage to 'beloved papa'. The diary peters out in a rapt silence. 'Wrote & read. Rather tired. Bed at 11.45. . . .'

Others had expected to find the coronation an even more 'terrible ordeal' than did King George. Their reaction foreshadowed changes in the monarchy which were deeply to affect King George's descendants.

General Louis Botha and his wife were to attend the coronation, representing the Dominion of South Africa. Dominion, not colony. The change had come about at the Imperial Conference of 1907, six years after the *Bacchante* had found the 'colonists' of the Empire so 'good natured'. Good-natured they still might be but since 1907 the colonial label had been ripped off. 'This was the opening move in the long campaign for equality of status', writes the Commonwealth authority, Professor Hancock. Now Botha wondered whether the Imperial Conference of 1911, marked by the King's coronation, would not halt the advance. He grumbled over the uniform which he must wear on all official occasions by royal command. It was uncomfortable, costly and stiff. The nadir of his visit would be 'eight hours of purgatory' in Westminster Abbey.

Yet lo and behold, the glamour got him, and he was moved to write back to his colleague Jan Smuts in South Africa: 'I and my wife had good seats. . . . You will understand my feeling . . . but one must admit that they understand how to make this sort of thing beautiful, tasteful and brilliant and so orderly too. . . .' The monarchy had scored another victory. And at the Imperial Conference Botha was impelled to report optimistically on the state of the self-governing Empire: 'Decentralisation and liberty have done wonders.' But at home in South Africa the simple, Bible-reading farmers, who would never see the Abbey in all its glory, did not want to hear how tastefully 'they' splashed their money about over there. Not for them the role of children gaping admiringly at the splendour of a mother-country. They had liberty. They wanted equality.

King George himself was in for a year of pomp and circumstance. The Coronation Durbar at Delhi in December stretched his imagination as never before, sending him home a changed man. The Cabinet's coolness – what about the expense? the security risk among thousands of Indian nationalists? – was ignored. It was his own idea. Even 'Motherdear's' verdict that a visit to India was 'inconceivable' in the chaotic state of Europe was disregarded. (She was right about Europe. The Agadir crisis occurred while the King was away.) He was in an exalted mood, strengthened a thousand times by the sight of his Indian Empire *en fête* for him and Queen Mary: the two silver thrones, the coronation robes brought out once more, the new imperial crown costing the Government of India £60,000 and destined to be worn only once, the review of 50,000 troops, the salute of 101 guns, the death of thirty-one tigers, fourteen rhinos and four bears.

Two mishaps were vaguely symbolic: the state banquet came to grief in the kitchen, so that all but the King and his immediate neighbours left the imperial board hungry; and a light bulb hanging in the roof of the great tent began winking during the investiture like an evil eye. Would it fuse, catch fire and roast all the imperial guests alive? Like the Empire, it went out.

King George's ever-brimming emotions choked him as he neared the end of his farewell speech at Bombay. His fine resonant voice broke. 'To you, the representatives of Bombay, I deliver this our loving message of farewell to the Indian Empire. . . .' He had had a sudden intuition that he would never see India again. Nor did he.

Nevertheless the brief, scintillating confrontation was enough to change the King, if not India. He felt himself a King-Emperor at last, felt it in his very bones. A royal progress can create a 'mist' which is as potent for the sovereign as for the subject.

A country throbbing with unsolved problems welcomed back the tired envoy of empire in 1912. A coal strike was only one symptom of industrial distress. Instead of the peacock fans and golden maces of Delhi, there were suffragettes marching, meeting, picketing the House of Commons. For the New Woman on her bicycle, at her office, in the senior common-room of her college was still as voteless as ever. It was not the monarch's business to 'warn', far less 'encourage' these ladies, and Mr Asquith was decidedly allergic to their disturbing presence at his political meetings; but King George v was revolted by their punishments. He was to denounce the forcible feeding of these 'insensate' women, as 'something shocking, if not almost cruel'.

To heal industrial bitterness had always seemed to King George his paramount duty. Now in 1912 Cosmo Lang, Archbishop of York, advised him to visit the provinces and see the people in their own surroundings. The royal pair warmed to this congenial task, and Lang overheard a characteristic commentary from south Yorkshire:

'Na then, which is t' King?'

'It's t' little chap i the front wi' a billycock hat.'

'Nay, he ain't seech a fine man as Teddy.'

'Well, anyway, he's gotten him a fine oopstanding wife.'

It was tours like these, small though they were in numbers compared with the ceaseless peregrinations of George v's successors, which caused the socialist Professor Laski to give up all hope of a republic in his time. This King, he wrote, had become identified with the needs of ordinary people, 'an emollient, rather than an active umpire, between conflicting interests'. Two years of bitter struggle over Ireland, however, from 1912 to 1914, were to demonstrate the limitations of emollients.

Thanks to the Parliament Act, the Liberal government had high hopes in 1912 of getting Home Rule for Ireland on to the statute book. Their Bill passed its second reading in the Commons on 9 May. But at once the Conservative and Unionist party went into passionate opposition. This time the King saw their point.

Mr Gladstone's remedial land laws of the last century, the King held, had removed the wish for Home Rule except on the part of agitators. Even the Church of Rome, in his opinion, was at heart hoping for things to be left as they were. Why stir up the Ulsterman's black fear that 'Home Rule meant Rome Rule'?

Soon the King found himself exposed to a protracted and fierce cross-fire. The Unionist leader, now Bonar Law, a Canadian of Northern Irish birth and desperate to defeat the Government, produced a secret weapon from his armoury.

The Government had dragged the crown into politics, said Law to the King after dinner one day in 1912. 'Your only chance is that they should resign within two years.' If not, he must choose between giving the Royal Assent to Home Rule or appointing new ministers to quash it; 'and in either case,' continued Law menacingly, 'half your subjects will think you have acted against them.'

The King flushed with chagrin.

'Have you ever considered that, Sir?' pursued his tormentor.

'No, it is the first time it has been suggested to me.'

Triumphantly Law then rammed home his novel political theory: that the Parliament Act, by destroying the Lords' veto, had resuscitated the veto of the monarch.

'They may say . . . the prerogative of veto is dead. That was true as long as there was a buffer between you and the House of Commons, but they have destroyed this buffer. . . .'

Bonar Law's implication was that the throne itself had now become the buffer, the only buffer left between a malignant House of Commons and the country. Well satisfied with his night's work, Law boasted afterwards to Austen Chamberlain, Joe's son, 'I think I have given the King the worst five minutes he has had for a long time.'

No one would have dared to speak like that to King Edward VII.

Later that year, 1912, the Home Rule debate produced such uproar that after the House had been twice suspended a book was thrown by a Unionist MP at Winston Churchill's head. The King gently reproved Mr Asquith for forgetting to inform him of this event. Next year Asquith countered Law's 'buffer' bombshell with a powerful conventional weapon of his own. The King must steer by constitutional precedents, take his ministers' advice. Nothing had shaken that pole-star. The Parliament Act? It did not affect the crown. It had changed nothing but the relations between the two Houses. If H.M. acted as Law wished, he would become 'the football of contending parties'.

Buffer or football, which was the King to be? Could he avoid being either?

While King George tortured himself, Europe and Ireland rushed on towards full-scale hostilities. Two Balkan wars were fought between October 1912 and August 1913. Ulster launched its Protestant Covenant against Home Rule, and by November 1912 half a million signatures had been collected. The signatories bound themselves to adopt 'all means' to defeat 'the present conspiracy'. Their own conspiracy, meanwhile, went darkly ahead and within a year included a powerful armed body calling itself the Ulster Volunteer Force. Before the end of that same period Dublin had retaliated with its National Volunteers.

At Westminster the Home Rule Bill had passed its third reading in the Commons, had been rejected by the peers and now awaited the Parliament Act to make it law. That Act should function by the summer of 1914. The King had a haunting conviction that the ominous date would mark the opening of a civil war. Already serious trouble had broken out in March at the Curragh Camp near Dublin, where the threat of 'mutiny' by British Army officers against an anticipated order to coerce their Ulster brothers seemed to bring civil war hideously close. Next month there was gun-running from Germany by the Unionists into the Northern Irish harbour of Larne. Yet how could the King prevent the explosion? There had been rumours that he would abdicate. His mother, ready as always with the wrong advice, begged him to 'speak out and put your foot down'. But if he 'intervened personally', as he was implored to do in thousands of letters from Unionists in England and Ulster, he would be dragging the monarchy back to the days of Queen Anne, when it was still possible – but only just – to refuse the Royal Assent.

Royal intervention in 1914 could take the form either of forcing Asquith to resign or dismissing him, after which H.M. would grant a dissolution to Bonar Law and hope the electors would then overwhelm both Asquith and the Home Rule issue in one resounding defeat. A fine prospect – except that the King would be up to his ermines in party politics. Moreover, he liked and trusted Asquith.

On the other hand, surely it was 'un-English', wrote the King plaintively to Asquith, to coerce Ulster? Asquith appeared not to disagree. Which led the King to his solution. Acting neither as buffer nor as football, he would call an inter-party conference at Buckingham Palace. With luck, a settlement would be negotiated on the basis of Ulster's partial or temporary exclusion from the new Irish Parliament.

During the long Irish crisis Asquith had variously called his Sovereign excitable, *émotioné* and hysterical, while the King had accused Asquith of 'drifting'. But now these two were united in mutual affection, almost in hope. Alas, there was to be no change in the luck.

The Buckingham Palace Conference began to sit on 21 July. It broke up three days later. For Europe itself was breaking up.

Immediately behind King Edward's coffin had walked his fox-terrier, 'Caesar', on a lead. But the real 'Caesar' marched behind the terrier. He was the German Emperor William II. Unfortunately no one had him on a lead.

On the eve of war, 3 August 1914, King George was implored by telegram to intervene. King Albert pleaded with him to save Belgium's neutrality at the eleventh hour; Raymond Poincaré, the French President, announced that Germany had invaded Luxembourg. The harassed King replied to Poincaré that events were changing too quickly for it to be possible to prejudge his ministers' views. '*Paralysé par les règles constitutionelles*,' was Poincaré's sour comment on the position of '*le Roi George*'. But in fact the King was protected rather than paralysed by the constitutional rules, both as they applied to foreign and home affairs. Throughout the rest of 1914 he was to be inundated with letters of grievance and gratuitous advice, ranging from the scandal of society ladies at Army H.Q. in France to the treachery of the headmaster of Eton, who apparently wanted to give up Gibraltar. All of them he was able to hand over to the state department concerned.

And so on 4 August 1914 the King, the Queen and their eldest son showed themselves to the people on the balcony of Buckingham Palace. As Lord Grey, the Foreign Secretary, imagined the lights going out all over Europe, the Royal Family saw a sea of happy faces and heard ecstatic cheers.

This is not the place to try to compress the oceanic events of 1914–18 into a pint

King George presents Edward, Prince of Wales, to the people, after
the investiture at Caernarvon Castle in 1911. But there had been
'a family blow-up' beforehand when the Prince objected to his
'preposterous rig' which would make all his naval friends jeer.

LEFT: An invitation to the coronation, 1911, designed by Bernard Partridge.

BELOW: King George (centre figure) on a tiger-shoot in Nepal during the tour of India, 1912. The King emerged unscathed even by the Press from his hunting expeditions. But years later Prince Philip was criticised in some quarters for tiger-shooting during the royal tour of 1961.

TOP RIGHT: Prince Albert (second left inside the carriage) arrives at Devonport for his training cruise aboard HMS *Cumberland*, January 1913.

RIGHT: Prince Albert (second left) below decks in HMS *Cumberland*. The faces of Labour ministers who were later to serve him had been no blacker.

TOP LEFT: When war broke out in 1914 Prince Albert was a midshipman aboard HMS *Collingwood*. Despite increasingly bad health he manned turret 'A' as a sub-lieutenant during the battle of Jutland, 1916.

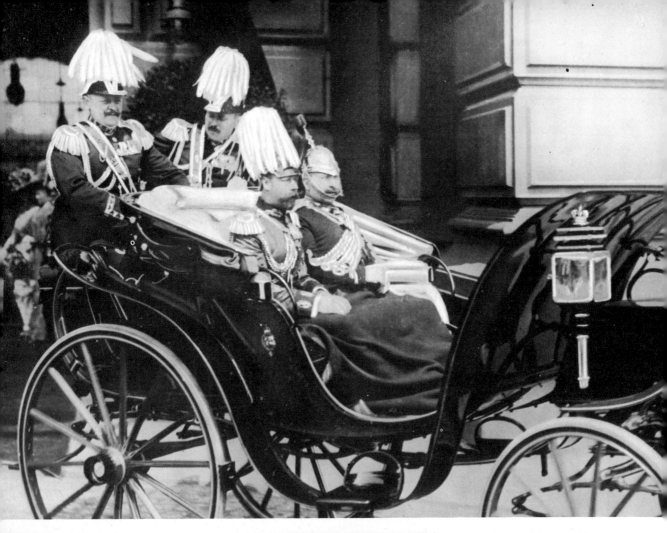

ABOVE: George V in the uniform of a German general rides with his cousin the Kaiser during the King's visit to Berlin in May 1913 to attend the marriage of the Kaiser's daughter. Kaiser William II was the son of Queen Victoria's eldest daughter, Victoria, Princess Royal, who had married the Emperor Frederick III.

LEFT: The Battenberg family, c. 1912. From left to right: Prince Louis of Battenberg, his children: Prince Louis (later Earl Mountbatten of Burma), Princess Louise and Prince George, and his wife, Princess Victoria of Battenberg. Princess Victoria was a granddaughter of Queen Victoria through the Queen's daughter Alice who had married Louis IV, Prince of Hesse.

The King as a focus of loyalty on a naval poster of the First World War.

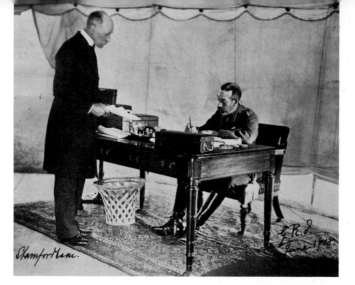

RIGHT: The proclamation of the House of Windsor, 17 July 1917.

TOP: The King with Arthur Bigge, Lord Stamfordham, who was his invaluable Private Secretary for thirty years. His grandson Michael (now Lord) Adeane was Private Secretary to Queen Elizabeth II.
ABOVE: The King and General Haig meet French leaders in France, August 1916, to discuss the disaster of the Somme offensive. Left to right: Joseph Joffre, French commander-in-chief until December 1916, President Raymond Poincaré, King George, General Foch, General Sir Douglas Haig. The King, as titular head of the Army, considered it his duty to back Haig against the politicians.
RIGHT: A silhouette of Edward, Prince of Wales, in army uniform, by H. Oakley. The Prince served in France during the War in the Grenadier Guards, where his height of only 5 feet 6 inches made him 'a pygmy among giants'.

BY THE KING.

A PROCLAMATION

Declaring that the Name of Windsor is to be borne by His Royal House and Family and relinquishing the use of all German Titles and Dignities.

GEORGE R.I.

WHEREAS WE, having taken into consideration the Name and Title of Our Royal House and Family, have determined that henceforth Our House and Family shall be styled and known as the House and Family of Windsor:

AND WHEREAS We have further determined for Ourselves and for and on behalf of Our descendants and all other the descendants of Our Grandmother Queen Victoria of blessed and glorious memory to relinquish and discontinue the use of all German Titles and Dignities:

AND WHEREAS We have declared these Our determinations in Our Privy Council:

NOW, THEREFORE, We, out of Our Royal Will and Authority, do hereby declare and announce that as from the date of this Our Royal Proclamation Our House and Family shall be styled and known as the House and Family of Windsor, and that all the descendants in the male line of Our said Grandmother Queen Victoria who are subjects of these Realms, other than female descendants who may marry or may have married, shall bear the said Name of Windsor:

And do hereby further declare and announce that We for Ourselves and for and on behalf of Our descendants and all other the descendants of Our said Grandmother Queen Victoria who are subjects of these Realms, relinquish and enjoin the discontinuance of the use of the Degrees, Styles, Dignities, Titles and Honours of Dukes and Duchesses of Saxony and Princes and Princesses of Saxe-Coburg and Gotha, and all other German Degrees, Styles, Dignities, Titles, Honours and Appellations to Us or to them heretofore belonging or appertaining.

Given at Our Court at Buckingham Palace, this Seventeenth day of July, in the year of our Lord One thousand nine hundred and seventeen, and in the Eighth year of Our Reign.

GOD SAVE THE KING.

LONDON. Printed by EYRE AND SPOTTISWOODE, LIMITED, Printers to the King's most Excellent Majesty

ABOVE: The King and Queen with their sons and others, digging for victory at Windsor in 1917. But they could not quench their thirst with a glass of beer since the Palace had gone 'dry' for the duration to set an example.

OPPOSITE: George V pictured at the helm of his yacht and, at the bottom of the plate, as a naval cadet.

H.M. THE KING   AS A YACHTSMAN.

pot. Suffice it to say that from the King's point of view, as he faced crisis after crisis and seemed at times to flounder, he nonetheless emerged from the total ordeal with a prestige greater than his father had ever enjoyed. In this sense, war strengthened the monarch. It also changed the monarchy, as it changed everything else.

Any personal criticism of the King's conduct during the First World War mainly concentrated on his tenacious loyalties, whether to displaced or threatened commanders and politicians or to his ideal of common humanity. His attitude, already noted, to the enemy Garter Knights and to aliens in general was an example of the latter. Other examples were his advocacy of humane treatment for German prisoners and his opposition to reprisals against submarine crews. Again, there was his visit to a hospital containing some casualties from poison gas. 'I found one was a German,' wrote Sir Frederick Ponsonby, a private secretary who accompanied H.M., 'and regretted the pity I had wasted on him, but the King rebuked me and said that after all he was only a poor dying human being, in no way responsible for the German horrors.'

Anything which damaged national unity was to anger King George, anything which strengthened it, to please him. One brilliant civil servant, Maurice Hankey, succeeded in reconciling the War Office and Board of Trade over a manpower dispute: he was rewarded with three brace of pheasants from Sandringham and a KCB. The King's anger was first aroused by 'those politicians' – disruptive Unionists, who criticised him for giving his assent to the Home Rule Bill in September 1914, though its operation was to be held in abeyance. Next month he assented most unwillingly to Admiral Fisher as Battenberg's successor: the Navy had no confidence in Fisher, who was seventy-four; therefore he would prove a divisive influence. That the King's judgment was sound emerged from Fisher's later bizarre and quarrelsome career. His arbitrary resignation in 1915 finished off the Liberals and brought about the formation of the First Coalition Government. This might be excused; but not the ranting letter he addressed to Churchill, who had been dismissed over the Dardanelles failure in 1916:

... THINK IN OCEANS! SHOOT AT SIGHT! ... Go in and WIN! Don't Falter! 'AUT CAESAR aut nullus' ... Every War always wants a Man!

The King did not want an inspired madman.

Nor could he enter with zest, like his Hanoverian ancestors, into the changes and chances of war. No George IV imagining himself leading the charge at Salamanca, no Queen Victoria longing to be a man and give those Russians 'such a beating', George V hated war. He would tour industrial or bombed areas as well as hospitals, in order to get close to his people. He took it all very seriously and no jokes have survived about his visits. Queen Mary, on the other hand, attracted comedy. In one maternity ward she was said to have been struck by a golden-haired mother with an

OPPOSITE: A miniature of Edward, Prince of Wales, in army uniform, painted by R. G. Eves.

extremely dark baby. 'Is the father very dark too?' asked the Queen innocently. 'Sure Ma'am, I don't know, he never took his hat off.'

At other times the King suffered vicariously for his friends, especially the great war-lord, Kitchener, when the Cabinet criticised him for clam-like autocracy, and Sir John French, Commander-in-Chief, campaigned with the press to get Kitchener out. The King admired Kitchener but 'K' did not admire the politicians. 'I never knew that there were such people – did you?' 'Did you know what these people were? I had no idea before,' he would say in mingled scorn and bewilderment. 'They did not get much out of me,' he boasted in October 1914. 'I just turned my swivel eye on them.' King George, as titular head of both the Army and the State, was again in a dangerous crossfire: this time between soldiers and politicians.

After French had been supplanted by Sir Douglas Haig (December 1915) and the sea had swallowed up Lord Kitchener (June 1916) H.M. transferred all his keen affections to the new Commander-in-Chief, Haig, and the new Chief of the Imperial General Staff, Sir William Robertson. During the last year of the War the King was battling – unsuccessfully – to maintain Robertson in his command. But it was in February – March 1917, less than a year after Haig's appointment, that H.M. began to feel acute sympathetic pains at Haig's position. The Cabinet (over whom Lloyd George now presided) had secretly agreed to put Haig and his dead-locked British force under the supreme command of the French. It had been found that the 'unanimité de l'indignation', which M. Poincaré eloquently proclaimed in his best Académie Française French to be the binding force of the Allies, needed sustaining by some more potent form of unanimity if the War was to be won. Though the proposal for a French supremo had been sprung on him, Haig accepted it; but he afterwards told the King he suspected there was 'something *behind* it'. Ought he to resign?

Caught between his Cabinet and his Commander-in-Chief, the position was as difficult as any a constitutional monarch would have to face in wartime. King George's loyalty to Haig was not diminished by the fact that the Cabinet had failed to consult H.M. himself about the new military agreement.

The King had by now studied Walter Bagehot's *English Constitution* to some purpose. He knew that he possessed 'the right to be consulted, the right to encourage, the right to warn.' Any ministerial failure to 'consult' him caused vexation, as being a slur on the monarchy. For instance, three months after the Haig affair, Lloyd George failed again. It was June 1917, just when the King was worried by the state of his fellow-monarchs, the Tsar of Russia and the King of Greece – the one under arrest, the other in exile – as well as over the change in his own 'alien' family name. Lloyd George announced an amnesty for Irishmen imprisoned after the Dublin 'Easter Rising' of 1916. As always, the King greatly favoured conciliation. But he had not been consulted. 'I see it is to be announced in the House today & I have never been asked for my approval,' he wrote to Stamfordham. 'Usual way things are done in present day. I better join the King of Greece in exile!'

Returning to Haig, his suggestion of 'something *behind*' Lloyd George's proposals was bound to put the straightforward King even more against the Cabinet. Ignored and suspicious, he nevertheless tried to do his duty. Through Stamfordham, he advised Haig not to resign, 'not to worry', to be sure that H.M. would 'do his utmost to protect your interests . . . continue to work on the most amicable and open terms' with the French, and 'all will come right'.

All came wrong, at Passchendaele. And to make matters worse, the military disasters provoked a violent agitation against all aliens and a demand for their wholesale internment. The outraged King invited the Prime Minister and Mrs Asquith to luncheon and poured his anger into their sympathetic ears. Margot Asquith, in a passion of loyalty, described the scene afterwards: 'I was moved to deepest admiration by his revolt against this alien stunt. "Intern me first" he said – and showed fairness and Christianity and real moral indignation over the whole low business.'

In May King George's old and trusted friend Lord Hardinge was censured, as Viceroy of India, in the Mesopotamia Report. The King – successfully this time – defended Hardinge, thus earning Lloyd George's angry comment on pressures which were brought from 'influential quarters' to stop necessary measures against 'inefficiency'.

But by far the deepest wound inflicted on the King's loyal nature was the ousting of Asquith by Lloyd George himself. The King like everyone else realised that the War was going badly; but as usual he did not blame Asquith. Cynthia Asquith, the Prime Minister's daughter-in-law, heard on 5 December 1916 while the battle for the political leadership raged that the King, 'terribly distressed', had actually said, 'I shall resign if Asquith does.'

However, it was one of those royal abdication threats which nobody took seriously. The demands of national survival made Asquith's resignation inevitable. Whether Bonar Law or Lloyd George should lead the new coalition was the only real question.

The King correctly sent first for Bonar Law. Their interview was unpropitious. Law held that Robertson was 'all wrong' and the King that politicians should leave war to experts: Law wanted the promise of an election if he took office, the King refused to give one in advance. Next day, 6 December, the King again tried his hand at a Buckingham Palace conference. After a sharp one-and-a-half hours it was clear that this conference also would fail, Asquith refusing to serve under Law, Lloyd George refusing to serve under Asquith and no government being possible without Lloyd George. In the end Lloyd George got what he wanted, including a war council, two new ministries (food and shipping), the first Cabinet secretariat in British history, with a system of Cabinet minutes, and the chance, eventually, to win the war.

Nevertheless King George V's sympathy for the fallen Prime Minister was not a bad thing at that traumatic time. It brought an element of humanity into the knacker's yard. King George VI was to do the same for Neville Chamberlain when he fell during a critical moment of the Second World War.

The King's loyalty to Haig is the only one of his great wartime devotions which has got him into serious trouble with history. He has emerged unscathed from the Asquith–Lloyd George duel. When memoirs and diaries came to be published, the prime mover in that drama turned out to be a very different person from the bluff but sensitive monarch, always anxious to do his duty both to fellow human beings and to the constitution. The spot-light settled on a brilliant little Presbyterian gnome from Canada who, after capturing a large slice of the popular press, found himself able to assist the Welsh wizard to the top of the tree, while depositing on the next branch, as Chancellor of the Exchequer, his great friend and compatriot, Bonar Law. The monkey-like charm and delight in mischief of Max Aitken, soon to be Lord Beaverbrook, were to reappear later on in the reign of King George v and also of his eldest son.

Over Haig, however, the King did sanction a dangerous phrase. His promise to Haig to 'do his utmost to protect your interests' was nearer to the forbidden ground of interference than to the permitted area of encouragement. That does not mean one must go so far in condemnation as a more or less convinced republican like Kingsley Martin. He has argued that the Haig–Lloyd George battle was waged between 'a democratically chosen Premier and a military junta, powerfully and secretly supported by the King'.

There are two answers to this kind of criticism. First, on psychological grounds: the implication that King George v was happy to operate in secret was far from true. He preferred a straightforward course. In 1915, for instance, Kitchener had invited Haig to keep him secretly in touch, and he would see Haig's ideas 'given effect to', rather than French's; but Haig must 'profess ignorance when that happened!' Kitchener revealed this plan to the King and the resulting dialogue was characteristic of both.

'If anyone acted like that,' said the King, 'told tales out of school, he would at school be called a sneak.'

'We are beyond the schoolboy's age!' was Kitchener's reply.

Second, on historical grounds, the King, as titular Head of the Army, had a special relationship with his commanders. At that time, writes John Terraine, Haig's biographer, this relationship 'meant far more to Regular officers than is easy to imagine today. . . .'

And even now, traces of it can still reappear. A Guards officer was asked during the Suez crisis how he would feel if a government ordered him to take part in operations which he deplored. 'I don't take orders from the government,' he replied, 'I serve the Queen.'

Two quite different episodes – one serious and the other comic – are probably the most vividly remembered of the King's war record. During the second of his five visits to the Western Front he was injured in an accident after which he was never physically the same. Friends said that he suddenly looked ten years older. While he was reviewing troops on 28 October 1915 a burst of cheering sent his terrified mare on to her hind legs and then over backwards on to the King. His pelvis was broken in two places, he was deeply shocked and agonisingly bruised. Ironically, the mare had been lent to him by his friend Haig.

The King's accident, hideous though it was, nonetheless seemed to associate him with the monarch's ancient right to run the risks of battle at the head of his soldiers. The other episode was the somewhat ludicrous result of an attempt to set a royal example to civilians. The King was 'conned' – there is no other word for it – by the ebullient Lloyd George in the spring of 1915 into becoming a teetotaller for the duration, as an inducement to munition workers to work more and drink less. 'I hate doing it', wrote King George in his diary, 'but hope it will do good.' The Household were privileged to share in this self-denial, but no one else of note volunteered except Lord Haldane. As a result he was said to have lost his zest. The House of Commons decided to take no such risk. In Nicolson's words, 'Mr Lloyd George's crusade left His Majesty and his Household high and dry.'

And all to no effect. The supply of munitions continued to give acute anxiety and the 'King's Pledge' did not always win the kudos it deserved. Worldly-wise people reported that Queen Mary's fruit cup was laced with champagne, while the King's withdrawal to his study after dinner 'to attend to a small matter of business' meant 'a small glass of port'. This genial exaggeration probably arose from a misunderstanding. The King's doctor, Sir Bertrand Dawson, prescribed a temporary daily dose of something stronger than water after his accident that autumn. As late as summer 1917 the King and Queen were still abjuring delicious French wines when visiting the front. But an offering of aperient water disguised as mineral water drew from the King a sharp comment. He finally summed up Lloyd George's part in the 'Pledge' as a 'scurvy trick'.

The War ended for King George V, as it had begun, on the balcony of Buckingham Palace. His was a trim, upright figure, even a little stiff, with the flawlessly correct uniform and not a hair of the head or beard out of place.

Some in that crowd may have heard that King George's court was stiff. There was the story of Rosie Boote, that most respectable ex-chorus girl married to Lord Headfort, the Irish peer. In 1916 the Viceroy's secretary had imitated King George's horror when asked if an invitation to the viceregal court might be sent to Lady Headfort.

'Rosie *Boote*, Rosie Boote come to my court!'

Yet King George thought he knew the difference between a rigid court and a correct one, and his was not meant to be stiff – at least, not compared with, say, the Viennese court which he had visited in youth. He had loved being among his troops in France precisely because 'It was not stiff, the men often following me round the town.'

75

As regards dress and decorations, his father would have agreed with him. 'Some people are surprised that my father and I are so particular about these things,' he once said. 'But wouldn't it be peculiar if in ordinary society people turned up with their shirts outside their trousers?'

The picture on the balcony is not of a relaxed king, and it might be wooden but for the sensitive human being underneath. So highly-strung was he that he had burst into angry tears when the American President, Woodrow Wilson, accompanied his 'Peace Note' of 1916 with the insulting remark that 'the objects which the belligerents on both sides have in mind are virtually the same'. The huge multitude looking up at the famous balcony on Armistice Day in 1918 certainly did not think the two opposing monarchs had been 'virtually the same'. Indeed *The Times*, in analysing the reasons for King George's ovation, laid stress on the crowd's spontaneous wish 'to mark the contrast between popular sovereignty and German autocracy'. *The Times* added that the monarchy, on this tremendous occasion, became a focus for joy, a symbol for unity and the epitome of all who would never give in. Sir Maurice Hankey, whether or not remembering the pheasants, named as three architects of victory Asquith, Lloyd George, 'and at the very top our beloved Monarch, King George V . . .' If a constitutional monarch's practical contribution could hardly be so decisive, the qualities which Hankey ascribed to King George were not exaggerated: 'His steadfast faith, his ceaseless devotion to duty and his inspiring leadership.'

The Versailles Peace Treaty was signed on 28 June 1919. 'Please God', wrote the King in his diary after a final tumultuous appearance on the balcony at 11 p.m., 'please God the dear old Country will now settle down & work in unity.'

Five months later the first anniversary of Armistice Day came round. There was to be a 'Two Minutes' Silence' of remembrance. The King and Cabinet, except for the Foreign Secretary, Lord Curzon, favoured this ceremony. Curzon apparently understood the silence was to last for one hour.

But even if the silence had lasted for one hour, or two hours, or two years, there would scarcely have been time to do the necessary thinking: to think of all the dead of the Great War and all the living of that 'dear old Country'. The dead had perhaps settled down. Who among the living were ready to 'work in unity'?

4

The first great constitutional monarch

'He asserted few or no rights, but he was nevertheless the centre of constitutional government. He was, in my opinion, the first great Constitutional Monarch.' Sir Robert Menzies, Prime Minister of Australia, on King George v.

ORGIVE me for talking so much of myself but . . . it is my hour now!' This was Queen Marie of Rumania writing to her cousin King George in November 1918, after being liberated at last from the German occupation. 'My hour now!' It was King George's hour also; but an hour of exultation which was to pass away even more quickly than most glorious hours do. There was growing unrest both on the King's domestic front and among the country's workers. Since little has as yet been said about King George as the father of future kings, we may look first at the scene inside the Palace.

The King, as has been seen, would tie on an apron with naval panache and 'make a very good lap' at the babies' bath-time. He did not make a very good papa to adolescents. Indeed, if his sons could have straightway become married men with delightful wives to be his daughters-in-law, he would have been much relieved. This despite the fact that, in his phobia of jazz, bobbed hair, short skirts, lipsticks and week-ending, he professed to dread the coming of daughters-in-law.

When peace was signed in 1919 the four surviving Princes were all within the age-span which their father disliked. Prince Edward (David) was twenty-five, Prince Albert (Bertie) twenty-four, Prince Henry (Harry) nineteen, Prince George seventeen. Prince John, an epileptic, had died that year aged thirteen and was buried at Sandringham beside his baby uncle of the same name.

The two eldest Princes, David and Bertie, were already showing the effects of their father's censorious brusqueness. Prince Albert was as sensitive as his father, as shy as both his parents and afflicted with a most hampering stammer. A glamorous elder brother and a father who showed his anger in roars and his affection in 'chaffing' did not help.

It could not be denied that the fair, smiling Prince of Wales, dressed in khaki and posted beside his parents on the Palace balcony, had glamour. That he often felt frustrated was also plain. There was the tiff with his father in 1914 over running the risk of capture by getting too close to the front line. But if he might not take risks, why should he take war medals from the Allies? His father rebuked him for this 'silly' misunderstanding of his royal role.

The Prince of Wales, however, soon felt that it was his father, not he, who misunderstood monarchy in the post-war age. Visiting his mother's friend and lady-in-waiting, Lady Airlie, one day in March 1919, he discussed with her the new hazards to which kings everywhere were prone. (Three dynasties had already fallen, the Romanovs, the Hapsburgs and the Hohenzollerns.) 'I shall have to work to keep my job,' he told her. 'I don't mind that, but the trouble is, they won't let me have a free hand.' His powers were not stretched until the King, with some misgivings, allowed him to undertake prolonged royal progresses abroad as a young ambassador extraordinary to a changing world.

Signs had appeared by 1919 that his sister Mary also was repressed at home. At a charity matinée, wrote an observer, she hardly laughed, but 'her mother *rocked*'. Fearing that the King hoped to keep her permanently at home unmarried, the Prince of Wales begged Queen Mary to tackle his father on this delicate subject. When she failed to do so, the Prince included his mother in his general criticism.

King George v had every intention of doing his duty by the family as well as by the country. It was not easy. The time has come to attempt a deeper probe into the causes of his failure.

First, he was profoundly conservative, far more so than his father or any of his successors. Moreover, he had views on the need of discipline for those brought up in a court. The Duke of Gloucester once returned from a world tour to find that the family had just gone in to luncheon. King George's first words of greeting were, 'Late as usual!' 'Quarterdeck' discipline came naturally to him and he applied it.

Second, it is often suggested that consuming admiration for his father, King Edward vii, led him to apply uncritically the parental methods of one generation to another. 'Beloved Papa' had chaffed his sons unmercifully and kept them in a state of considerable awe. This technique, Prince George had noted, made him love and obey his father. What had worked with one generation was surely appropriate to the next? 'I was always frightened of my father; they must be frightened of me.'

There is another aspect, however, of King George's relations with his father which, understandably, has not been investigated in the past. It is impossible to doubt that he regretted his father's spectacular unfaithfulness to an adored mother. Georgina Battiscombe's *Queen Alexandra* lifts a corner of the veil. 'Alas, Mrs K. arrives to-morrow and stops here in the yacht,' wrote Prince George to his wife from Cowes in 1895; 'I am afraid that peace and quiet will not remain.' His wife replied with the directness of one to whom the subject was no mystery: 'What a pity Mrs G.K. is again to the fore! How annoyed Mama will be.' Mrs K. and Mrs G.K. were Mrs George Keppel, and Mama was of course Queen Alexandra. It is to James Pope-Hennessy that we owe a further vital clue. Prince Eddy, we are told, was 'demoralised by the example of his father's private life'. Prince George must have endured the same strains, though reacting to them in a wholly dissimilar way. The presumption is that the awe in which he held his father's majesty contained an element of disapproval for his father's frailty. This took the form of shyness. He was never quite natural with King Edward, never indeed wrote to him a really unstilted letter in his life, though King Edward's letters to him were completely normal and relaxed.

The potential for inner conflict was thus only too apparent: intense love of a parent whose example, nevertheless, he did not wish his sons to follow. Both his biographers, Gore and Nicolson, dwell on the immediate change in the King's attitude to his sons once they had married. No more nagging criticism making for difficult relations. The point is not only that King George considered the married state itself a talisman, incidentally releasing him from responsibility, but also that he had perfect confidence in the individuals his three sons had chosen: Lady Elizabeth Bowes-Lyon, Lady Alice Montagu-Douglas-Scott and Princess Marina of Greece. As for the wish to keep his daughter at home, this was not selfishness so much as personal observation of what could happen to a girl who looked for fidelity in her husband and did not find it.

If King George v disapproved of post-war youth, there were other war-time and post-war social developments which he disliked far more. Indeed, he sometimes showed a certain startled sympathy with the expedients of the young. One day during the War Princess Marie-Louise said to her much older cousin:

'George, do you object to my going by bus?'

'What would Grandmama have thought!' exclaimed the King with a grave look. 'But I think you are quite old enough to travel by bus. Do you strap-hang?'

The conferring of peerages on press lords was among the new developments which made strap-hanging seem relatively harmless.

The monarch was traditionally the 'fount of honour'. King Edward vII, with his love of giving pleasure and his feeling that honours were a personal gift from himself, had begun to make the fountain work with extreme energy. King George was indignant when politicians turned it into a 'pump' or the wrong people tried to dip in it. He had unsuccessfully opposed Sir Max Aitken's baronetcy in 1916 (Aitken had been knighted five years earlier) as also his peerage (Beaverbrook) in 1917, the latter on the ground that Sir Max's public services did not call for 'such special recognition'. A fresh opportunity to thwart Beaverbrook presented itself soon afterwards, when Lloyd George proposed to appoint him Chancellor of the Duchy of Lancaster. Again the King's opposition was overridden. Undeterred, he next rejected a step up in the peerage for Lord Rothermere, another press baron to whom Lloyd George found himself indebted. Beaverbrook's peerage, said the King, had already created a storm, and he was not now going to provoke a tempest. Bonar Law had to be called in to work upon the King before Rothermere's viscountcy could be gazetted. Fifteen years later it was Lord Beaverbrook and Viscount Rothermere who combined to present King Edward vIII with his chief organs of propaganda in his bid to give an entirely new direction to the monarchy.

Industrial distress or 'unrest', as writers have preferred to call the chief phenomenon of the post-war years, had an immediate effect upon the House of Windsor. Together with the Europe-wide onslaught upon monarchies, it weakened the popular appeal of the throne. This was not at once realised by all those attached to the court. Lady Airlie, for instance, freely admitted having been deceived by the cheers welling up beneath the Palace balcony in June 1919. However, there were those like Lord Cromer who as early as 1918 had seen the red light. He wrote:

In spite of the unceasing labours and devotion to public duty of the King and Queen during the last three years, the fact remains that the position of the Monarchy is not so stable now, in 1918, as it was at the beginning of the War.

The King's formal sanction of the lamentable 'Coupon Election' in 1918, with Lloyd George's beguiling slogan of 'Homes Fit for Heroes', was perhaps the start of the trouble. But it has been convincingly demonstrated by Sir Harold Nicolson that a constitutional monarch could not refuse the Prime Minister a dissolution without being prepared to accept his resignation. After the ministerial crisis of only two years before, the risk of dismissing the Lloyd George coalition was prohibitive. Nevertheless the King did warn Lloyd George against holding the election before the soldiers had got their voting papers or the women their votes. Lloyd George stood these warnings on their heads. He wanted his election to take place before the discontent of ex-soldiers could become articulate and while the voteless women were, as he put it, still 'sane'. As a result he got his majority and a notorious Parliament filled, according to the economist J.M.Keynes, with 'hard-faced men who had done well out of the War', and according to Bonar Law's private secretary, J.C.Davidson, 'hard-headed men, mostly on the make'.

King George was neither hard-faced nor hard-headed; level-headed, rather. He realised at once that the first post-war King's Speech must show understanding of the workers. (The Labour Party had withdrawn their support from Lloyd George before the election.) Accordingly the King, after seeing the draft of the Speech which had just left the hands of the Cabinet assistant secretary, Thomas Jones, suggested 'the allusion to labour troubles ought to be strengthened' – in a democratic sense. This was a shock for certain elder statesmen in the Cabinet. But they enthusiastically adjusted themselves to the Monarch's lead, all but Bonar Law, 'who appeared to be suffering great pain throughout the meeting'.

Thomas Jones (knighted later) was the brilliant Welsh assistant secretary of the recently appointed Cabinet secretariat. A life-long Labour man and described by Churchill as 'the liberal conscience of the party', he has left behind him a spicy *Whitehall Diary*, which illuminates the backroom scene. Physically he was small and stocky, with the face of a ram. But he was never caught in a thicket.

The King's hope, expressed in 1918, that the country would quickly 'settle down and work in unity' showed no sign of fulfilment three years later; rather the opposite.

The artificial peace-time boom rapidly collapsed into slump, and by mid-1921 there were two million unemployed. An indignant letter was sent to Lloyd George on 1 September 1921 in which the King made four salient points: that the unemployed wanted work, not doles; that public works 'although unremunerative' were necessary in the emergency; that people could not be expected to live on a weekly dole of fifteen shillings (75 pence) for men and twelve shillings (60 pence) for women; and that a government which had afforded the 'enormous daily cost of the war' could afford to be liberal in this crisis.

Despite their hardships, King George had found the working classes amazingly loyal. After a football match, a huge crowd cheered him and sang the national anthem. He responded with his own *Jubilate*: 'There were no bolsheviks there! At least I could not see any. The country is alright . . .'

That football match had been played in April 1921. Two months later, on 22 June, the King was to be more than a spectator at the centuries-old struggle between the two sides in Ireland.

At this point the briefest of summaries must bring events in Ireland up to the year 1921. The Easter Rising of 1916 has been mentioned. It was savagely repressed and proved a most bloody turning-point. Two Irish leaders, De Valera and Cosgrave, were exempted at the last moment, but the sixteen executions, the 122 convicts, the three thousand internees made sure that the South would fight for independence. Sinn Fein took over. 'Now it was farewell in earnest to constitutional agitation, farewell to everything but arms.' The arms were borne by the IRA – the Irish Republican Army.

Nevertheless, both Asquith with a personal visit and Lloyd George with his release of prisoners and 'hand-picked' Convention still hoped to bring a vestige of peace to Southern Ireland and to wring a hint of concession from the North. The Coupon Election of 1918 showed how futile their hope had been. The old Irish Parliamentary party was swept away. Sinn Fein, holding almost three-quarters of the seats for all Ireland, boycotted Parliament, declared a Republic for the whole country, appointed De Valera its President and continued to ride forward for the next two years on mounting waves of violence perpetrated by both sides. Meanwhile Ireland was partitioned by Britain, a separate Parliament established in Belfast and retaliation officially organised against the IRA through the 'Black-and-Tans' a brutal force of hired mercenaries who did not stop at murder, robbery, arson, torture and mutilation.

King George declared his revulsion from such terrorism by asking in May 1921 'if this policy of reprisals is to be continued and, if so, to where will it lead Ireland and us all?' Where indeed. The King often told his equerry Lord Granard, an Irish peer, that the excesses of the Black-and-Tans would only strengthen the IRA; that for every day Terence McSwiney, mayor of Cork, continued on hunger strike a hundred men would join the IRA, and that McSwiney ought to be accorded political treatment (the Home Secretary turned down the King's proposal). Though a rigid conservative, King George had an inner sense that the British Government's policy was going to fail.

Suddenly he forged for himself an opportunity to be of positive service to Ireland. The Government had arranged for him to open the new Ulster Parliament at Stormont in Belfast on 22 June. At first the court had been shocked. King George felt such an act would further antagonise his Irish subjects in the South, especially if he were asked to declaim the speech drafted by Sir James Craig, the Ulster Prime Minister. Queen Mary and Stamfordham feared for King George's safety. But a seminal conversation between the King and General Smuts changed the focus of the whole enterprise.

Smuts had become a post-war statesman of immense prestige far beyond the borders of South Africa, partly through his own character and partly through the advances of the Empire and Commonwealth – a feature of King George's reign which will be examined later. By 1922 the Dominions had outgrown their 'daughter-hood' while Ireland was ruled as if she were a Crown Colony. Surely fellow members of the Commonwealth, Smuts asked himself, should help one another in an emergency? The chance came when Smuts called on King George at Buckingham Palace and found him 'anxiously preoccupied' with the coming speech. Smuts then made his creative suggestion: that the speech should be addressed not solely to Ulster but to all Irishmen in a spirit of general reconciliation.

Fired with enthusiasm for an idea that matched his own, the King agreed to Smuts preparing a five-sentence draft speech as a guide-line for the Cabinet. But neither Balfour nor Chamberlain, wrote Jones, liked what they called the 'gush' of Smuts's draft. 'It will not do as behind it all lurks the innuendo of oppression.' Balfour therefore withdrew to make a fresh attempt. Finally a distinguished civil servant, Sir Edward Grigg (afterwards Lord Altrincham) used the drafts of both Smuts and Balfour to produce a final speech of which the King highly approved.

Notwithstanding all these labours, the royal party set off in piano mood for Belfast on 21 June, Queen Mary having decided at the last minute to go too. A fine drizzle fell as they drove through subdued streets to Euston station. Two women who recognised them commiserated, 'Poor things.'

In Belfast next morning the sun shone, but no more brilliantly than the King. As he pronounced the memorable words of what has since been called the 'Forgive and Forget' speech, no one ever forgot the pure emotion which flooded his peroration:

. . . I appeal to all Irishmen to pause, to stretch out the hand of forbearance and conciliation, to forgive and forget and to join in making for the land which they love a new era of peace, contentment and goodwill.

Forgive and forget . . . it was no coincidence that the words which Smuts had used in a letter to his wife at the Peace of Vereeniging after the Boer War had been 'forgive and forget'.

The next few lines of the King's speech went further and foreshadowed Dominion Status for the South:

It is My earnest desire that in Southern Ireland too there may ere long take place a parallel to what is now passing in this Hall; that there a similar occasion may present itself and a similar ceremony be performed.

Homeward bound, the royal party said goodbye to Sir James Craig, the Prime Minister, on the quay. The British Home Secretary, longing to be safe home, looked up at the sky and imagined a bloody epilogue.

'Michael Collins could get me with a bomb dropped from an aeroplane.'

'They could have got you at any time today, old boy,' laughed Craig, giving small credit to the Black-and-Tans who had guarded the route and whose 'desperate expression' had greatly struck Lady Airlie.

'They could have got any of us,' chipped in the Queen.

THE KING'S TRIUMPH. GREAT WELCOME IN BELFAST. The press rejoiced next morning when the King arrived safely back in London, but the 'new era of peace' which he had prayed for did not materialise. Despite the Government's *volte face* of June 1921 and the subsequent establishment of an Irish Free State by treaty, civil war broke out in the South. For Ireland was partitioned by an unacceptable boundary and full independence was denied. This Michael Collins gloomily accepted. This De Valera made war in vain to prevent. Nevertheless the change in British tactics from the Black-and-Tans to the Treaty negotiations had been as abrupt as it was revolutionary. 'No British Government in modern times', wrote Churchill, 'has ever appeared to make so sudden and complete a reversal of policy.' Lloyd George no doubt carried it through, by over-riding the doubters in a divided Cabinet. But who or what inspired Lloyd George? To this day there is an unexplained gap, an invisible man.

If that man was King George v it would not be surprising. We know from Lady Airlie's memoirs (not published until 1962) that King George was furious to find London still intransigent when he returned from Belfast. A copy of *The Times* reporting a ministerial speech in the Lords which threatened 'full force' against Ireland was hurled by the King across the room.

Assuming there is something in such a view, the Belfast speech and Treaty negotiations will turn out to mark the first major intervention in policy by the House of Windsor. We shall soon see that it was not the last.

The King's health was running down and the Labour party was coming up. That was to be one theme of the next six years, 1922–8, with a fascinating because unexpected interplay between the Palace and the people.

By autumn 1922 Lloyd George had lost his grip on the Conservatives. Moved by Stanley Baldwin's eloquence, they broke up the Coalition. Lloyd George resigned, Bonar Law became Prime Minister and the Conservatives won the October election. More significant, Labour came second with 138 seats, as against 117 for the Liberals. The King's passion for continuity led him to make one of his rare false predictions: that Lloyd George would some day come back.

Seven months later Bonar Law was dying from cancer of the throat. He resigned on 20 May 1923 and King George made his second positive incursion into politics when he chose Law's successor. Again the position of the Labour Party was a significant factor.

From the limbo of lost prerogatives the royal right to choose the Prime Minister stood out intact. King George exercised it with his eye on the official Labour Opposition. Labour's whole strength was in the Commons. Therefore the leader of the Government must not try to face them from the Lords. This was the King's own view. After elaborate confidential enquiries, it turned out to be supported by Bonar Law, who gave his opinion 'in a loud whisper' to Thomas Jones and sent a message to Stamfordham through his private secretary. It was also the opinion of three Cabinet ministers. It was opposed by the Lord Salisbury of the day. Lord Balfour was thereupon called in as elder statesman. By now the competing candidates were reduced to two: Lord Curzon and Mr Baldwin, peer and commoner. Balfour loftily surveyed them both, the first an old friend whom he could not bear, the second in his opinion a nobody. Then he too adopted the constitutional precept: the Prime Minister ought to be in the Commons. He added cheerfully that this would result in the brilliant George Curzon being superseded by Stanley Baldwin, a man with an 'uneventful' career behind him (what about ousting Lloyd George?) and no signs of 'special gifts' or 'exceptional ability' ahead. This mission performed to his satisfaction, Balfour arrived back home to find a bevy of eager society ladies awaiting him.

'And will dear George be Prime Minister?'

'Dear George will not.'

Stamfordham broke the news to a crushed and tearful Curzon and at once King George appointed Baldwin. As one of history's cruellest blows to personal ambition, it was paradoxical that it should be dealt by King George v, the kindest of men.

Meanwhile Labour watched and had not long to wait.

After only five months of battling with post-war economic problems, Baldwin decided to ask the King for a dissolution. The election issue should be the adoption of Protection. King George's common sense told him that an election would be the end of the Conservatives. He warned Baldwin against it. Baldwin in fact lost his overall majority and the Liberals, despite their fighting as a united party, were again defeated by the ever-growing forces of Labour. The figures were Conservatives 258, Labour 191, Liberals 158.

The very thought of three-party combinations and permutations was enough to make any British heart sink. Panic broke out in many quarters. While most people thought the King should send for Baldwin (though Baldwin disagreed), others suggested the Labour leader, yet others proposing one of the Chamberlain brothers, Austen or Neville, and Balfour sacrificially proposing himself. Panic reached its zenith when the *Spectator* made its proposal for a 'Government of National trustees'. King George was not attracted by fancy solutions. Finding no precedent to guide his choice of Prime Minister, he wrote, 'I must use my own judgment.' That was in fact his prerogative.

The day after the election, 9 December 1923, Lord Esher had told Thomas Jones of the Cabinet secretariat that he and Stamfordham, though 'much concerned' about the King's duty in the present crisis, were

eager that Stamfordham should not have to go scouting from one person to another in secret trying to find out who should be sent for to succeed Baldwin. That is what happened when Bonar Law resigned. The King should be guided either by a [Conservative] Party Meeting or by the meeting of Parliament.

Jones promised Esher to 'put this strongly' to Baldwin before he went to the Palace next day, hoping for an immediate dissolution.

No Conservative party meeting having been convened to elect a new leader, the King used his own judgment. He left Baldwin no choice but to face Parliament again as Prime Minister. And when Baldwin was defeated in Parliament on 21 January 1924, the King sent for the leader of the next strongest party. It was Ramsay Macdonald, Labour's first Prime Minister.

To some Labour people it still seemed too good to be true. George Lansbury for one had issued a warning as recently as 5 January to all those sinister courtiers who were sure to be plotting to keep Labour out: 'Some centuries ago a King stood against the common people and he lost his head.'

From each side of the fence, Palace side and Parliament side, the prospect was regarded with bated breath. How could the King deal with socialists? demanded an uncomprehending foreign press. Long ago the Kaiser had ridiculed King George's father for 'boating with his grocer' (cruising on Sir Thomas Lipton's yacht). Now it seemed that King George was summoning his executioner. Indeed the thought may have crossed even the King's mind. During Macdonald's first audience the King recalled Lansbury's threat about Charles I and took the opportunity to deny 'intrigues at Court'. He explained that after consulting his private secretary according to constitutional usage, he always 'formed his own judgment'. In fact when one benighted courtier commiserated with him on the 'tiresomeness' of his new Labour contacts, he turned his back on the sympathiser. But after Macdonald had gone he wrote in his diary: 'Today twenty three years ago dear Grandmama died, I wonder what she would have thought of a Labour government.'

On the Parliament side, Labour leaders were astonished by their position: working men from industry and the mines now members of H. M. Government. Herbert Morrison, a Labour leader, devoted a colourful passage of his memoirs to the miracle of Ramsay Macdonald. That a man from a desperately poor Scottish home, who had once addressed envelopes in London for a living, augmented by oatmeal posted to him by his mother and mixed rather than cooked in tepid water – that this man should be appointed 'His Majesty's principal minister' – a 'momentous occasion' indeed.

The King, whose face in youth had been as grimy as any of his ministers' when his ship was coaling, reacted favourably to the man from Scotland: 'He impressed me very much, he wishes to do the right thing.' Macdonald had formed the same opinion of this constitutional monarch.

The King took immense pains to make his first Labour government feel reasonably at home. Knee-breeches were excused and Stamfordham investigated the cheap wonders of Moss Bros. They stocked 'a few suits of Household, Second Class Levée Dress from £30 complete'. This, though under half price, included a 'cock-hat, and sword'. But hardly had they found out which way round to wear the hat, stem to stern or broadside on, before the party's romantic sympathy with Russian communism was used by their enemies to unseat them.

The 'Campbell Case' gave the impression during August that Macdonald, yielding to his extremists, had interfered in the course of justice in order to save J.R.Campbell, a communist editor accused of sedition. By October the 'Campbell Case' had become the subject for a vote of censure. Macdonald lost. Not heartbroken to escape from the strait-jacket of a minority government – office without power – Macdonald asked for a dissolution. Reluctantly the King agreed, having found that neither the Conservative nor Liberal leader was willing to wear the strait-jacket himself. When polling day was less than a week away, the press published a notorious document known as the 'Zinoviev Letter', in which a Russian politician of that name allegedly discussed the means by which British communists might promote class war and bloody revolution. 'I suppose there is *no doubt* that Z's *letter* is genuine?' enquired the King of the Foreign Office. 'I see the Communists say it is a forgery.' It was a forgery. But the evidence was only to dribble out over the years. At the declaration of the poll both the Labour and Liberal parties were found to have lost heavily. Baldwin had a huge overall majority of more than two hundred.

'Un-English' was an expression which King George often found himself using. It could not be applied to Stanley Baldwin, now again Prime Minister. Baldwin's

OPPOSITE: The coronation portrait of King George VI by Sir Gerald Kelly.

genius was as shrewd, pragmatic and English (despite Highland blood) as Lloyd George's was sizzling, inspirational and Welsh. Baldwin did not go in for grand designs; he had failed as soon as he tried one, Protection, in 1923. But King George found him an ideal leader when the chronic post-war sickness suddenly came to a head on 4 May 1926 with the General Strike. (Churchill had ushered in 1926 with a famous speech known as 'The Broadening Hope'. It belonged to that well-known brand of economic optimism which sees the country 'poised for prosperity' just before a resounding crash.) Baldwin was no theorist but good on symptoms and always on call.

It could almost be said that in retrospect King George v enjoyed the General Strike. Everyone seemed to have behaved so well. No frightful tales of bloodshed came to his ears, just a few of those buses smashed up in which Marie-Louise might have done her strap-hanging. And it was all over in nine days. 'Our old country can well be proud of itself,' he wrote characteristically, 'it shows what a wonderful people we are.' He let fly when a few less 'wonderful' people like Lord Durham, an enormously wealthy coal owner, called the miners 'a damn lot of revolutionaries'. 'Try living on their wages,' retorted the King, 'before you judge them.' He personally intervened to deprecate both Churchill's announcement of 'full support' for the military if they were called in, and also a Cabinet proposal to tamper with strike pay. Nor did he see why the starving families of miners who stayed out of work long after the General Strike was over should not be relieved by Russian gold. Baldwin agreed.

After such a display of good feeling it is hard to believe that 'peace' was finally restored not by a substantial rise in wages, but on a basis of further cuts.

The unfortunate King found himself filling in the quiet interval after the storms of 1926 (and before the unguessed tempest of 1931) with a shattering illness. He had been forced by his doctors to go on a Mediterranean cruise in February 1925 after bronchitis. Having hated every moment, he was still below par in July when the 1925 coal strike began. 'I never seem to get any peace in the world. Feel very low and depressed.'

The note of self-pity was unlike the jovial King, so ready to dispense his own chaff and to enjoy other men's broad humour. But the note reappeared in November 1928 when he was stricken with an appalling chest abscess and laid low for the best part of a year. If he was permanently weakened by the accident of 1915, he was left with a fading sunset mellowness by his illness of 1928–9, often broken, however, by shafts of vivid petulance or indigo banks of boredom.

Sent away to convalesce at Bognor, he longed for home. Nevertheless there were compensations. He got to know well and enjoyed playing with his favourite grandchild, the Yorks' daughter Elizabeth. 'I am devoted to children and good with them,' he once said.

OPPOSITE: The coronation portrait of Queen Elizabeth by Sir Gerald Kelly.

But they grow up, and you can only watch them going their own way and can do nothing to stop them. Nowadays young people don't seem to care what they do or what people think.

If he had lived to watch his 'sweet little Lilibet' grow up, he might have judged the young differently.

The interest in the King's illness had been remarkably widespread. Vincent Massey of Canada was asked by lift boys in Louisiana, 'Have you got any word today about "the King"?' Public anxiety showed itself in strange offerings, such as a Tudor cough mixture, and in unlikely criticism of his doctors. One story about the devoted Dawson, whose dramatic location of the fluid on 12 December saved the King's life, suggested that no doctor had ever been such an ass. He was supposed, writes Dawson's biographer, to have given a man six weeks' treatment for jaundice before discovering he was Chinese.

The King's recovery despite two operations and two relapses was phenomenal. For the first time an X-ray unit had been brought into the Palace. Thanks to modern nursing (so unlike that accorded to his ancestor Prince Albert) he was able to attend St Paul's Cathedral while still far from fit. 'Fancy a Thanksgiving Service,' he said to Dawson, 'with an open wound in your back.' But his recovery was not attributed to the miracles of science by his ribald crony J.H.Thomas, the Labour politician: 'I was surprised to see him looking so well,' said Thomas. 'But we all know that's his bloody guts.'

The return of another minority Labour government in June 1929 did not strike foreign observers as the surest aid to King George's convalescence (Labour 287, Conservatives 261, Liberals 59). But King George was glad to have 'Jimmy' Thomas back, even though one of his risky jokes brought on such a gale of laughter that it caused the second relapse and operation (15 July). And the dream-like sinuosity of Macdonald's thought must often have been soothing.

Nevertheless the last great ordeal of the King's life was intimately connected with Labour rule. It has provoked fiercer accusations of unconstitutional conduct than any other event in the House of Windsor's history.

Baldwin had lost the election on his slogan 'Safety First', and Labour had won it on bold plans to cure unemployment. By 1931 it was clear that there was to be no safety and no cure. The Great Depression had swept over the world, its course marked by the Wall Street crash of 1929, the build-up of panic in Europe and its spread to the banking systems in summer 1931. The Cabinet were warned by Britain's own Big Five banks that unless they took drastic measures the crisis would ruin them all.

Like small craft wrecked simultaneously by 'natural' causes, three beloved old friends, Dalton, still a canon of Windsor at $91\frac{1}{2}$, Sir Charles Cust, an equerry for

39 years and, alas, Stamfordham himself all died between January and June 1931. King George's depression seemed to match the world's; when his doctors insisted he was better he retorted, 'I don't feel so.'

What sort of doctor's mandate was required for Britain? The possible remedies were loans, taxation and cuts. Suppose drastic economies meant cuts in unemployment pay? This in turn would drive millions of families below the subsistence line. Impossible for a Labour government. Yet the May Report on economies of 31 July 1931 announced a budget deficit of £120,000,000. As in all periods of crisis, the air reverberated not only with flappings and croakings but also with ideas for coalitions and 'national' rescue operations, such as the *Spectator* had proposed just before the first Labour government of 1924. By August the unhappy Cabinet realised that American bankers would not raise loans to refloat the British economy, and so rescue the country from a sinking pound and roaring inflation, until the deficit had been dealt with. This meant raising £50,000,000 in taxation and minimal cuts in wages and salaries of £76,000,000, including specifically 10% off the dole. Would even this suffice? Macdonald wondered miserably. The Bank of England telegraphed New York on 22 August to find out.

At 10 a.m. next morning, Sunday the 23rd, Macdonald put the King in the picture. (H.M. had travelled overnight to Balmoral on the 21st and rushed back overnight on the 22nd.) Macdonald's message was that Labour would probably resign. No doubt he also discussed the resultant possibilities including coalition.

From 7 p.m. till nearly 9 p.m. that evening an agonised Cabinet waited in the garden – where else? – of No. 10 Downing Street. When at last the answer came from New York, 'pandemonium' broke out. For the American bankers wanted to know, before finally making the loan, whether the City of London really considered that the proposed cuts were big enough. After half an hour of furious protest ('Bankers' Ramp'), when a majority of the Cabinet showed themselves to be against any dole cuts whatever, Macdonald was instructed to hand in their resignations forthwith to the King. Telling them that he would advise H.M. to hold a conference next morning between himself, Baldwin and Sir Herbert Samuel (standing in for Lloyd George who was on indefinite sick-leave) Macdonald dashed off to the Palace looking, according to various eye-witness accounts, distraught, agitated, scared and unbalanced.

Meanwhile the die had already been cast. After Macdonald's warning, the King had quite correctly consulted Baldwin and Samuel. By chance Samuel was available first. He put the case persuasively for a National Government of all three parties, headed by Macdonald. The King was deeply impressed by Samuel. When Baldwin arrived it was to be asked by the King to serve under Macdonald in a National Government. Baldwin agreed, though he had little love for coalitions.

Now came Macdonald armed with the Cabinet's resignations. The King begged him fervently to think again about the situation: backed by Baldwin and Samuel, he was the man to save the country. Macdonald responded by asking the King to 'confer' with all three of them next morning.

The last Buckingham Palace Conference of King George v's reign was held at 10 a.m. on 24 August 1931. It seemed to be a dazzling compensation for all the previous failures. The three party leaders arrived as an incipient National Government, thanks to the King's previous 'encouragement'. All was satisfactorily concluded by noon. The final act remained to be performed in the afternoon. 'The Prime Minister came at 4.0,' wrote the King, 'and tendered his resignation. I then invited him to form a National Government which he agreed to do.'

Macdonald had perforce filled in the interval between noon and luncheon with a traumatic scene at No. 10. A stunned silence fell upon his late Cabinet when he gave them the news. Arthur Henderson let out a long whistle.

The extreme bitterness of Labour at subsequent developments – their party split into those few who followed Macdonald and the majority who did not, their proud political edifice reduced to rubble after an October election when Macdonald got his 'Doctor's Mandate' to make whatever cuts were needed – all these miseries had their repercussions on King George v.

Most people at the time had taken it for granted that King George was within his rights when he asked his ministers to form a National Government. And indeed he was. Once the Labour government had disintegrated under the threat of the crisis, it was the King's prerogative to choose the Prime Minister and appoint the administration he wished. Harold Laski, however, an eloquent Labour propagandist and republican, set to work to prove that the King had exerted undemocratic pressures to achieve a so-called 'national government' and so dish the socialists. The pamphlet Laski produced had some influence on the frustrated Labour parliamentary rump, who had found one villain in Macdonald and were not sorry to find another in the Monarch.

Herbert Morrison, the Labour Cabinet minister, wrote in 1960 that he thought George v had been mistaken in urging Macdonald to be Prime Minister in the Coalition. The natural constitutional course was to ask Baldwin as leader of the Conservative party to form a government with Liberal support, which would have been forthcoming. As it was, continued Morrison, the King's action was 'conducive to' a split in the Labour party, and in all the controversy during the 'Doctor's Mandate' election, 'the name of the King became involved'.

Some two years after this election Sir Stafford Cripps, a future pillar of Churchill's wartime coalition and Attlee's post-war Labour government, used the occasion of a political meeting in Nottingham for an attack on the King.

When the Labour Party comes to power we must act rapidly. . . . There is no doubt that we shall have to overcome opposition from Buckingham Palace and other places as well.

Hubbub broke out in the press. Official Labour disowned Cripps and J.R.Clynes paid tribute to His Majesty's 'friendly help and willing cooperation' while he was a minister. Cripps himself tried to make amends for what was in truth an unpremeditated *gaffe* by saying that he had meant 'Court Circles' and the officials who surrounded the King, not the crown itself. Upon which Jimmy Thomas commented: 'I suppose his next statement will be that it was the Palace door-keeper he was talking about.' The King, delighted with this riposte, was soon repeating it to Anthony Eden. 'What does he mean by saying that Buckingham Palace is not me? Who else is there I should like to know. Does he mean the Footman?'

It is now over forty years ago that King George v exercised his constitutional right in such a dramatic fashion. So much controversy has since arisen that a balanced verdict must be attempted.

Labour criticism of the King in the Thirties provoked defensive passages from the pens of writers like Gore, Nicolson, Samuel, Eden, Hoare and Churchill after the Second World War. Most of them were content to emphasise that King George had had the constitutional right to 'encourage' his ministers to sink party differences and form a coalition of 'Individuals' or 'Personalities'. (This of course was true but superfluous as a line of defence. The situation had already passed beyond the stage of mere 'encouragement' and presented the King with his constitutional right to exercise 'choice'.) The only question that arises is this: did King George act wisely? Even Morrison did not suggest that his conduct was unconstitutional, but he wrote censoriously: 'The action of the Throne was the action of King George v and he must be held responsible for what happened.' Churchill and many others, though approving of King George's action and holding his ministers as finally 'responsible', also regarded the King's influence as decisive:

There is no doubt [wrote Churchill] that he used his influence, now become so great, to bring about the formation of a national, or so-called national Administration, to save the country from unnecessary collapse, and unwarrantable bankruptcy.

Churchill conceded that in the whole of King George's political career his conduct of 1931 was 'most disputable' – 'But in no way did his action go beyond the boundary of the Royal Function.'

That was so. Moreover, it must be remembered that the National Government was intended to be a temporary government of individuals, assembled purely to save the pound. That it neither saved the pound nor was temporary had nothing to do with the King.

If the King acted unwisely, it was in another respect. He invited Macdonald to be Prime Minister without first ascertaining that he still had the Labour party behind him. This was what split the party, giving the impression of royal prejudice. But on the major issue of a coalition there can be no constitutional debate. Indeed the present House of Windsor, if faced with a similar crisis, might well act in the same way.

5

Progressing with the people

*'He knew and understood his people and the age in which they lived,
and progressed with them.'* C.R. Attlee, M.P., on King George V.

IMPRESSIVE changes marked King George V's reign. Some of these must now be enlarged upon, before the glitter of his Silver Jubilee fades out in the quiet of his death.

The year 1931, if judged by permanent rather than ephemeral change, should be the year of the Commonwealth. While the quick-change artists of the National Government were taking the stage in November, the Statute of Westminster was starting its momentous journey towards enactment, which it reached on 12 December. The Empire and Commonwealth would never be the same again after this famous statute.

The resolute tramp of the 'white Empire' towards independence has already been heard in these pages. During the First World War it gathered momentum. Two Imperial Conferences, in 1917 and 1918, registered the accelerated pace when 'Liberty, Equality, Unity' became its watchwords. An 'exultant chorus' burst from its leaders as they chanted the new creed in antiphonal joy. 'We are a League of Free Nations.' 'We are an Imperial Commonwealth of United Nations.'

The creed carried a conscious message of experiment. It was no coincidence that another experiment with a 'League of Nations' was also absorbing the minds of the Allies. But Smuts declared to the Empire in 1917:

> Yours is the only system that has ever worked in history, where a large number of nations have been living in unity. Talk about a League of Nations – you are the only league of nations that has ever existed.

Let them exercise greater and nobler influence on mankind than ever before, concluded Smuts, by remaining true to their 'tradition of self-government and freedom'.

'Commonwealth' had nothing to do with Cromwell's interregnum but suggested the old 'common weal', an ancient community of interest. It was as if 'Fraternity' had been added to the magical trinity of 'Liberty, Equality and Unity'; though in no French revolutionary sense. The fraternity of the Commonwealth meant brotherly love. And in this was included love of the Sovereign.

By 1923 there were several testing opportunities for the Commonwealth to show its fraternal faith.

That ordeals would come had been recognised by all. While calling for 'absolute out-and-out partnership' in 1919, Lord Milner, Colonial Secretary and a curious King Arthur of the Round Table group, rubbed in the enormous difficulties of the task. 'I am not afraid of it,' he added. But clearly he was afraid. And 1923 showed why.

Trouble broke out as soon as the Imperial Conference began to draft its loyal message to the King. The Irish were dismayed to find that the Canadian delegate, Vincent Massey, had inserted two words into the draft which seemed to contradict the new emphasis on 'freedom'. One was a reference to H.M.'s 'subjects'; the other spoke of H.M. strengthening the loyalties which were said to 'firmly bind' the Commonwealth. To Massey's annoyance, the word 'subjects' was struck out and 'firmly bind' was changed into 'unite'.

Two violent racial clashes of that year demonstrated the lurking contradiction between self-government and partnership, liberty and unity. In Kenya the white settlers were recommended from Whitehall to accord full civil rights to their Indian immigrants. In reply they threatened to kidnap the King's representative, the Governor, and set up a rebel state with the bizarre slogan, 'For King and Kenya'. There was indeed much singing of God Save the King as the rebels prepared to kick the crown from the top of Kilimanjaro. (Ulster loyalists had once been ready to 'kick the King's Crown into the Boyne'.)

In India intense anguish was felt because their brothers were denied equality in South Africa. On their behalf Sir Tej Bahadur Sapru demanded from the Imperial Conference a place in the House of King George, of whom they were all subjects, rather than 'a place in his stables'. South Africa retorted that 'common Kingship' represented no more than a binding link between the parts of the Empire, and conferred no rights on individual citizens. India thereupon denied that different grades of citizenship could coexist in the same Empire ruled over by a single monarch. This damaging quarrel was eventually settled 'behind closed doors' at the Imperial Conference of 1926. Closed doors were not an auspicious symbol.

The 1926 Conference represented another striking advance in the creation of Empire and Commonwealth lore, trumpeted forth in the famous report of the Balfour Committee. Its grand object was to proclaim anew the principle of equality. This was achieved by 'redecoration' of the old Empire through the gilding of words like 'friendship' and 'refreshment of the spirit'. Most important for the House of Windsor, the crown in sonorous phrases was found to be the symbol of unity; literally the crowning symbol.

Redecoration might also involve some changes in the furnishings. When Vincent Massey of Canada arrived for the Conference, he asked about dress for his audience with the King. King George's insistence on correct dress was well known. He once flew into a rage when he saw Lady Cynthia Colville's husband walking down the

Mall in a top hat and short black jacket instead of the regulation morning coat. Massey was told that though frock coats were not obligatory, H.M. preferred visitors to wear them. Duly frock-coated, Massey arrived at the Palace, to enquire further if the ceremony of 'kissing hands' was to be taken literally. 'By Jove, I don't know,' exclaimed the lord-in-waiting who received him. 'I'll ask Reggie.' 'Reggie's' answer was that you really did kiss the royal hand. But when Massey obliged he noticed a look of surprise on the King's face. Afterwards a different Reggie explained, 'You only kiss when sworn of the Privy Council.'

It was possible that a little illogicality and puzzlement did not come amiss when dealing with this symbolic crown which now stood for so much. It has been pithily said that the old Colonial Empire was governed in the last resort by 'Mister Mother Country', an obscure clerk in a back room of the Colonial Office. By 1926 the new independent Commonwealth was united under the monarchical symbol of 'H.M. Mother Country'. Soon the last two words – Mother Country – were to be eliminated, leaving nothing whatever to stand between Majesty and the peoples overseas.

Meanwhile the King's 'Style and Title' had to be changed owing to the establishment of the Irish Free State as a Dominion. Instead of being styled 'of the United Kingdom of Great Britain and Ireland, and of the British Dominions beyond the Seas, King . . .' he became henceforth 'King of Great Britain, Ireland and the British Dominions beyond the Seas' – the old 'United Kingdom of Great Britain' having ceased to exist when Southern Ireland joined the Dominions, leaving the 'Ireland' of the King's new title to refer to Northern Ireland alone.

Such sensitivities of style were not in the King's line but he accepted the inevitable with the muted complaint, 'It is a bore having to change one's title . . .'

Finally, there were always complications to be ironed out concerning the vice-regal post of Governor-General.

What if a Governor-General seemed to perform his functions with bias? The year before the 1926 Conference Lord Byng, Governor-General of Canada, had refused a dissolution to the Liberal Prime Minister and granted one ten days later to the Conservative. Conference declared apropos of this resounding constitutional fracas that the Governor-General of a Dominion must behave 'in all essentials' like the King of Great Britain. Broadly this emphasised that there were to be no more arbitrary Governors-General as in the old Colonial days; specifically it pointed to the fact that King George rarely if ever refused a dissolution.

Before the great landmark of 1931 was reached, another 'Governor-General' row had blown up, this time with the King personally, to be settled in London at the 1930 Conference. It concerned the delicate question of appointments.

As long ago as the 1921 Conference on Ireland Thomas Jones had reported that one of the Irish delegates 'raised the question of the election of Colonial Governors'. Must they continue to be appointed from the Palace on the advice of the British Prime Minister? Lloyd George replied that any change 'would be a cut against

King George and his four sons out riding in May 1923. From left to right: the King, Edward, Prince of Wales, Albert, Duke of York, Henry, Duke of Gloucester and George, Duke of Kent.

The Prince of Wales was equally at home wearing cowboy dress on his ranch in Alberta (left), or steeple chasing in formal attire (below).

RIGHT: The Prince of Wales (in tartan) with the Duke of Kent and Mr and Mrs Baldwin during his Canadian tour of 1919. The Duke of Kent was the Prince's favourite brother. Baldwin got the impression that he was a favourite politician but afterwards the Prince wrote of him as a prosy bore.

BELOW: The Prince at Auckland Domain during his tour of New Zealand, 1920. He was the darling of the crowds wherever he went.

ABOVE: The Duke of York playing golf against Frank Hodges, leader of the miners' union, who had invited him to play on a miners' course in the Rhondda Valley, 1924.

LEFT: The Duke playing in the Wimbledon championship of 1926; he and his partner, Sir Louis Grieg, were beaten in the first round of the men's doubles.

BELOW: At his boys' camp near Romney in 1927 the Duke of York watches water sports.

LEFT: Lady Elizabeth Bowes-Lyon as a child. She was the ninth of the ten children of the fourteenth Earl of Strathmore.

BELOW: The Duke and Duchess of York shown leaving Buckingham Palace after their wedding reception in 1923. King George wrote to his son, 'You are indeed a lucky man to have such a charming and delightful wife as Elizabeth.'

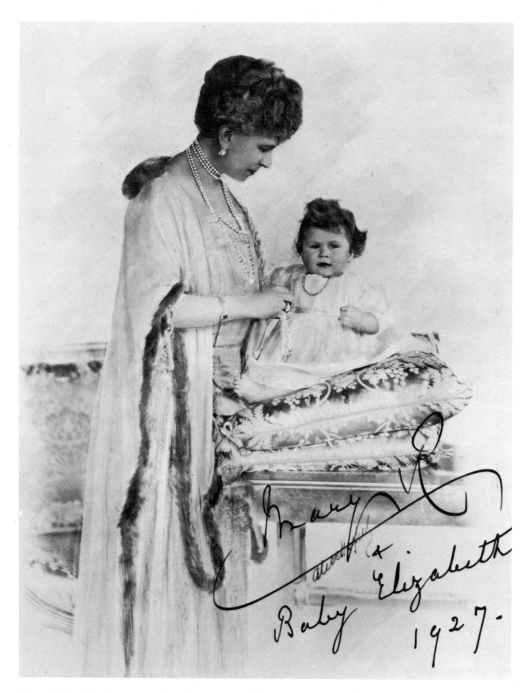

Mary R
Baby Elizabeth 1927.

When the Duke and Duchess of York visited Australia in 1927, the baby Princess Elizabeth, born 1926, was left in Queen Mary's care. The Duchess said that, leaving her baby for so long, 'quite broke me up.'

ABOVE: The Duke of York outside
Parliament House, Canberra, on the occasion
of its official opening in 1927. It was his
particular wish to speak to the crowds
gathered outside the Parliament building
before he went inside for the speech from the
throne.

ABOVE RIGHT: The King and Queen and
Princess Elizabeth appear on the balcony of
Buckingham Palace with the Duke and
Duchess of York, on their return from the
Australian tour.

RIGHT: Princess Elizabeth riding a tricycle,
1931.

royalty'. But by 1926 the Dominions of Australia and South Africa claimed the right of appointing their own Governor-General – perhaps some local worthy instead of a royal duke or British aristocrat – and submitting their choice to the King direct. It now transpired that the Australian Prime Minister had chosen as Governor-General one Sir Isaac Issacs, a radical compatriot of seventy-five years. The King distrusted his background and denounced his age. As Isaacs was to work hard and live on happily to be over ninety, the King's objection on the score of age was to fall to the ground. Eventually that magical process called 'informal consultation' bridged the gap between the King's prerogative of choice, hitherto vested in the British Prime Minister, and the Dominions' freedom. Meanwhile, rather than 'fan the flame of agitation', King George accepted Sir Isaac.

It is doubtful whether even Lord Stamfordham, if he had been alive, could have got King George to master the details of the Statute of Westminster. Its main point was plain: to crystallise an optimistic decade of Commonwealth growth. This seemed the appropriate moment for writing down the creed of unity in difference, partnership through freedom. But as in so many human institutions, the moment of fruition suddenly pin-pointed the possibility of decline. Freedom to cooperate would involve freedom to secede. Nevertheless the ageing King-Emperor found in the Preamble to the Statute of Westminster a thrilling new justification for his own existence. Now that the Dominions were absolutely free, what held them together? It had 'rather taken H.M.'s breath away', wrote Lord Stamfordham in 1927, when Canada sent her own separate diplomatic missions to France and Japan. The Dominions would have their separate ambassadors next. They did. But something still overcame their separateness. It was nothing but their common allegiance to the crown. They recognised the crown as the symbol of their free association.

The crown's exalted position under the Statute of Westminster, however, was not quite as inevitable as many excellent royalists have suggested. This was indeed the position of King George v in 1931. But the Dominions might decide to do without any symbol of their free association; or choose a different symbol; or insist on the crown being their symbol but not on all being kingdoms; or regard the crown as symbol but not as the object of legal allegiance. 'There might be thought to be a limit to this,' wrote Professor Wheare with characteristic wit – and continued to conceive of even more remote logical possibilities: a crown as symbol of free association, yet all the members republics; a king without any kingdom. 'It might approach the inconceivable, but it would be rash to conclude that so absurd an anomaly could not happen in the Commonwealth.'

Nothing could have been further from King George's natural bent than this kind of speculation. Perhaps we may leave him and the Statute of Westminster with a striking thought from Professor Mansergh, another incomparable authority on the Commonwealth. The position of the crown and Commonwealth in 1931 was at first sight something of a paradox. An age of equality which had swept away so many imperial institutions had 'left the Crown not only unimpaired but exalted'. How could this be? 'Because the Dominions all stood in the same and equal relationship to the Crown.'

Up till now little has been said about King George and the imperial jewel which he loved so deeply, India. During the Twenties there had been a happy belief that India and the rest of the non-self-governing Empire would in due time reach independence under the crown. By the Thirties, India's pilgrimage towards that Mecca had not become noticeably rapid. It was impeded in the King's opinion both by 'the Conservatives, egged on by the retired die-hards from India' and by Gandhi and his Congress party, and their campaign of civil disobedience. Nevertheless King George was persuaded to receive Gandhi at Buckingham Palace in September 1931. What happened there gives a vivid picture of the early House of Windsor at home to the Eastern Empire. Sir Samuel Hoare, as Secretary of State for India in the just-formed National Government, had the preliminary duty of getting Gandhi an invitation.

'What!' roared the King, 'have this rebel fakir in the Palace, after he has been behind all these attacks on my loyal officers?' But by the end of the interview King George had accepted that the rebel fakir would receive an invitation, undeserved though it was: 'the little man . . . no proper clothes on, and bare knees'. At the party there was a nervous moment for Hoare when King George looked at the knees resentfully, but the moment passed thanks to Gandhi's 'beautiful manners'. When the time came to depart, Hoare again held his breath, for the King had decided it was his duty to warn the rebel.

'Remember, Mr. Gandhi, I won't have any attacks on my Empire!'

Gandhi replied, to Hoare's immense relief, 'I must not be drawn into a political argument in Your Majesty's Palace, after receiving Your Majesty's hospitality.'

Four years later the King showed himself equally critical of the Indian princes who were sabotaging federal proposals.

'I won't see them when they come to London,' he announced to Hoare. (It was the year of the Silver Jubilee.) 'Why should they come to London at all and spend a lot of money?' Then in the tones of his grandmama, who had always stood up for her poor Indians:

'Tell them to stay in their States and look after their own subjects.'

The House of Windsor was born in battle and grew up in the angry aftermath of war. Dedicated to stability and a loving preservation of the past, King George v reigned for twenty-five years over a nation in perpetual flux. When he came to the throne Britain called herself a democracy, but it was only a courtesy title. Women formed half the population but were not free even to vote for the male government who ruled them. The radical or socialist half of male voters were constantly thwarted in their wishes by the veto of the House of Lords. Vote and veto: by 1928 the women had won completely and seventeen years earlier the Lords had lost their main battle.

At the same time constitutional 'usages' had grown up since the beginning of the century which changed and restricted the monarch's power: such as his selection of prime ministers only from the House of Commons, and his almost invariable consent to a dissolution. Though King George never ceased to be King-Emperor, the changed post-war Empire was a familiar if not agreeable thought to him. Nor were there any signs that the changes had ceased – or ever would cease. 'The historian who writes today,' declared Professor Hancock in his book on the Commonwealth published in the year after King George's death, 'cannot look back upon a completed journey.'

The journey for many foreign dynasties had already been completed, either by death or banishment. This tended to isolate the British monarchy, though the effect was not necessarily weakening. After the fall of so many worthless monarchies, King George v should have felt the same relief as Britain in 1940: 'We stand alone.' Perhaps he did, which would explain why, by 1926, King George was telling Lord Stamfordham that 'State Visits have ceased to be of any political importance', though he was always glad to invite exiled royalties to shoot at Sandringham.

Aristocracy as well as royalty had not always surfaced after the First World War. Three-mansion families (two in the country and one in town) were becoming rarer. Lady Airlie's brother, Lord Arran, expatiated to her on the folly of indulging one's nostalgia for pre-1914 halcyon days. Why stick up family portraits in small London flats?

. . . even were I able to afford to live again as I did then it would be impossible owing to the march of democracy. To live that life demanded that domestic servants should be slaves and contented with their slavery. It was only by slavery that the old regime could be carried on.

One statesman who particularly liked to dilate on the changes in George v's reign was C.R. Attlee, a moderate Labour politician who was to reach the leadership of the Labour party in 1935 and the premiership in 1945. Attlee nominated the 'advances of science', the 'spread of education' and 'ideas of self-government', all played upon by a fountain, or rather geyser of 'economic forces', as the causes of inevitable change which the First World War accelerated.

Through these innovations, Attlee saw King George as both 'a rallying point of stability' and a focus for 'sympathy with new ideas'. Attlee, whose words were part of an encomium delivered in the House of Commons on the King's death, may have exaggerated the warmth of welcome which new ideas received from King George. Nevertheless Attlee was right in his summary of King George as a democrat: 'He knew and understood his people and the age in which they lived, and progressed with them.'

The judgment of Herbert Morrison, Attlee's contemporary and later rival for party leadership, was not so favourable. His audiences at the Palace led him to conclude that George V was 'a monarch of a rather old tradition, and perhaps a little out of date' – with an 'affable' personal attitude but the official approach of 'Royalty which by divine right had to keep the commoner at a distance'. Morrison did not deny King George's 'profound knowledge of his constitutional position', but summed him up as 'a Tory of the *Daily Mail* school during the Northcliffe regime'.

It might have surprised Morrison to know that King George's avid reading of the newspapers stopped short at the *Mail* and *Express*. It is probably true, however, that Sir Clive Wigram, Stamfordham's successor as private secretary, did not discourage the King from airing his Tory opinions. In the Eden *Memoirs* we read that Wigram told Eden he hoped 'S.B.' (Stanley Baldwin) would win the 1935 election and hand over in a year or two to Eden himself and the younger men. 'That I know,' added Wigram, 'is what the King wants to see too.' It was lucky that Sir Stafford Cripps did not overhear this confidence.

Duty, well understood and well performed, was the badge of King George V. It was mainly because of his obedience to this call that he could become 'the rallying point of stability' in a distracted age. The kind of stability which he himself favoured, however, was not always calculated to please the world of Mr Attlee or even Mr Baldwin. He once had to be reproved by Baldwin for political interference when he complained of recumbent figures on the benches during an all-night sitting – 'Members of Parliament now include ladies,' Stamfordham had pointed out to Baldwin, 'and such a state of things as you describe seems to His Majesty hardly *decorous . . .*'

The King's standard of decorum was sometimes too much even for the Household. Females had to carry gloves at meals, and when one lady-in-waiting shortened her ankle-length skirt with a view to Queen Mary following suit, King George showed that the experiment must not be repeated. His loud, uninhibited complaints became legendary. Queen Mary would shut windows or doors if the criticism got too intemperate, as when a Bank Holiday crowd was parading under his windows at Windsor and she is said to have 'called on him peremptorily to be silent'. One hopes that she had said, 'Shut up, George!'

In Buckingham Palace, habit and decorum made him breakfast every day at 9 a.m. precisely, always entering the breakfast-room while Big Ben was actually striking the hour. It was not that he loved ceremonial. He disliked it intensely, though feeling it his duty to keep it up at Windsor and Buckingham Palace. His ideal life was the domestic simplicity of York Cottage.

But even in York Cottage the blustering of a sudden gale could raise the roof. He would damn and blast his doctors for the 'muck' they offered him; indeed the promise of a risky joke after a nasty dose was often the only way to make this endearingly child-like monarch take his medicine.

One of these jokes he passed on to Sir Anthony Eden in 1935, after the unpopularity of the Hoare–Laval plan, concocted that year in Paris, had forced Sir Samuel Hoare to resign. 'I said to your predecessor [Hoare]' remarked the King to Eden, ' "you know what they're all saying, no more coals to Newcastle, no more Hoares to Paris." The fellow didn't even laugh.'

The King was kinder to 'the fellow' than his joke suggested. 'Now you are free,' he said consolingly, 'you will have more time for shooting. Go and shoot a lot of woodcock in Norfolk.' Those were the last words of King George to Hoare, and incidentally one of the last autumns for shooting lots of woodcock in Norfolk. The Second World War was four autumns away, but its shadow already overhung the Silver Jubilee, at least for King George.

'I am an old man,' he had said to Hoare. 'I have been through one world war. How can I go through another?' He did not have to. And the Silver Jubilee was for many thousands a moment of fragile joy suspended like a dewdrop in a cobweb.

Jubilee Day – Monday 6 May 1935 – drew forth the eclectic but brilliant powers of a new social diarist, Sir Henry ('Chips') Channon. New, at least, to historians, since the diaries were first published in 1967.

We are standing with 'Chips' and his wife Honor in St James's. A thunder of applause heralds the royal carriages – the Yorks 'with two tiny pink children' (Princess Elizabeth and Princess Margaret), the Duchess 'charming and gracious, the baby princesses much interested in the proceedings, and waving' – the Kents, 'that dazzling pair', Princess Marina wearing 'an enormous platter hat, chic but slightly unsuitable – She was much cheered' – the Prince of Wales 'smiling his dentist smile and waving to his friends, but still he has his old spell for the crowd. . . .' Suddenly the coach with Their Majesties. Channon, quite carried away, feels that Queen Mary in her 'white and silvery splendour' eclipses even the King: 'She has become the best dressed woman in the world. . . .'

Sir Robert Menzies of Australia decided to sound out the people after the Thanksgiving Service at St Paul's.

'Do you believe in all this royalty business?' he asked a barber in the Strand. The barber admitted that in his local pub after work he and his friends had great arguments – 'but *we're all for the King*'.

At the close of Jubilee Day the King broadcast a message of thanks to his 'very very dear people'.

Broadcasting was one of the new ideas to which he was highly sympathetic. His Christmas messages have often been described nostalgically by contemporary listeners who dwell on the rich deep voice. One might be forgiven for thinking of plum pudding – until one hears the recordings. His Christmas messages were perfection.

On Jubilee Day he dedicated himself anew to his people's service 'for all the years that may still be given to me'. There were in fact to be months not years.

Far into the May night the crowds milled round the floodlit balcony of the Palace cheering and calling for the King.

'I had no idea that I was so popular,' he said to his friend Menzies; and to his hospital nurse, Catherine Black, 'I am beginning to think they must really like me for myself.'

It was typical of the King's humility that he should have taken twenty years to find out that he was beloved. As long ago as 1918 Mr and Mrs Asquith had been invited to lunch at the Palace and Margot had afterwards written lyrically about him to Lord Stamfordham. 'As you know, I've loved him since he was a little middy . . . he has come on immensely – *au fond* has always had goodwill, simplicity and fine courage.' In the next seventeen years he had continued to 'come on' and now he had definitely arrived. The letters he received after his Jubilee showed what all kinds of people felt.

Lord Salisbury wrote immediately after listening to the broadcast that the Jubilee was an 'astonishing testimony to the deeply founded stability and solidarity of this Country and Empire under Your Majesty's authority'.

The Most Reverend Cosmo Gordon Lang, Archbishop of Canterbury, showed himself capable of a light touch. 'The crowds in the streets,' he wrote to King George, ' – so orderly, cheerful, eager – were far more striking than any decorations. As a very plain "man in the street" said to me today "There may be a bit of fun and excitement but make no mistake, the king himself is at the bottom of it all." '

At the convent of the Holy Child Jesus near Sevenoaks, the nuns sat round listening, and their Reverend Mother thanked the King next day for 'the great example and devoted Service You have given us these twenty-five years'.

A minister from the slums of Liverpool thanked their Majesties on behalf of the very poor for a great range of benefits beginning with their 'perpetual concern' and ending with 'That vibrating "God bless you" on Christmas Day'. 'You have played a splendid game,' concluded the Reverend W.B. Williams, for the 'courage with which these poor people face their difficulties is derived largely from the THRONE. *The poor really love you both.*'

Finally an anonymous letter to Queen Mary from 'an old English Woman' who desired only to tell Her Majesty how happy last Monday had made her. She had seen three Jubilees, and used to think that Victorian cheers were unsurpassable. 'But Monday was even greater, and I long to tell you how beautiful you were, and how we love you, and the king, who too looked so well. . . .'

But he was slowly failing. Bronchitis in February had set him back. The death of his deeply loved sister Victoria in December broke him up. 'How I shall miss her,' he wrote, '& our daily talks on the telephone.'

One of their daily talks had begun with the old Princess ringing up her brother and saying affectionately, 'Is that you, you old fool?' The operator replied, 'No, your Royal Highness, His Majesty is not yet on the line.'

He began to feel ill on 15 January and on 20 January 1936 the end came. As he sank, Dawson wrote out his famous bulletin at 9.25 p.m. – 'The King's life is moving peacefully to its close' – and the spirits of those who listened to it being repeated at intervals on the wireless sank too. He died at 11.55 p.m.

One of his dying whispers had been, 'The Empire?' 'It's absolutely all right, Sir,' replied his private secretary.

During the last tumultuous weeks of his eldest son's reign which were so soon to follow, he was often remembered as 'King George the well-beloved'.

The debonair Prince of Wales in the uniform of the Welsh guards, 1932.

ABOVE: George V making his last broadcast in 1935. He was the first British king to speak to the people by radio. His voice and manner were perfection.

RIGHT: The funeral procession of George V passes through the lower ward of Windsor Castle, 1936. During the earlier procession to the lying-in-state at Westminster, the Maltese cross on top of the crown – then inherited by King Edward VIII – fell off.

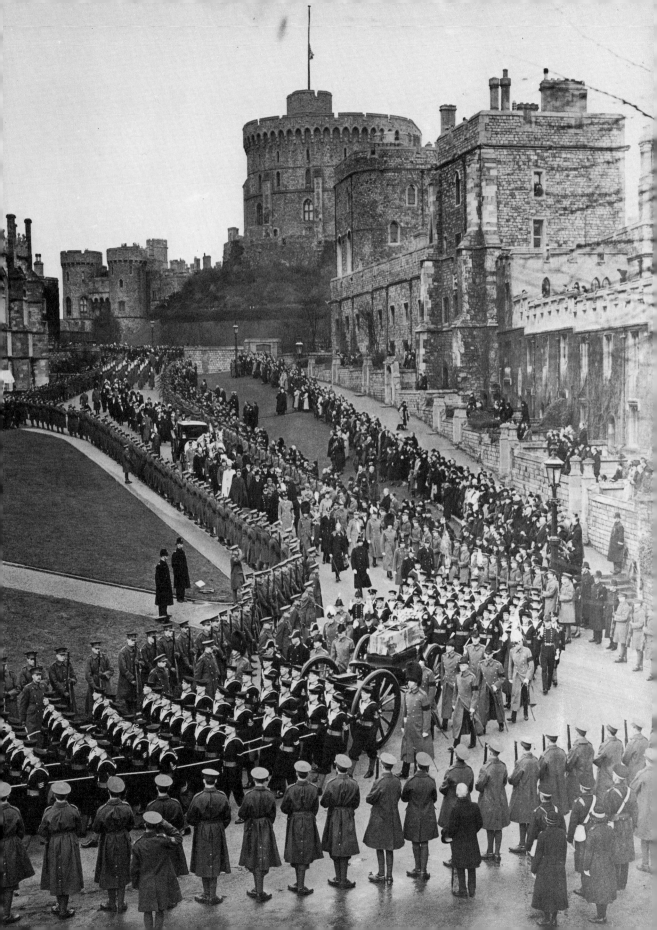

LEFT: An informal picture of the new King, Edward VIII, walking through the rain with Admiral Sir Lionel Halsey, caused a stir in Establishment circles. 'We can't have the King doing this kind of thing,' commented an M.P. to Mrs Simpson. 'He has the Daimler.'

BELOW: The King's visit to depressed areas of South Wales in November 1936, and his oft-reported words 'Something must be done' boosted his popularity during the Abdication – but not with the government.

ABOVE: The picture the British public never saw: King Edward and Mrs Simpson sightseeing at Trogir during their Adriatic cruise in the *Nahlin* during the summer of 1936.

ABOVE RIGHT: The King exercising on board the yacht *Nahlin*. Exercise was one of his obsessions.

THE CHOICE

THE PRIME MINISTER. "ALL THE PEOPLES OF YOUR EMPIRE, SIR, SYMPATHISE WITH YOU MOST DEEPLY; BUT THEY ALL KNOW—AS YOU YOURSELF MUST—THAT THE THRONE IS GREATER THAN THE MAN."

INSTRUMENT OF ABDICATION

I, Edward the Eighth, of Great Britain, Ireland, and the British Dominions beyond the Seas, King, Emperor of India, do hereby declare My irrevocable determination to renounce the Throne for Myself and for My descendants, and My desire that effect should be given to this Instrument of Abdication immediately.

In token whereof I have hereunto set My hand this tenth day of December, nineteen hundred and thirty six, in the presence of the witnesses whose signatures are subscribed.

SIGNED AT
FORT BELVEDERE
IN THE PRESENCE
OF

Edward RI

Albert

Henry

George

OVE: The instrument of Abdication signed by Edward and three brothers, the Dukes of York, Gloucester and Kent.

OVE RIGHT: A Punch cartoon on the Abdication.

FT: A photograph by Cecil Beaton of the Duke and Duchess Windsor on their wedding day, 3 June 1937, at the Château Condé, France.

A signed photograph of the Duke and Duchess of Windsor after the
Abdication.

PART
3

EDWARD VIII,
DUKE OF WINDSOR

6

The first royal communicator

'*I am sure you won't mind when I tell you that I'm out the
whole of every day seeing & visiting* the troops, *i.e. "the people*"!!!!
The Prince of Wales to King George V, 1918.

NEVER has a monarch's temperament so stamped itself upon every month of his reign as did that of King Edward VIII. True, the months added up to not quite eleven. Nevertheless the King's story was the story of his temperament. A duller man would not have reached the end of the road so rapidly; a less attractive one would have been relinquished sooner. The key to his short-lived encounter with destiny – from January to December 1936 – lies in his own nature.

He was the first royal communicator. Observing his unique *rapport* with the masses while on tour, a *Times* correspondent once described his performance as that of an artist. The Aga Khan fervently agreed:

There lies the real secret of his temperament, of his tragedy as much as of his achievement; he was a born artist.

Today we should say that he was a born communicator. Moreover, one born to parents who found reciprocation almost impossible. Much of the tragedy had been prepared during the forty years or so before he came to the throne.

His memoirs, *A King's Story*, written as Duke of Windsor, bring out the temperamental gulf between himself and his father. The book opens with King George V reading *Pilgrim's Progress* on 23 June 1894, while anxiously awaiting his child's birth. The son, writing fifty-seven years later, doubts whether 'this ponderous classic' was suited to distracting a father-to-be. Yet John Bunyan's masterpiece, hailing from King George's beloved East Anglia, was surely an inspired choice. He could reflect upon Vanity Fair and the young pilgrim about to start along the trail.

'At 10.0 a sweet little boy was born', wrote the father that evening. Once more, doubts assail the son. Did his father ever again call him 'sweet'? The note of bitterness, though lightly struck, is present on the first page.

Sweet the prince undoubtedly was, and in time every photograph, every pressman was publicising this fact. His slightness, his piquant nose, blue eyes, fair skin and yellow hair shining like a buttercup made him a dream prince with all the sweetness of unfading youth. One of the best impressions was to come from a politician, Duff Cooper, after watching the State Opening of Parliament:

The scene in the House of Lords is the most delightful thing in the world, the most like a fairy story. The King and Queen sitting on their thrones ... The Prince of Wales on a smaller throne in the robes of the Garter, looking most like a fairy prince, his pink face and golden hair rising out of ermine, beautiful as an angel....

His impossible youthfulness struck everyone: 'looking like a child of eight', decided Duff Cooper's wife Lady Diana, when the Prince appeared aged forty-two in shorts on a cruise. Towards the end, it was the television screen which seemed to be lying when it showed such an entanglement of lines on so young a face.

His actual youth had not been entirely serene. One of little David's earliest recollections was of a sadistic nurse regularly twisting his arm as he entered the Sandringham drawing-room. Fate seemed to have been twisting his arm slightly ever since. His incursions into the parental zone were sufficiently daunting. Papa's footfall, recalled the Duke of Windsor, was 'noticeably heavy', even 'ominous': 'the Library became for us ... the place of admonition and reproof'. A place of reproof it remained, though David meanwhile left the schoolroom to savour the Navy at Osborne and Dartmouth as Prince Edward, to acquire culture in Europe as 'Lord Chester' and, as Prince of Wales, to endure the to him 'dreary chore' that was Oxford University. 'Bookish he will never be', wrote the head of his college, softening this blow with a compliment about his 'learning more and more every day of men ...'.

The young student of men, however, never learnt to handle his own father. Considerable edginess developed over dress, since each thought dress immensely important while aiming at diametrically opposite effects. King George believed that correctness was next to godliness. Knowing this, the Prince was tactless to confront his father at breakfast in American-style trousers with 'cuffs'. Turned up trousers, except to cross a puddle, were taboo. 'Is it raining in *here*?' demanded the King. But if sarcasm was permissible, Lady Airlie thought King George went too far in calling his son the worst dressed man in London and setting traps for him over the wearing of decorations.

On the other hand, both agreed in disliking formality. When the Prince denounced State visits as 'rot & a waste of time, money, & energy', he was only echoing his father's view in fiercer language. But whereas George v understood the place of formality in kingship, it was Edward viii's charm but also his misfortune never to do so.

This defect must be kept in perspective by looking at it first in relation to Prince Edward's virtues.

Who does not sympathise with his resistance to his first suit of white-tie-and-tails? The youth who protested 'I shall look an ass' was engagingly honest. No less sympathetic was his yearning for responsibility. 'Oh!! that I had a job,' he exclaimed on the outbreak of the First World War. That was no unworthy wish. Indeed there is nothing but admiration for his stubborn and courageous fight to get to the Front. 'What does it matter if I am killed?' he asked Lord Kitchener. 'I have four brothers.' He badgered everybody. 'When shall I be sent out? It is terrible for me to sit here and see all my friends being killed or wounded.'

As the years passed his craving for responsibility only sharpened. 1915: 'It is sad to have to say it, I have no *real* job except that of being Prince of Wales. . . . Oh! not to be a prince.' 1919: 'the Prince of Wales's traditional role of leader of society . . . agent for the Monarch.' 1924: 'chained to the banquet table'. 1925: 'The Prince of Wales is the king's deputy, the "King-in-Waiting", so to speak. But he has no specific, routine job in the sense, for example, that a vice-president has a job. . . . I actually possess no prescribed State duties or responsibilities.' This was a convincing picture of vacuum; especially as his father repeated Queen Victoria's mistake in neither unlocking the red State boxes for the heir, nor admitting him to audiences. Even his four remarkable Empire and foreign tours were an advance in degree not in kind, for Queen Victoria and King Edward VII had sometimes allowed their heirs to represent them abroad.

However, when the Prince moved on to wider criticisms of his position, his grasp was less firm.

A first sign of confusion appeared during his investiture as Prince of Wales in 1911. Any boy of seventeen might be expected to shake with nerves; this particular boy of seventeen could be relied upon to call his Investiture robes a 'preposterous rig'; but what was this about 'recoiling' from 'homage'? He confessed to having made a painful discovery about himself:

It was that, while I was prepared to fulfil my role in all this pomp and ritual, I recoiled from anything that tended to set me up as a person requiring homage.

Here indeed was a fatal weakness in a future monarch. Homage was not being paid to one sort of 'person' or another – one 'requiring' homage, another not – but to the ancient institution of monarchy. No one was abased; the monarchy was honoured. It was honoured, moreover, in a manner hallowed by history. Taken out of its historic context, the act would be meaningless if not repellent. In short, the young Prince had failed to distinguish between the person and the office.

Unfortunately his mother smoothed things over without once getting to the point. 'You mustn't take a mere ceremony so seriously,' she said with the best intentions but the worst results. Her son continued to regard ceremony as 'mere', and perhaps himself as rather less 'mere' because he had seen through it.

There was one adult who could have put the matter in perspective: his father. King George had never been tempted to confuse his exalted office with his humble self. No need for him to 'discover' that he was an ordinary person. His first thirty years had made it obvious. Thus he was well equipped to teach his son the facts of common humanity. But when it came to the other side of the coin – symbolism, ceremony, homage – he seems to have given his son little guidance.

In the son's further defence it must be admitted that abroad he was sometimes treated like a totem. 'Touching mania' would suddenly seize a crowd. 'I touched him! I touched him!' triumphant Australian voices would shrill in his startled ears, busy Canadian fingers rip off his buttons and whip out his handkerchief. There was something about him which bewitched them. One of his milder compliments was to be called 'Sir Galahad'. Even his father would say, 'I must concede that you have done very well.' But there again, success itself was perilous. It reinforced his view that the person counted, not the institution.

There is in fact a superficial contradiction in the monarchy, one which his impressionable mind grappled with again and again but never solved. For the person clearly did count. Loyalty would indeed be stronger towards a human prince than a pompous one. After the Prince of Wales visited Sydney *The Times* correspondent reported that Labour, 'so critical of the Monarchy as an institution', was fair-minded enough 'to judge the heir to the Throne as a man'. But when the press added that 'the Prince had silenced criticism of the Monarchy for current life times', reality had succumbed to romance. Untrained as he was to judge between them, the Prince could only grope his way towards the throne along an unmapped path, irregularly paved with good intentions.

The Prince of Wales's progress, though somewhat circular, had its milestones. He passed an important one at twenty-five, when he left Buckingham Palace to live at York House, St James's. At last, a roof of his own.

His arrival at this state of relative independence can be traced to several impulses working in his life. There was the Twenties' sense of release and frenetic gaiety, epitomised by fancy dress, cocktails and bottle parties. If all these forms of entertainment did not equally engage the Prince, the total atmosphere of the time enchanted him. Bodies were perhaps vile, but the life of the élite was not. It may be of significance that burlesque clerical costumes were universal favourites. The clerical 'establishment' was much mocked during the Prince's heyday.

There is general agreement that the Prince 'craved' for violent exercise like polo, running and steeplechasing as well as for parties – both being ways of siphoning off his surplus vitality. While on his South African tour in 1925 he would stop the royal train in the middle of nowhere and, accompanied only by his valet, go for a cross-country run. 'Craving' is a word applied to him with odd consistency. It suggests a vehement but unsatisfied nature.

The Prince's interest in social work, though not exactly a craving, was strong and genuine. And it formed another outlet for tireless energy. His industrial tours through the 'sad and poverty-ridden places' of Britain struck a special chord both in his own heart and the people's. But he was no radical. During the General Strike his sympathy for the workers was probably less vivid than his father's. He hung around amateur action-stations, longing to join in, and lent his car and chauffeur to carry the Government newspaper, *The British Gazette*, to strike-bound Wales.

It was a fine inspiration which drove him to set up an informal Housing committee at York House under his chairmanship; but it was not quite such an innovation as he thought. His grandfather as Prince of Wales had served on (but not initiated) a Royal Commission on Housing in 1884. Socially, his aim was not so much to encourage reform as to forge new links between the monarchy and the people. As long ago as 1918, when the Russian Revolution convinced the young Prince that all monarchies must henceforth change their approach, his eyes had been fixed on personal relations. 'I am sure you won't mind', he wrote to his father, 'when I tell you that I'm out the whole of every day seeing & visiting *the troops* i.e. *"the people"*!!!!' As time went on, the press began to exaggerate and sentimentalise his visits: he had sat in a miner's cottage and held the hand of a woman in childbirth; he had kissed a mutilated face in hospital ... But he also founded King George's Jubilee Trust for Youth, and the Feathers Club; Lady Astor, a dedicated social reformer, noted the veins of true gold in his varied activities. 'You know, Sir, that you and I do not always agree', she began with characteristic pugnacity, but went on to congratulate him on giving a modern punch to the idea of monarchy, and making 'the way easier for your successors'.

The Prince did not make the way easier for himself – at least, with his father. But it was one of these attempts to get closer to '*the people*' which had finally brought him to his first milestone away from home. The disagreement was as usual over dress. King George had reproved his son for wearing a bowler hat at provincial civic functions instead of the orthodox 'topper'. Having failed to convince his father that a bowler would bring him closer to the people, the Prince carried his problem to that old and tried courtier, 'Fritz' Ponsonby, now Lord Sysonby. To the Prince's dismay, 'Fritz' whole-heartedly supported the King's general attitude, adding that H.R.H. had become 'too accessible'.

'The Monarchy must always retain an element of mystery. A Prince should not show himself too much. . . . The Monarchy must remain on a pedestal. If you bring it down to the people, it will lose its mystery and influence.'

'I do not agree,' retorted the Prince. 'Times are changing.'

At any rate he himself changed his establishment from Buckingham Palace to York House. There was to be an ironic epilogue. Two years after this dialogue, 'Fritz's' daughter Loelia held the first bottle-party. The venue was St James's Palace. Times had changed.

The next landmark was passed when the Prince was thirty-four. King George v's serious illness brought Prince Edward hurrying home from a tour. He described his arrival in a chapter of his memoirs entitled 'A Prophetic Date' – for he reached England on 11 December 1928, eight years to the day before his final exile. His brother Prince Albert met him at Victoria Station. With his habitual brevity and truth, Prince Albert summed up first their father's, then their mother's situation: 'You will find him greatly changed.' 'She has been wonderful.' But – 'she is really far too reserved; she keeps too much locked up inside her'.

The time had long since passed for Prince Edward to help his mother find the key. For he was about to pass another milestone cutting himself off still further. In 1930 the King gave him a castellated royal folly on the edge of Windsor Great Park, at Sunningdale. Its name was Fort Belvedere. This time a retreat of his own. 'What could you possibly want that queer old place for?' asked the King. 'Those damned week-ends, I suppose.'

With the 'chaff' curtain between the Prince and his father, and a curtain of reserve between him and his mother, how delightfully uncurtained was life at The Fort. Its brand new American-type showers and its wild shrubberies for him to tame, sometimes wearing his bearskin cap while he dug, in order to break it in for a military occasion – all this was to turn The Fort and its garden into his Land of Heart's Desire.

On that 'prophetic' 11 December 1928 Lord Esher had made an accurate observation about the Prince of Wales. 'He takes violent likes and dislikes.' Now he was about to take the most violent liking of his life. In this year of The Fort, 1930, he met Mrs Simpson.

The Prince's love for Mrs Simpson was his grand passion. That does not mean he had felt no deep commitment until he was nearly forty. On the contrary, he had been devoted to Mrs Dudley Ward from 1919 till 1934 – when she was dropped for Wallis Simpson dramatically and, some might think, callously. However, despite all his first love's unique charm, he realised Mrs Dudley Ward would never go away with him, as he often suggested. She gave him everything else: devotion, gaiety, intelligence. Perhaps it was this which drove him into sporadic unfaithfulness. Nevertheless until the spring of 1934 he had telephoned to Mrs Dudley Ward every single day. Then came a silence; and when she, puzzled, rang him, a telephonist's voice at the other end said, 'I have orders not to put you through.' Spiritually if not in fact it was Mrs Simpson who was now at the other end. But before we can understand Mrs Simpson's rocket-like ascent, it is necessary to look at the Prince's previous emotional development.

Arranged marriages repelled him. They were boring and loveless. He showed his feelings by calling the conventional marriage-market the 'grab bag' – a rag-bag of titles and heiresses trying to grab you, or you them. Lady Cynthia Asquith's picture of London society in 1918 emphasises his point. 'No girl is allowed to leave London', she wrote, 'during the three weeks of his leave and every mother's heart beats high.'

Soon, however, there were jokes about H.R.H. falling in love only with married women, and at least one husband declared his *unaccommodatingness*'. The reason for

Prince Edward's preference was not far to seek. Psychologically he had rejected his father and his mother had rejected him. Yet he craved for a supportive relationship. His biographer, Frances Donaldson, believes that 'in his relationship with first one and then the other of the two women for whom he cared deeply' he was 'actively seeking a dominating, quasi-maternal partner'. Mrs Simpson seemed to have all he needed consciously or subconsciously. She was exciting, resolute, ambitious, amusing, gifted, American – and childless. She was also phenomenally interested in his great career, though in this she was destined to resemble the wolf in *Red Riding Hood*.

Wallis Warfield Simpson was born in Baltimore. She afterwards provided many remarkable insights in her memoirs, *The Heart Has Its Reasons*. Her aunt, Mrs Bessie Merryman, remembered little Wallis insisting on a red rather than a blue sash at a children's party 'so the boys would notice you'. Yet there was never any need to hang out such flags. She swept Earl Winfield Spencer, a naval lieutenant, into matrimony. Unable to cope with her social panache, he temporarily broke down. After the divorce she led a 'lotus-eater's' life in Peking with her friends Mr and Mrs Herman Rogers, perfecting her skill at poker. In a sense she was to break away from a conventional upbringing as completely as the Prince of Wales himself. Meanwhile the once-divorced Ernest Simpson, an American-born, naturalised British citizen, had married this dazzling poker player and, after a Paris spree, brought her to England. They were introduced to the Prince of Wales by his current favourite, also a once-divorced American, Lady Furness, born a Vanderbilt. The place of America in Edward VIII's life is so vital as to merit a detour.

His first visit had been on his own initiative. To him, America stood for a new world where 'nothing was impossible' – not even a twice-divorced Queen of England. No more than Wallis did he like the old America of which his father might doubt-fully have approved. The Prince was criticised in America itself for encouraging 'social climbers'. This was in 1924. Later, King George retorted to what he considered scurrilous American newspaper reports by forbidding his sons to visit the place again. Prince Edward, however, had come home humming an American song to which young Wallis, unknown to him, was dancing: *A Pretty Girl is Like a Melody*. In 1930 he still hummed it in his heart, and for him pretty girls and attractive things proved quite surprisingly often to be American.

Mrs Simpson's story is one of challenge and response. Her first recollected con-versation with the Prince set the tone. He enquired about American central heating and she tartly replied: 'Every American woman who comes to your country is always asked that same question. I had hoped for something more original from the Prince of Wales.' He responded to the challenge. He kept in touch and by 1933 he had given her at least one 'more original' thing, a potted orchid which took a full year to bloom. It bloomed in 1934. That was the year when he decided to marry her. In April his love for Freda Dudley Ward had died and in May his affair with Thelma Furness ended. Wallis's orchid alone was blooming.

Since her first raw-boned encounter with the Prince, Mrs Simpson had indeed become something of an exotic. In 1935 Cecil Beaton, with his artist's eye, noted her amazing transformation: 'immaculate, soignée, fresh as a young girl; her skin was as bright and smooth as the inside of a shell, her hair so sleek she might have been Chinese'. Or Red Indian? She was said to be descended from Princess Pocahontas.

Undoubtedly the Prince had been good for her. Was she good for him?

With reservations, the contemporary diaries of both Channon and Nicolson agree that she had improved him. Frances Donaldson, however, points out that she was far from good for his reputation. 'The couple's ecstatic indiscretion, her flaunting of jewels he had given her, his infatuated delight in exhibiting in public his prize orchid, splashed him with more scandal in two years than he had known in the previous forty. Nevertheless she was 'good for him' in ending his discontent, giving him confidence and imposing the equability and good manners born of happiness. For Prince Charming had his moods. Not everyone was privileged to bask in his sunshine. In Australia Robert Menzies had at first been 'high-hatted' (despite the Prince's contempt for the headgear which had given its name to the behaviour); J.C.C. Davidson, a Cabinet minister in 1934, had always regarded him coldly; 'Chips' Channon clearly felt Wallis was too good for him. At any rate, beneath Mrs Simpson's stimulating spell, supplemented by judicious kicks under the table, he too was beginning to flower like the orchid.

In 1935 came the break with Ernest Simpson, after Mrs Simpson's holidays with the Prince on the yacht *Rosaura* and in Switzerland, during neither of which her husband was willing to be present. Under the Mediterranean moon and friendly chaperonage of Mrs Bessie Merryman, the Prince declared his love. Mrs Simpson advised her husband to return to an earlier love, Mary Kirk Raffray, now liberated by a divorce of her own. He eventually took the advice; but without ever denouncing his royal supplanter. In his eyes the monarchy was above criticism. Ernest Simpson had served George V in the Guards during the war and fortunately for Edward VIII was more British than the British. The nearest Ernest Simpson ever got to sourness was when he capped his wife's ecstatic description of herself as 'Wallis in Wonderland' by calling the Prince 'Peter Pan'.

Her husband's percipience annoyed her, for she was indeed living with the Prince in Never-Never Land, not England, a country she scarcely understood. Sir Samuel Hoare had seen at once that though she was very bejewelled, attractive and intelligent, she was also 'very American and with little or no knowledge of English life'. As for the Prince, the pipings of Pan were endemic in his forebears, as we have seen: Queen Alexandra, young Prince George his father, and now himself. The trouble was that he expected the Never-Never Land suddenly to materialise inside Buckingham Palace.

Mrs Simpson had been inside Buckingham Palace to be presented. In 1935 the orchid wilted momentarily when she was invited again and felt the King's eyes resting on her as she danced. She gave a premonitory shiver. No doubt the King did too. The Prince had never confided in his father, beyond casual references to 'my friend Mrs Simpson'. But King George knew. In melancholy vein he wrote after the Duke of Gloucester's wedding: 'Now, all the children are married but David.'

Long afterwards the Duke of Windsor told his lawyer and friend, Lord Monckton, that he would have spoken to the King but for his illness. His brother Bertie, however, was probably nearer the mark in citing their father's tendency to 'go for' David as the main barrier. Nor must one forget the Royal Marriages Act, by which the reigning monarch can oppose an unsuitable marriage in his family. King George V might conceivably have used it, through Parliament, despite his son's age.

Death supervened. The Prince's picture of his father dying in the arms of the 'Establishment', so to speak – 'Lord Dawson, as much courtier as physician . . . the Archbishop of Canterbury, a noiseless spectre in black gaiters' – reflects his own rebellious mood. His refusal to distinguish between the man and the office caused him to blench at his mother's first act beside the death-bed. She kissed her son's hand. It was that homage again. The time had come, he felt, to change all this. An unprecedented royal love-match, beyond protocol and beyond dreams, would be a good start.

Like all celebrated love-stories, this one had its share of prophecies, premonitions and coincidences. If few believed in them, the very fact that they have been observed is of interest. It is only during a time of great drama that people remember the small things.

We have already noted Mrs Simpson's 'shiver'. Mr Baldwin, the Prime Minister, seems to have had the first recorded premonition. Having accompanied the Prince during part of a royal tour, he had become as he believed *persona grata* to H.R.H. He met him at Folkestone in 1928 on his sudden recall when King George fell ill. The Prince, half expecting the worst, told Baldwin never to forget he could always speak freely to him about anything. A strange feeling swept over Baldwin that some day he would have to speak to him about a woman. 'Sir,' he said, 'I shall remind you of that.'

Mrs Simpson had taken the flowering of the orchid to be an encouraging symbol. With the accession of Edward VIII, the sombre omens predominated.

As the new King walked behind his father's coffin from King's Cross station to Westminster for the lying-in-state, the sapphire and diamond Maltese Cross on the top of the Imperial Crown broke off and rolled on to the pavement. Though a sergeant-major retrieved it with extreme deftness, the King had time to note the omen and say,

'Christ! What's going to happen next?'

'That will be the motto of the new reign,' said Walter Elliot to Robert Boothby, two MPs who had overheard the King's exclamation from their places in the crowd. Wallis Simpson was peculiarly impressed by the royal women in Westminster Hall,

all heavily veiled. (She told 'Chips' Channon afterwards that she had not worn black stockings since she gave up the can-can.) The veils between her and them were a good deal thicker than black gauze.

King Edward performed two symbolic acts on his accession. At Sandringham he immediately ordered the clocks to be put back. Edward VII and after him George V had kept the clocks half an hour fast. When King Edward VIII had the clocks put back within minutes of his father's death, Archbishop Lang wrote in his diary: 'I wonder what other customs will be put back also!'

King Edward then flew to London from Sandringham, the first reigning monarch to fly. The poet John Betjeman instinctively read much into that Sandringham flight, and pictured the older men of King George's generation staring,

> At the new suburb stretched beyond the runway
> Where a young man lands hatless from the air.

Notwithstanding the hatless arrival, King Edward VIII was proclaimed with medieval splendour. In London the five heralds read the proclamation in turn at St James's, Whitehall, Charing Cross, the Royal Exchange and Temple Bar. Their tabards were tied with crimson satin bows on shoulders and sides, and embroidered with the leopards of England and lion of Scotland in golden thread upon scarlet. The harp of Ireland was of gold on an azure ground. The trumpets shrilled, the people cheered. Not everything, however, was medieval. For the first time in history they heard the proclamation through a loudspeaker.

The presentiments continued. Buckingham Palace gave the new King strange 'feelings'. He wrote: 'One never tinkers much with palaces: like museums, they seem to resist change. Besides, a curious presentiment induced me to leave the rooms as they were. Somehow I had a feeling that I might not be there very long . . . I never got over the feeling of never quite belonging there.' In fact he never moved into his father's old rooms at Buckingham Palace but occupied the 'Belgian suite', in which he made just two innovations: a private line to The Fort and a single bed.

The 'Belgian suite', as he pointed out afterwards in his memoirs, had been so called from its having become the guest-suite for Queen Victoria's beloved 'Uncle Leopold', King of the Belgians. King Edward did not point out, or perhaps even remember, the salient pieces of advice on kingcraft which 'Uncle Leopold' had given to his young niece on her accession: to be extremely discreet; and constantly to express devotion for the Established Church.

The King's unloved Primate, Archbishop Lang, had 'glided' into his office at Buckingham Palace for a first visit, and 'glided' out again. He had uttered some enigmatic words about having tried to make his father see his conduct in the best possible light. After he had gone, the King felt 'the air in the room was heavy with portent'. And the Archbishop himself, agonised by the idea of consecrating '*him*' as King, began to believe that he might never have to do it. 'I had a *sense* that circumstances might change.' Even the little Duchess of York was conscious of a certain sultriness in the atmosphere: 'everything is different', she wrote to Lord Dawson, ' – especially spiritually, and mentally. . . . I mind things that I don't like more than before.'

There were things that Cabinet ministers also did not like. 'King Edward looked very nervous and ill at ease' was Mr Attlee's impression at the Accession Council. Attlee must have opened up the subject with Baldwin, for the Prime Minister replied by expressing his own 'anxiety for the future and his doubts as to whether the new King would stay the course'. They both meant that the royal rider was hampered by the loose horse galloping beside him. (The Earl Marshal's staff were to speak of 'the Loose Box' when preparing a kind of royal box for Mrs Simpson at the Abbey, in case she were not crowned.) However, there were others more buoyant at the Accession Council, such as Lord Beaverbrook. Not having got on with King George, he felt hopeful about the new monarch. And the country as a whole was blissfully ignorant of everything but their Prince Charming's previous record of sunshine and service.

True, one spectator who watched him in the funeral procession from Westminster to Paddington station expressed doubts. 'He looks as though the weight on his shoulders were just as much as he can bear.' But the *Daily Mirror* replied cheerfully on behalf of the people: 'They know his task to be a hard one; they are confident that he will not fail in it.' And someone remembered an encouraging prophecy about the English crown: 'a "King David" would reign over us for many years'. As for the man who had once foreseen a British republic following on the Russian Revolution, H. G. Wells was now prophesying about a different future. In February 1936 the film of his *Shape of Things to Come* depicted a handsome well-scrubbed couple, not altogether unlike the King and Mrs Simpson, about to take off in a space-yacht for a cruise round the moon.

Herr Hitler, General Goering and Dr Goebbels later attended a memorial service in Berlin for King George v. In Britain 'Patience Strong', the people's poetess, had written in his memory:

> His meekness mocked the vulgar pomp of military power,
> A selfless life is greater than a tyrant's blazing hour.

The tyrants, Mussolini and Hitler, were to be the new king's inheritance. Lord Beaverbrook had been elated to see the Russians transformed into 'respectable' potential allies against the tyrants, by wearing high hats at King George's funeral – 'we need Russia'. But King Edward's philosophy, in so far as it had crystallised on foreign affairs, moved along totally different lines.

What was this attitude which the Duke of Windsor would later call 'my philosophy'? It is not easy to pin it down. He often defined it by negatives. He hoped to be Edward the Innovator, not Edward the Reformer, though he claimed only a couple of inno-vations: he created the 'King's Flight' and made beards for Beefeaters optional. His philosophy was anti-'Establishment' and anti-officialdom. It was anti-League of Nations and anti-war. Indeed, as Prince of Wales he was believed to have conveyed to Hitler the idea that Britain would not fight when the Nazis occupied the Rhineland in March 1936 – a private *détente* which would not have assisted Anthony Eden, the Foreign Secretary, at a time of extreme diplomatic finesse. King Edward was also anti-State control and in favour of private enterprise, a balanced budget and the gold standard – all of which made him 'Gladstonian' rather than 'modern'. He insisted nonetheless that he had always wanted to be 'a King in a modern way'.

This note of 'modernity' amounted to two things: first, a general desire to let in fresh air on the monarchy; second, a particular resolve to get the 'hypocritical' attitude to divorce changed.

He rightly describes himself as having been 'acutely conscious of the changes working in the times', and 'eager to respond to them'. His response, however, was mainly limited to trivia. He preferred to walk to his office wearing a bowler hat and carrying an umbrella rather than ride in his Daimler – which the family had any-way christened mockingly 'the Crystal Palace'. Many of his business appointments were made direct by telephone instead of through a court official. Both these changes were in principle admirable, though the latter could cause irritation. James Frere, then Chester Herald of Arms, describes how the King would ring up the College and say abruptly, 'King speaking. Fetch Garter.' Once he dropped into Vandyke's photographic studio unheralded, thereby dislodging a sitter who was there by appointment.

His first (March) broadcast to his people was recognised, rightly or wrongly, as a challenge to the old order, in Compton Mackenzie's phrase, 'as the first stone from David's sling'. He told them he was that same man whom they had known better as Prince of Wales. This meant the man who worked overtime and played, some thought, overmuch. Above all it meant, though they did not yet know it, the man who loved Mrs Simpson. There were two million listeners to that broadcast, the greatest number so far in history.

As for the second aspect of the King's philosophy – divorce – he criticised the custom which barred many 'otherwise worthy and blameless people' from places like the Royal Enclosure at Ascot simply because they had been guilty parties in divorce. His aim was to reinterpret the church's teaching on marriage, by royal example at the coronation. Sitting beside Wallis Windsor, he on his throne, she on hers, he meant them both to be anointed, she as Queen, he as King and 'Defender' of the Christian faith. He saw himself 'defending' that faith against a too-literal interpreta-tion of the words 'for better for worse'. He intended to be a *Christian* King 'in a modern way'.

Here were patent sincerity and candour. Here also, it must be admitted, was an element of special pleading. For his 'circle', as it later came to be called, had had more than its fair share of divorces.

King Edward's ideas may have been right or wrong. His method of carrying them out was not that of a realist. He remained the dazzled child. No care, no caution. In Lady Diana Cooper's vivid phrase, The Fort was still 'a Walt Disney symphony toy', with the Prince in a white kilt and Wallis in 'tiny blue glass slippers' – a Cinderella hoping that the clock would never strike twelve and those smiling people round them never turn into timid mice or treacherous rats. Yet only six months were to pass before 'Chips' Channon was lamenting: 'The rats, oh, the rats.'

Meanwhile, as soon as the King ventured out of toyland into the real world, he was to make a series of fatal mistakes.

Channon's diaries were full of gossip about 'the "new Court"' (meaning the King's inner circle), which Channon also referred to as 'the royal racket'. In May 1936 he wrote:

It appears that the King is Mrs Simpson's absolute slave, and will go nowhere where she is not invited. . . .

From the start Channon had doubted whether the King would continue the 'same old round' as his father, of Sandringham, Ascot, Cowes and Balmoral. King Edward revelled in pleasure-cruises abroad as much as his father had detested them. Since he would indeed 'go nowhere' without Mrs Simpson, a Balkan holiday together that summer on a chartered yacht, the *Nahlin*, seemed the ideal choice. How wrong he was.

The cruise of the *Nahlin* was a riot of indiscretion on the part of the King. The foreign press and populace were not taken in by suggestions that he was working for good political relations with Turkey under cover of a private holiday. It was the other way round. Photographers snapped their cameras at the radiant pair and the King snapped his fingers at the photographers. No concealment was attempted. Pictures flew around the world, especially the United States. Crowds mobbed them shouting 'Cheerio!' and 'Long live love'. If the King had been criticised at home by the 'Establishment' for wearing a bowler and carrying an umbrella, how would they react to his going through the Corinth Canal on board the *Nahlin* wearing nothing but 'spick-and-span little shorts' (another of Lady Diana Cooper's inimitable descriptions) and binoculars? Deliriously happy, he had dispensed with even his 'tiny blue-and-white singlet'.

But his subjects at home still did not know. By common consent the British press averted their eyes from the Ruritanian romance. 'The relatively few photographs taken of him during his holiday,' lied the *Weekly Illustrated News* loyally, 'show a carefree holiday-maker with camera, short sleeves, hatless . . . [*sic*] the younger type of English tourist to the life.' The three dots in that quotation no doubt represented the invisible Mrs Simpson, who was not shown along with the carefree holiday-maker only because the *Weekly Illustrated News* had cut her picture out. The very day after the Abdication, 12 December 1936, this magazine was to publish a photograph of the pair hand-in-hand, admitting that many such pictures had been taken during the cruise.

When they returned home Mrs Simpson was dismayed to see her American press-cuttings. The slugs had got at the orchid. The King, however, was unflappable. 'It doesn't mean a thing.' He had been through it all before on his first visit to Long Island. Anyway, the British press were 'ignoring this nonsense'.

So now he invited her to Balmoral – and made his second mistake. 'By another of those unfortunate coincidences,' wrote the Duchess of Windsor long afterwards, her arrival at Aberdeen was on the very day of a grand hospital fête which the King had been unable to open because of court mourning. Court mourning, however, did not prevent him from meeting her at the railway station, a fact noted by angry Scots. The Scottish servants up at the Castle added their own complaint: American three-decker toasted sandwiches were required to be served, at Madam's suggestion, last thing at night. Queen Victoria, who had ordered even the smoking-room to be locked betimes in order to save the legs of John Brown and the other servants, would have turned in her mausoleum.

Worse still, the King had the names of his guests, including Mrs Simpson and Mr and Mrs Rogers, published in the Court Circular. Again, his great-grandmother could have told him that Court Circulars were inflammatory material. Had not *Punch* drawn attention to John Brown's position in a mock Court Circular?

> Balmoral, Tuesday.
> . . . In the evening, Mr John Brown was pleased to listen to a bag-pipe. . . .

Through the Court Circulars of September 1936 some members of the public began to suspect. But the King was as 'pleased' as John Brown had been to march round the Balmoral dining-table playing the bag-pipes himself. Piping, it might seem, while the Royal House smouldered.

He had resolved not only to marry Mrs Simpson but to marry her as soon as she was free. Alternately panic-stricken and confident, she filed a divorce petition against Ernest Simpson: 'It was too late for me to turn back.' At last, however, the King did take one precautionary step. He 'handled' (the Duchess's word afterwards) the British press on 16 October through the vital co-operation of Lord Beaverbrook and Esmond Harmsworth, the future Lord Rothermere. A 'gentleman's agreement' ensured that neither the divorce should be run as a front-page story nor the King's affair mentioned. Unfortunately for him, this latter agreement was to prove a great if understandable mistake. He rightly wanted to shield Mrs Simpson from a whirlwind of scandalous speculation which would have been caused, after all, by his own impetuosity. But the result was permanently to 'shield' their joint enterprise from any favourable winds as well. An opportunity to put his case to the public was thus thrown away, never to return.

Mrs Simpson obtained her decree *nisi* at Ipswich on 27 October, after she had duly testified to her accidental discovery of a letter from Mr Simpson to 'the other woman'. A fortunate coincidence this time. But a portentous new factor had meanwhile appeared on the scene. The King had had his first important interview with Baldwin.

7

Nine days' wonder

'God grant him peace and happiness but never understanding of what he has lost.' Mrs Baldwin.

THE interview between King Edward and Baldwin was not a success, perhaps because it was the first invasion of toyland and neither side was quite sure how to proceed. It took place at The Fort on Tuesday 20 October at 10 a.m. A date had been urgently requested by Baldwin as soon as he heard (on the 15th) about the forthcoming divorce. He had been in Wales recuperating from nervous exhaustion due to the international situation and returned to deal with a spate of angry letters about the divorce from overseas. But once inside The Fort he failed to advance. Though Mrs Simpson was mentioned and her divorce deprecated – 'Must the case really go on?' – the question of marriage was skirted in favour of an abstract lecture on kingly duties.

For his part, King Edward had not looked forward to the interview. Baldwin, in retrospect, had bored him with prosy John Bullish monologues during the Canadian tour. Now Baldwin irritated him by arriving in an undersized 'black beetle' of a car and delivering a king-sized lecture. He also had mannerisms. Did King Edward know how much the mannerisms of Sir Robert Peel had annoyed Queen Victoria? Baldwin would click his fingers, stretch his arms, silently wag his tongue inside his open mouth and polish his pipe on his nose. King Edward was happy to score a psychological victory. When Baldwin unexpectedly asked for whisky and assumed the King would follow suit, H.M. replied, 'I never take a drink before seven o'clock in the evening.'

Baldwin departed with the comment that 'the ice had been broken'. Only the ice in his whisky glass, thought the King sardonically. He concluded with the stipulation that he and Baldwin should settle the affair alone. 'No one else must interfere.' This was a warning by the suspicious king against consultations with the Dominions or church.

Mrs Simpson felt at last thoroughly uneasy, and Lord Beaverbrook, soon to be one of the King's outstanding supporters, afterwards reflected how shockingly both monarch and prime minister had fluffed their interview. They should have got down to bedrock, i.e. marriage.

At least the King began to invoke aid. On the 23rd he gave lunch at The Fort to an extremely able friend, Walter Monckton, KC, and having outlined the problem, touched on one possible solution. If 'they' really wanted someone more like King George v, 'Well, there is my brother Bertie.' Over The Fort had fallen the shadow of abdication.

At the King's suggestion his devoted lord in waiting Lord Brownlow, gave a dinner on 7 November for Beaverbrook to meet Mrs Simpson. Beaverbrook did not until this evening suspect that the King wanted to *marry* Mrs Simpson. Up till now he had assumed that another merry monarch was amusing himself along conventional royal lines. Instead the King was defying a convention accepted by his own grandfather and, not content with the prospect of a suitable mistress, wanted an unsuitable wife. This was the paradox inherent in the King's story. Whereas all his departures from convention were anathema to the 'Establishment', in this single case he was defying a convention which no member of the 'Establishment' could openly defend.

Next night (8 November) Mrs Simpson went to the opera 'dripping with emeralds' as a guest of Lady Cunard in the Royal Box – *absit omen*. On the 10th Channon detected a bad tone in the House of Commons. Why discuss the coronation, demanded a Socialist member, when 'there will not be one?' Cries of 'Shame! Shame!' only provoked shouts of 'Yes' and mention of the fatal name, 'Mrs Simpson'.

That same day Baldwin's high command was being formed. For the first time he took four of his senior colleagues fully into his confidence. A day later Channon got into an acrimonious argument in the members' dining-room at the House. 'Prince Charming charms his people no more,' he decided, the monarchy was slipping and might well crash over 'dear Wallis'. Only the jokes still made him smile: the American paper which headlined the Ipswich divorce as 'King's Moll Reno'd in Wolsey's Home Town'; and the cab driver who had given the Balmoral visit a bright send-off by saying, 'I'm sorry, lady' when Wallis told him 'King's Cross'.

That night the King travelled to Portland where he arrived in a storm at 4 a.m. on the 12th. That day he inspected seven warships in pouring rain. One of his admiring biographers, Lewis Broad, was to narrate that whereas Hoare, the First Lord of the Admiralty, wore a waterproof, the King did not. 'A small thing,' wrote Broad, 'but sailors take note of small things, and in this they saw the real difference between the Politician and the Monarch.'

Elated and exhausted by a strenuous job well done, the King arrived back at The Fort to recharge his batteries on Friday 13 November. The superstitious would be gloomily impressed. For on that fell date he came into collision with a man who was to compete with the Archbishop for top place in the royal demonology.

Major Alec Hardinge (afterwards Lord Hardinge of Penshurst) had been a loyal servant of the old court and as such marked down by 'Chips' Channon as one of the 'dreary narrow-minded fogies' due to be sacked. Nevertheless he was accepted by King Edward as his principal private secretary. In a sense it was a mistake. Despite Hardinge's devotion to the monarchy, his attempts at guiding the new king failed through an appearance of rigidity.

After the decree *nisi*, with its foaming wake of rumours, Hardinge realised that it was only a matter of time before the restraint of the press collapsed. But there was a sure defence: 'that is,' he wrote on the 13th to his unsuspecting master, 'for Mrs Simpson to go abroad *without further delay. . . .*'

They wanted to send her away. Feeling shell-shocked, the King made for a warm relaxing tub. He soon began to experience an upsurge of blazing wrath. But he had learnt enough self-control to say nothing whatever to Hardinge then or later. In a bemused state, the wretched Hardinge was to follow his master on a tour through the Welsh valleys, wondering if the letter had ever been received. Finally he found out. He had been superseded as an intermediary by Walter Monckton.

The King meanwhile acted swiftly. He summoned Baldwin on the Monday (16 November) to Buckingham Palace and this time broke the ice himself with a mighty crack. He hurled at Baldwin the two challenging words 'constitutional crisis'. Was that what Baldwin and the inner Cabinet feared as a result of 'my friendship with Mrs Simpson'?

'Yes, Sir, that is correct.' Baldwin then launched his own two challenging words, 'marriage' and 'divorce'. The Cabinet were alarmed, he said, at the idea of the King marrying a divorced woman, for whoever he married would have to be Queen. 'I believe I know,' he continued in his role of John Bull, 'what the people would tolerate and what they would not.' Baldwin then delivered another of his homilies on kingship, to the accompaniment of much emphatic finger-snapping, 'with a quick flip of the hand past his right ear.'

The King promptly dealt one last devastating blow with his ice-axe: 'I intend to marry Mrs Simpson as soon as she is free to marry.' And if the Government opposed him he was '*prepared to go*'.

Baldwin gave a jump, emerged from his smoke-wreath to announce, 'Sir, that is most grievous news . . .', and beetled off in the squat black car.

By now the King was doubly obsessed. He sensed Lang's 'shadowy, hovering presence' moving 'invisibly and noiselessly' about, though the Archbishop was in fact to play no part in the crisis (the King refused to see him). Next day the King hurried round to see his mother, before anybody else 'padded off to her' with a distorted account of the last Baldwin interview. Clearly it was Lang who might 'pad'. These two obsessions, the second of course being with Mrs Simpson, illustrated the polarisation of emotions which came so naturally to this strange man. Baldwin himself was to sum up this second obsession most vividly. During the interview of 16 November, he had found the poetic side of his own nature responding to the King's exalted state. 'His face at times wore such a look of beauty,' Baldwin told his son long afterwards, 'as . . . might have lighted the face of a young knight who had caught a glimpse of the Holy Grail.'

Before the final crisis, a last burst of manœuvres began with the famous visit of 18–19 November to South Wales. The King's heart was always moved by suffering and now was wrung anew by the patient hardship he saw. He began to wonder about his words, *'prepared to go'*. Was he not *prepared to stay*, if his people needed him? At any rate he would say something heartening. His relatively mild remarks to the miners on departure and arrival – 'Something ought to be done,' 'Something will be done' – were converted by legend into a dramatic and minatory message to his ministers: 'Something *must* be done.' A few Marxists did not like the sound of this regal interference in economic affairs; the right-wing were indignant. But thousands of simple and sincere people responded to their King's compassion. Out of their enthusiasm and gratitude would be formed a 'King's party' – if formed it were.

King Edward returned to London, again requiring to be recharged. This time his need was spectacularly met. Harmsworth, not Hardinge, proposed a new solution. His marriage to Mrs Simpson should be morganatic. She would be consort but not queen.

The King's hopes bounded, though Mrs Simpson thought the proposal somewhat 'inhuman'. A woman found fit for bed but not for state was surely little better than a mistress. Moreover, the King's circle were mistaken in thinking that English precedents existed for this entirely different Continental practice, which was based on a legal concern for blue blood. English law knew no such concern. And the oft-cited 'morganatic marriages' of the old royal dukes, Sussex and Cambridge, were not strictly legal marriages at all, since they had never been submitted to the Royal Marriages Act.

When the King put the proposal to Baldwin he was non-committal, but pointed out that the Dominions as well as the British Cabinet would have to be consulted. Neither he nor the King was aware that under the Preamble to the Statute of Westminster the sovereign's consultation was direct. So Baldwin promised, in answer to the King's request, to give him the Cabinet's 'advice' on the morganatic marriage, and also to act as intermediary with the Dominions.

As soon as the door shut behind his Prime Minister, King Edward realised that he had fallen into a trap. Having asked for 'advice' he was constitutionally bound to accept it. His more colourful course would have been to come out boldly for the right of every British citizen, however high, however humble, to marry according to personal choice provided the marriage was legal. But that bold appeal to the people, over the heads of the Cabinet, involved a 'King's party' to support him. This initiative, as we shall see, the King himself repudiated. A new initiative, however, was essential.

Lord Beaverbrook had left England after helping to silence the press. He hoped to relieve his asthma in Arizona. Suddenly an urgent cable arrived from the King imploring him to return and relieve the equally obdurate royal malady. 'He's not worth it,' advised Beaverbrook's friend Lord Castlerosse, the heavy-weight Irish peer and journalist. But Beaverbrook felt the King was worth it, and so was the cause.

The cause was political. Beaverbrook passionately desired an abdication – that of

Baldwin. He had no love for the Socialist 'establishment' either. If a 'King's party' could destroy both the old caucuses, Britain would be governed at last by a new party under her new King and Queen from the New World. Years later when Randolph Churchill asked Beaverbrook why he had fought so hard for the King he replied: 'To bugger Baldwin.' This was the supremely agreeable if ultimately barren pastime to which the incorrigible imp would often refer nostalgically: 'I would not have missed it for anything. I never had such fun in my life.'

As for the morganatic scheme, Beaverbrook knew his Dominions as well as Baldwin knew his Britain. The Dominions would never even look at it. 'Sir,' he expostulated, 'you have put your head on the execution block. All that Baldwin has to do now is to swing the axe.' The King muttered something about having to put his head somewhere.

The idea of an immediate 'King's party' was romantically seductive to Churchill but abhorrent to Monckton and others, who did not relish fighting shoulder to shoulder with 'royalist' Blackshirts and Communists. But there was yet another solution to which all the King's friends could agree. He must play for time. In any case marriage to Mrs Simpson was legally impossible until the following April, when the decree *nisi* would be made absolute. On 12 May 1937 he would be crowned. Let the 'King's matter' – as his marriage came to be called – rest for a year or so. Let Mrs Simpson go away. Once on the throne and with a longer record of popular rule, the King would be in a firmer position to marry the woman he loved. (Alternatively, his love for her might go away also. This was the secret hope of many of his friends.)

But the King could not bring himself to play for time; time spent apart from Mrs Simpson was limbo. Nor had he the ability or temperament to conduct a skilful game of manœuvre. As for playing at being the 'Archbishop's Anointed' during his coronation while in fact he intended to flout the church by promptly marrying a divorced woman – 'I refused to be crowned with a lie on my lips.' Such was the state of 'play' when a bishop of the church precipitated the crisis at the beginning of December.

As usual in this story the event seemed to be heralded by an omen. On its eve, 30 November, that celebrated Victorian glasshouse, the Crystal Palace, caught fire. Oddly enough the North Transept had been destroyed by fire on 30 November 1866. This time the whole thing was burnt to the ground, all but one great tower of strength, symbolising – whom?

On 1 December Bishop Blunt of Bradford initiated in his diocese a 'Recall to Religion', designed by Lang to be nation-wide and centring on the coronation. Blunt spoke somewhat critically of the new King, doubting his 'awareness' of the need for God's grace. The speech had been written several weeks ago, about the time of the King's first interview with Baldwin. Dr Blunt had not heard of Mrs Simpson by then, but knew about her now, as all the bishops did, from the Archbishop of

Canterbury. When Dr Blunt decided not to change his speech he only half knew what he was doing. In that sense his speech was truly 'a blow with a Blunt instrument', blunt as the Instrument of Abdication. In every other sense, the Bishop was keen-edged rather than blunt, being a fine scholar and an extreme socialist Anglo-Catholic.

Blunt or not, the speech was published prominently on 2 December by the northern papers, led by the *Yorkshire Post*. Its tough editor was called Arthur Mann, yet another name that seemed just right, for he spoke out like a man. Mrs Simpson's actual name did not yet stare from the editorial columns. But that too would come. The 'Nine Days' Wonder' had begun.

The Crisis or Nine Days' Wonder was destined to last from 2–11 December. News was handed out each day like bulletins from a sick room, wrote Vincent Massey solemnly in his diary. When the crisis ended he felt 'the patient had recovered'. There were rumours that Queen Mary would rule, the King being insane. Channon had pinpointed his 'insanity' already: 'The King is insane about Wallis, insane.' Many actual patients, however, were said to have received a shot in the arm. Evelyn Waugh's diary records: 'The Simpson crisis has been a great delight to everyone . . . pronounced turn for the better in all adult patients.' Quintin Bell tells us that his aunt, Virginia Woolf, liked problems presented in personal terms: she enjoyed the Abdication 'immensely'.

By Wednesday, 2 December, Baldwin knew the opinion of the Cabinet and Dominions. They had no use for the morganatic solution. South Africa was the most emphatic: abdication would be a sudden shock, morganatic marriage an ever-open wound. New Zealand was the most ingenious: not having heard of Mrs Simpson before, the Prime Minister would 'neither quarrel with anything the King did nor with anything his Government in the United Kingdom' did to stop him.

Armed with this ammunition, Baldwin reported to the Palace that three choices were open to H.M.: to renounce Mrs Simpson; to marry contrary to his ministers' advice and so force their resignation; to abdicate. The King answered tensely that at all costs he would marry, 'if necessary abdicate to do so'. But that evening, when he and Wallis paced in the cold dark garden of The Fort discussing the crisis, she totally rejected abdication. Temporarily she would leave England. Meanwhile she gave hope to the unhappy King by suggesting that he should imitate President Roosevelt and give a 'Fireside Chat'. The King at once thought of his father's Christmas broadcasts. He would ask the Cabinet to let him put his case to the people.

To the Cabinet, however, this proposal must have sounded like an offer by Mark Antony to praise Brutus – ' . . . *but* Baldwin *is an honourable man*'. In any case they could scarcely advise the King to put arguments of which they vehemently disapproved. So Mrs Simpson's project was to founder. But she herself was no longer at The Fort. On 3 December – 'that terrible day' – she fled from the press hubbub, escorted by Lord Brownlow, to the villa of Mr and Mrs Rogers in Cannes. Disguised as 'Mr and Mrs Harris', they endured a flight as wretched as any in history. Poor 'Mrs Harris' arrived with her head under a rug, crouching on the floor of the car. She was not to see England again for three years.

Meanwhile Monckton, Churchill, Beaverbrook and their team still worked feverishly for 'Mr James' (their code-name for the King, after St James's Palace) against 'Crutch' (Baldwin). But it was 'Mr James' who now needed the crutch. Desolate and alone, the King retained only one living link with Mrs Simpson, her dog Slipper. Gone were the days of the blue glass slippers twinkling round The Fort. His once peaceful retreat was beleaguered next morning by crowds of eager sightseers.

That Friday (4 December) Baldwin described Mrs Simpson's position to the House: if the King married her, she would have to be Queen like Queen Alexandra and Queen Mary – a shrewd analogy in its obvious fantasy. At The Fort late the same afternoon Baldwin himself rejected the King's cherished hope of a broadcast but made another formal appeal. 'There is still time for you to change your mind, Sir.' Time to jilt the woman whom he had promised to marry? The King told Baldwin equally formally, 'I will let you know as soon as possible.' But could there now be any answer except abdication?

Mrs Simpson for one thought there could. She had courageously tried to give him up. But her sacrifice was inaudible, being conducted on a shocking telephone line from Normandy, during her wild journey through France. In any case the King would have taken no notice, as was soon to appear. Moreover, the King's inner circle were still pinning their hopes on a policy of delay. The King had reluctantly become incommunicado to Beaverbrook ('Tornado') now that he expected to reach a settlement with Baldwin. But Churchill, Monckton and a few other intimates dined with him that night of the 4th. 'You must allow time for the big battalions to mass,' trumpeted Churchill, as if he saw himself as a new Prince Rupert, ready to take on Oliver Cromwell. The 'King's party', so-called, seemed to be gathering strength. Publicised vigorously by the whole Beaverbrook and Rothermere press, it burst out in graffiti, posters and slogans. 'God Save the King – from Baldwin', 'Flog Baldwin! B – the Bishops!' Notwithstanding all this, the King stuck to the most creditable decision of his life. He remained adamant against a 'King's party'. Anything was better than dragging the monarchy into politics. To that extent he was justified in writing afterwards: 'I abdicated because I chose the path of duty.'

On Saturday morning, 5 December, the King told Monckton of his final decision to abdicate. The news was passed to his other friends. 'Our cock won't fight,' said Beaverbrook. Monckton at once considered the King's personal position. Not only would his crown be lost to him for ever but his goddess also for many months. Monckton's own first marriage had broken down in 1934. Full of sympathy for his sovereign, he promised to ask Baldwin if Mrs Simpson's divorce could be expedited by special Act of Parliament. It seemed to them a small favour to ask for a king.

Sunday the 6th opened a calamitous week for King Edward. His Abdication Bill rolled inexorably forward, but a special Divorce Bill was rejected by the Cabinet. During MPs' weekend visits to constituencies they had found the provinces uncompromisingly pro-Government. Or as Channon would have said, all the 'Cavaliers' were in London while the country was profoundly 'Roundhead'. Lord Kemsley of the *Daily Telegraph* had told Baldwin as early as October that the Nonconformist conscience was still alive outside London. 'Every time I dipped into the bran-tub of provincial opinion during these days,' recalled the Labour leader Hugh Dalton, 'I pulled out a Puritan.' Baldwin was satisfied. 'I have always believed in the weekend,' he said; that weekend which King Edward had done so much to popularise. The 'Roundhead' news from the constituencies flashed round Parliament on the Monday. In the afternoon when Churchill tried to reiterate his arguments against 'any irrevocable step' he was howled down. 'Shut up! Sit down! Drop it! Twister!' Others, however, were still straining to prevent the irrevocable step.

That evening Mrs Simpson issued from Cannes a statement of her willingness 'to withdraw forthwith from a situation that was both unhappy and untenable'. The King did not take it seriously. Unknown to him, however, she was in the grip of a double 'plot' to make her give him up. This first plot had been hatched by Beaverbrook. Next morning, Tuesday, the second plot went into operation. In England there was fog. Over France, storm. Nevertheless Baldwin despatched Mrs Simpson's solicitor, Theodore Goddard, by plane to step up the pressure on Mrs Simpson for renunciation. Having a weak heart, Goddard took his doctor with him as well as his clerk. By one of those coincidences, Goddard's doctor happened to specialise also in gynaecology. Rumour promptly assigned the role of anaestheist to the clerk and the world waited for Mrs Simpson to give birth. It was a particularly cruel irony since her life-long regret was to have no children.

The King wound up the Tuesday with a memorable dinner-party at The Fort, including his two brothers and Mr Baldwin. Now that the irrevocable decision had been taken the King was no longer on the rack. Radiant in his white kilt, he quickly became the life and soul of a despairing party. 'Look at him,' murmured the brokenhearted Duke of York to his neighbour Monckton. 'We simply cannot let him go!' Baldwin, whom the King was never to see again, struck him as 'pasty and lifeless'; the King seemed to Baldwin like a man 'looking forward to his honeymoon'.

Wednesday showed how near the honeymoon was to vanishing for ever. Under Goddard's spur, Mrs Simpson once more prepared to renounce her lover. The King heard her saying over the telephone that she would go away. Back to Peking. Anywhere. He must keep his crown.

'But it's too late,' he cried triumphantly. The Instrument of Abdication was in being. 'You can go wherever you want – to China, Labrador . . . but wherever you go, I will follow you.' In his own way he was a hound of heaven. Again she seemed to surrender to him. That evening Baldwin informed him by letter that the Abdication Act, like every other Act, would require the Royal Assent. The traditional words *Le Roy le Veult* – 'It is the King's will' – would have a ring of special truth.

The dense fog had clamped down completely upon the English countryside. In this appropriate atmosphere Mrs Simpson came on the line for the last time begging the King not to renounce his throne. He replied that the only alternative was to renounce her for ever. Suddenly overwhelmed by the force of his pain, she capitulated.

The day of the Instrument had arrived. Always sensitive to atmosphere, the King noticed with pleasure that on this Thursday morning both the fog and the pressures outside The Fort had lifted. He was no longer beleaguered. He signed two Abdication documents involving many copies. They were witnessed by each of his three brothers. The King was almost eerily calm.

In a tense House of Commons the Prime Minister handed the Instrument of Abdication to the Speaker. He read it, his shaking fingers causing the three sheets of paper to whisper together. Then began the debate on the Abdication Bill. It was on the afternoon of this 10 December that Baldwin made the best speech of his life. He told the story as calmly as the King had signed the Instrument. Throughout, he insisted, the King had behaved as 'a great gentleman'. Baldwin did not add that Mrs Simpson had conducted herself like a great lady, as the King had stipulated in advance that he should. Baldwin, however, knew his people. To praise Mrs Simpson's part would have thrown the blame for the tragedy on the King. He was thinking not so much of the King as of the monarchy.

When Baldwin sat down members were too much moved to applaud: 'It was the silence of Gettysburg', wrote one MP, Harold Nicolson – an oration over the dead.

The debate continued. Historians have tended to remember the fulminations of the five who voted against Mr Baldwin rather than the 403 who followed him. True, a handful of Scottish Socialists spoke of a collusive divorce and outdated monarchy. But the Conservatives, Liberals and Labour party *en masse* supported the Bill. Morrison afterwards applauded the Commons' 'traditional policy of unanimity in time of major constitutional trouble'. The Bill of Abdication became law next day in the House of Lords. *Le Roy le Veult.*

All that morning the King had been polishing his farewell broadcast. No one could silence him after 1.52 p.m., for then he would have ceased to be King. Broadcast he would. He handed the speech to Churchill. This was not the first time he had wisely asked the mighty orator to improve a jejune draft. Earlier in his reign he records having shown a speech to Churchill for him 'to read and embellish'. Churchill embellished the famous broadcast with characteristic touches. His *chef d'œuvre* was to present the unlucky bachelor King as cruelly deprived of his human rights, compared with the Duke of York:

> And he has one matchless blessing, enjoyed by so many of you and not bestowed on me – a happy home life with his children.

It made the Archbishop very angry.

The owner of the matchless blessings, now King George VI, was summoned to The Fort by telephone, together with the Duke of Kent, Duke of Gloucester, and Prince Louis Mountbatten, shortly before the broadcast was delivered at the Castle. King George arrived first. The brothers bestowed on each other mutual encouragement and affection. Then,

'By the way,' asked King George, 'have you given any thought as to what you are going to be called now? . . . How about the family name of Windsor?'

'Duke of Windsor . . .' The elder brother nodded, liking the sound. The King had already decided he should be a *royal* duke who, by convention, could not speak in Parliament. Officials had thought of calling him 'Mr Edward Windsor', but his brother had pointed out that he could then sit for Parliament. 'Would you like that?'

Edward dined with his family at Royal Lodge. Before the end, Monckton arrived to take him up to Windsor Castle. The stones of the old place were about to absorb, quietly as ever, another historic scene. In the Augusta Tower, the director of British Broadcasting, Sir John Reith, made the introduction: 'This is Windsor Castle. His Royal Highness, Prince Edward.' The Prince moved across to face the microphone, accidentally kicking the table-leg with his foot. Some of the millions of listeners imagined the nonconformist Reith had banged the door disapprovingly as he went out.

> At long last I am able to say a few words of my own. . . . I have found it impossible to carry the heavy burden of responsibility . . . without the help and support of the woman I love. . . .
>
> I now quit altogether public affairs, and I lay down my burden. . . .
>
> And now we all have a new King. . . . God bless you all. God save the King.

When Prince Edward had finished he put his hand on Monckton's shoulder with the words, 'It is a far better thing that I go to.' The atmosphere seemed to call for quotation. Churchill had said goodbye to King Edward the day before, thumping his stick on the gravel and chanting,

> *He nothing common did or mean*
> *Upon that memorable scene.*

The unfortunate Archbishop, however, was to be less successful when he came to recite Shakespeare.

The family meanwhile reassembled at Royal Lodge. Soon the exhausted Queen Mary and her daughter went home. But midnight had struck before the moment came for the parting of the four brothers. The future Duke of Windsor bowed to the new King. This time an anguished cry broke from his brother the Duke of Kent:

'It isn't possible! It isn't happening.'

In the small hours of 12 December Monckton drove his friend to Portsmouth. As they crossed Harford Bridge Flats they both remembered training as young officers in 'this obscure part of England' during the summer of 1914. Actually Harford Bridge was once a busy posting-stage, and it was from here that the Duke of Wellington, living at Stratfield Saye, would receive his messages. The message which suddenly came out of the night to the future Duke of Windsor was a significant one. At twenty he had begun to train himself on these heaths for 'the real world' of the front line; now at forty-two he had freely chosen the 'real world' again. As he left his country's shores in the destroyer *Fury*, he knew that he had always seen the world of kingship as unreality.

The farewell broadcast had been something of a portent. Broadcasting itself was still relatively novel, the BBC not yet having reached its first decade. People were deeply touched by the skill and poignancy of the performance. A copy of the speech was swiftly on sale, its cover adorned with gothic lettering wreathed in roses, thistles and shamrocks. Entitled 'The Prince's Farewell to the Nation', the leaflet possessed all the Victorian pathos of *The Arab's Farewell to his Steed*. The young were not unmoved, though some felt surprised to hear words like 'the woman I love' on royal lips. It sounded more like a romantic novel. In America the young called him a 'decent guy' but 'a fool to throw in his mitt'. The sophisticated, such as 'Chips' Channon, squeezed the last drop of vinegar and sugar out of the situation. Channon listened to 'that unmistakable slightly Long Island voice', in a fellow politician's home, Oliver Stanley. 'I wept, and I murmured a prayer for he [*sic*] who had once been King Edward VIII. Then we played bridge.' One heart . . . two hearts . . .

Archbishop Lang delivered a broadcast on 13 December – ill-omened day – which was intended to be at once sympathetic and admonitory. Alas, he adorned a perfectly respectable thesis – the conflict between private happiness and public duty – with quite unacceptable rhetoric.

What pathos, nay what tragedy, surrounds the central figure of the swiftly moving scene.

Lang saw the central figure surrounded by an 'alien' social circle, whose fault it was that this once beloved and gifted sovereign had developed a hedonistic 'craving'. He reminded listeners that King James II – that other disloyal son of the Established

Church – had fled on the 11th day of December, 248 years before his equally benighted descendant did precisely the same thing.

In the darkness he left these shores . . . 'The pity of it, O, the pity of it!'

Lang concluded by committing to the infinite mercy of God this royal waif 'wherever he may be'.

Few thought Lang had shown any mercy himself. That 'wherever he may be' made the ex-King sound like a torn-up envelope blowing about Europe, cried the furious Compton Mackenzie. (It was a quotation from the prophet Jeremiah to the exiled Israelites, which Mackenzie must have known.) H. G. Wells said His Grace ought to be horsewhipped. Channon called him 'the most conspicuous rat of all'. But it was the writer Gerald Bullett who punished Lang most savagely for his blunders:

> My Lord Archbishop, what a scold you are!
> And when your man is down, how bold you are!
> Of Christian charity how scant you are!
> And, Auld Lang Swine, how full of cantuar!

When Lang's wonderful voice recited 'O the pity of it' from *Othello*, the result should have been pure oratory but it sounded pure cant. So did his ill-advised attack on the ex-King's 'circle'. Who formed this circle? Of course Lang mistily conceived of cocktail-parties, Long Island accents and divorcees thick as thieves in Vanderbiltia. But one of his suspected English targets, Lord Brownlow, afterwards challenged him to name names. Was it the Brownlows, the Edens, the Duff Coopers? He had learnt wisdom at last and made no reply.

For the rest, Lang was neither an insensitive nor a canting priest. Indeed his sensitivity was abnormal. Years ago, during the First World War, he had said a good word for the Kaiser in front of a throng of jingoes. He had been torn to shreds by the press, his thick black hair fell out and grew again pure white. That was a truer picture of Auld Lang Syne. Lang was right that the King had craved for something impossible: to marry a twice-divorced woman with two husbands still living and place her on the throne of Queen Victoria, Queen Alexandra and Queen Mary. American? That mattered not at all. A commoner? The Labour party and Dominions would have welcomed her. But string all three factors together – trans-Atlantic, twice-divorced, commoner – and you had the single devastating word, 'unsuitable'. As a cabby twice said to Kingsley Martin, 'It wouldn't have done. It wouldn't have done.'

The Royal House of Windsor has already passed in these pages through two transformations. A Coburg has become a Windsor, a king has become a duke. The character of the House is also emerging. It moves with the times. King George V 'progressed with his people'. King Edward VIII progressed to the edge of the stage and over. Was he, like her, 'unsuitable'? He often said so, and then again said the opposite. He wanted to reign – but only with her. He spoke of the 'drudgery' of kingship. If he had been president of a company he would have resigned his post and found another that suited him better. But he could not resign, only abdicate. He sometimes spoke of the hereditary principle as if it should have been made more presidential. Once think along those lines, however, and you invite the nation to install a president instead of a king.

These and like questions must wait until we finally consider the effects of the modern age on kingship. The effects of the Abdication on the next reign were immediate. It is hard not to hurry on into the reign of King George VI, treating the Duke of Windsor's middle and old age like that of the mythical Solomon Grundy, who was born on Monday, married on Wednesday, died on Saturday, buried on Sunday; 'That was the end of Solomon Grundy.' Nothing of his later years concerns this story directly. But a photograph taken during the day's work in his beloved French garden ironically recalls a speech once made by Baldwin, extolling his family firm. No one was ever sacked from Baldwin's, said the orator; and a large number of old gentlemen used to spend their days sitting quietly on the handles of wheel-barrows smoking their pipes. That was to be the Duke of Windsor to the life – except that he had been sacked.

When he died, Harold Wilson said on behalf of the Labour party, 'he bridged the generation from the Victorian age into which he was born to the hard hit, partly cynical, bewildered post-war generation.'

It is true that he and his friends seemed to have a 'post-war' look in common. A furrow between the brows, a wrinkling of the forehead; something quizzical and uncertain. Sitting side by side as man and wife, the well-groomed, flawlessly polished Duke and Duchess of Windsor are forever orphans of the storm.

PART

4

KING GEORGE VI
AND
QUEEN ELIZABETH

8

Merit not flairs

'*Starting at the top – the King and Queen are doing very well – they are basing themselves on real work and merit and not on flairs.*' Lord Dawson, 1938.

THE life of King George VI was eventful in a special sense. Time and again the outside world would change the direction of his development. His identity was hammered out from the very start by events, great and small, beyond his control. He has been fortunate in his biographer Sir John Wheeler-Bennett, an outstanding historian admirably equipped to gather a crowded half-century under the canopy of a single life. Though the canopy was necessarily tasselled and fringed with gold, the man himself was saved by the interaction of his inner and outer life from ever becoming a *roi soleil*. Few could have deduced from this monarch's inauspicious beginnings the fullness and dignity of his end.

The Abdication came more than half-way through King George VI's adult career. (He was twenty-one in December 1916, forty-one at the time of the Abdication in December 1936 and fifty-six when he died in February 1952.) There had been no opportunity for studying kingcraft. It was not until 17 November 1936 that he knew for certain his brother intended to marry Mrs Simpson. That left him precisely three weeks and three days to prepare. But to prepare for what? Hardly anyone was to guess the Abdication's effects correctly. Those who wrote memoranda seemed to hold as many different views as they held pens. There were the prophets of gloom, inspissated or moderate. In the Upper House Lord Salisbury viewed the Act of Abdication as 'almost desperate'. Among MPs, Duff Cooper was hardly less alarmed. He reflected that 'no such event had ever happened in English history'. (Richard II did not voluntarily abdicate his great inheritance and Parliament declared the throne void after James II's nocturnal flitting.) The monarchy would suffer from loss of prestige, the nation from loss of such a striking personality. This fear (afterwards described by Duff Cooper as 'groundless') implied doubts about the personality of the new king. No one shared those doubts more agonisingly than King George VI himself. Against Salisbury's word 'desperate' he could put his own word 'crumble'. For he had written to one of the King's secretaries as the Abdication drew inexorably closer:

If the worst happens & I have to take over, you can be assured that I will do my best to clear up the inevitable mess, if the whole fabric does not crumble under the shock and strain of it all.

It was only to be expected that those who had most fervently supported Mrs Simpson should foresee, as did 'Chips' Channon, a sudden void: 'Honor and I will be out of the royal racket having backed the wrong horse. . . .' Churchill regretted the public obsession with the Abdication and its sequel. Foreign affairs were forgotten. 'Our Island might have been ten thousand miles away from Europe'. As for Mrs Simpson's compatriots, it was hoped by Hugh Dalton that they would not be 'affronted'. But some of the American young saw it as a chance missed by the British to scrap 'a lot of out-of-date tradition that means nothing – and start running their country on American lines.'

From the Dominions came regrets for the lost leader. J.A.Lyons, Prime Minister of Australia, read King Edward's message of abdication to the House on 11 December and sat down on the following melancholy thought: '. . . how profoundly grieved we all are at this sudden termination of a reign which seemed so full of golden promise'. The promise of the new reign was leaden. Or, as Lord Beaverbrook saw it, there was no promise at all; nothing but foreboding and an unprecedented query:

With the existing King we knew where we were. We knew his defects and limitations. But with a new King we have to start all over again. And maybe we will find ourselves up against a new lot of defects of a different kind.

It is time to travel back over the previous forty-one years and begin to uncover the character of the Unknown King.

Prince Albert Frederick Arthur George of York managed to score two bad marks on the day of his birth. He elected to arrive on 'Mausoleum Day', 14 December 1895; he was a second son when his parents wanted a daughter. On the first point Queen Victoria graciously accepted the Duchess of York's apologies for having given birth on an anniversary dedicated to death: that of the Prince Consort's and Princess Alice's passing. Mollified, the old Queen hazarded a guess that the untoward coincidence might turn out 'a gift of God'. The baby's uncle Prince Frank of Teck went one better. 'I am glad they have got their king guarded,' he wrote, as if dynasties were a game of skill. He was thinking of Prince Eddy and Prince George, but the gnomic words were to apply even better to King Edward VIII and King George VI. As for little Bertie's failure to be a girl, his grandmother Queen Alexandra looked beyond him to a happier future: 'better luck next time!!!'

Ill-treatment by the baby's nurse laid the foundations for a delicate constitution. He was regularly given his afternoon bottle during the nursery carriage-outing which, in his biographer's words, resembled a Channel crossing, ' – and with corresponding results'. Acute gastric troubles in babyhood were followed by childish disabilities. He developed, like his father and all his brothers, except David, knock knees. This was treated by splints worn, to begin with, all night and part of each day. At eight he wrote to his mother with the artificial cheerfulness of the supervised child:

I am sitting in an armchair with my legs in the new splints. . . . I have got an invalid table, which is splendid for reading but rather awkward for writing at present,. I expect I shall get used to it.

At least the splints straightened his legs in due course. Something else, however, remained to be straightened out which never was, until his marriage. It went much deeper than the stomach or leg troubles, and emerged as an appalling stutter. Stammering can start from the wrong treatment of left-handedness. Since Prince Albert was left-handed and his stammering first showed itself between the ages of six and seven, there is a strong presumption that it was caused by his being forced to learn to write with his right hand. His father had instructed the little prince's tutor to break the left-handedness. A truly horrifying picture emerges of the eight-year-old child pinned by his legs to an invalid chair, while his 'awkward' right hand refuses more stubbornly than ever to control the pencil.

With legs, hands and tongue all in rebellion against parental attempts to make them conform, it is not surprising that their small master had his moments of total mutiny. His tears, rages and despairs angered his parents; the mimicking of his stammer by his siblings angered him. It is no wonder that he pulled his German tutor's beard while David, on the contrary, applied himself to his German studies. In most servant-run mansions there was usually at least one good-natured maid to favouritise the 'Master Bertie' of the nursery, while the top starch spoilt the 'Master David'. But at Sandringham there does not seem to have been anyone who loved Bertie best.

Sibling trouble has been mentioned. Prince Albert's place in the family did not help him. In the self-contained group of the three elder children, he occupied the withdrawn middle slot between a forthcoming elder brother and a petted, mercurial sister. Prince Albert's temperament, though desperately shy, was also mercurial; but in his case unlike Princess Mary's it was not indulged. The inevitable comparison of himself with his elder brother was probably as great as any of his handicaps. He was an ugly duckling, said a contemporary, to Prince Edward's cock pheasant. Not that the relations between the brothers were anything but affectionate. Actual coldness would have been unthinkable within the House of Windsor, where family feeling was always strong. Bertie as much as anyone admired and loved David. David protected Bertie, sometimes from parental criticism: as when he stoutly argued the case for rejoicing because Bertie's mathematical marks, though far from resplendent, had actually raised him two or three places from the bottom of the class.

It was not the occasional tiff but the permanent subordination which damaged the younger brother. Even in youthful wickedness, David must be the superior. 'Bertie and I,' the Duke of Windsor wrote in *A King's Story*, '– and mostly I – came in for a good deal of scolding. . . .' *Mostly I* was to be an alternative motto to *Ich Dien* which continued to operate right up to the Abdication. In games David must win. When they played an election race-game in 1906, David chose to back Sir Henry Campbell-Bannerman, 'no doubt because he led from the start' – while Bertie was born to be second.

And in so far as the elder brother both supported and faintly despised the younger, there crept in an element of patronage. Walter Monckton remembered that during the crisis King Edward VIII was continually referring to Bertie's convenient existence. Bertie gave him the excuse to abdicate. King Edward himself brought this to light in his memorable phrase, 'There is always Bertie.' It has the same whisper of insensitivity as appeared in 1915 when he claimed the freedom to be killed, if necessary, because 'I have four brothers'. Indeed this attitude finally caused him, in *A King's Story*, to picture Bertie in a guise which suited his own book but was far from true to life – as a reincarnation of King George V:

. . . my brother Bertie, to whom the succession would pass, was in outlook and temperament very much like my father. The patterns of their lives were much the same, with the steady swing of habit taking them both year after year to the same places at the same time and with the same associates.

In fact Lady Airlie remembered Prince Albert bemoaning the sameness of King George V's Ascot parties quite as forcibly as the Prince of Wales. There were differences between King George V and King George VI, as we shall see. It was by no means through all the same qualities that each became a good king. Nor did it assist Prince Albert's development that he should begin in parental splints and continue on a brotherly bed of Procrustes.

At this point it is necessary to heed a warning of Prince Albert's biographer: not to picture his youth in too sombre a tone. Sandringham was a cheerful place for children, just as it had been in the generation before. If Prince Albert had had no chance to develop strong affections, he could scarcely have achieved an ideal relationship with wife and children. Yet this he did.

Prince Albert followed his elder brother to Osborne and Dartmouth. There had seemed a real danger first, that his idleness would cause him to fail the written papers for Osborne, and second, that his stammer would prevent him passing the oral. Each time, however, a will to survive just carried him through. His Sandringham tutor looked forward to the discipline of Osborne bringing out new qualities in this 'very straight and honourable . . . very kind hearted and generous' twelve-year-old.

Naval discipline, however, could not light the spark in an unawakened mind. It did steady somewhat the volatile, easy-going, athletic and popular cadet, who could run much faster than he could add up. He left Osborne at fourteen with the position of 68th out of 68: 'P.A. has gone a mucker', wrote his Osborne to his Sandringham tutor. As a naval cadet still young for his age and lacking in confidence, 'P.A.' left Dartmouth at seventeen for a training period at sea with the position of 61st out of 67.

It is almost a relief to know that he had earned some high marks – for scrapes: 'skylarking' and talking, for which he was appropriately punished.

His final training as a cadet was on board the *Cumberland*. He benefited from entering a world for the first time which his brother had not already captivated. The ugly duckling was at last out of the cock pheasant's shadow. But alas, he found how completely he could be floored by popular fervour. Once while trying to make a short speech of thanks in Jamaica he was subjected to so much 'touching mania' that his stammer took control and almost brought him to a standstill. In face of adversity, however, the Prince's natural ingenuity and humour came to his rescue. He managed to cut down his public appearances, as distinct from speeches, by fixing with a fellow-cadet who happened to be his double, to stand forth and smile in his place. Whipping-boys had been known in the royal past. It showed a rare degree of shyness to require a 'smiling-boy'.

For the next four years, 1913–1917, 'P.A.' was to be 'Mr Johnson' in the Royal Navy. He joined HMS *Collingwood* of the First Battle Squadron in September 1913 and it was as an ordinary midshipman, sometimes black-faced like his father from coaling, often, unlike his father, desperately seasick, always developing the common touch, that he steamed round the Mediterranean on manœuvres and nearer and nearer to the First World War.

One day 'Mr Johnson' reported to H.M. that he had acquired a severe black eye: 'I fell out of my hammock, with the help of someone else, and hit my eye on my chest.' His father, a seaman himself, did not misinterpret the last phrase as a curious anatomical accident, but advised his son to 'do the same to the other fellow' on his sea-chest. In the great world, Austria was about to 'do the same to the other fellow' after the Sarajevo murders. By the end of July, thanks to the prompt steps of Admiral Prince Louis Mountbatten, soon confirmed by Churchill, the Test Mobilisation was extended and the Grand Fleet began its crucial moves from Portland to Scapa Flow. An eighteen-year-old midshipman on *Collingwood* noted that they had left Portland at 7 am on the 29th. He kept the afternoon watch alone. Later he went to 'night defence stations, the 4-inch guns bristling for enemy destroyers'. He kept the first watch. Around midnight they slipped safely through the Straits of Dover.

This should have been the atmosphere for his next twenty-two months: efficiency, secrecy, waiting at Scapa Flow with mounting excitement, pouncing, waiting again impatiently 'to see if the Germans could fight'. But before the end of August 1914 fate struck him amidships, as it were, with an agonising duodenal ulcer, so that it was a question whether the King's son rather than the Germans could fight. Even on the operating table his misfortunes dogged him. The acute pain – 'I could hardly breathe' – was diagnosed as appendicitis. After six deeply depressing months divided between sick-leave and staff work at the Admiralty – 'Nothing to do as usual' – he was at last allowed back to *Collingwood* and his friends, only to succumb three months later to fresh attacks of pain and vomiting. This time he was condemned to two months' severe treatment on a hospital ship for 'catarrhal condition of the stomach wall', followed by various ways of filling in time, including a visit suggested by his thoughtful brother to the Western Front. The suffering he glimpsed was horrific and the endurance magnificent, but it was not his war. He was pining for naval warfare. Apart from his own conscience and spiteful gossip about the King's son 'doing nothing', his whole heart and soul were bent on being there for 'the Day'. It came at last with the terrible and eerie Battle of Jutland on the afternoon of 31 May 1916, hardly more than three weeks after Prince Albert, now a sub-lieutenant, had rejoined *Collingwood.*

On 30 May *Collingwood* and the rest of the First Battle Squadron had put to sea, but the weather seemed to have no connection with the merry month, being a shredded nightmare of mist fit only for valkyries to ride. As ill luck would have it, the 21-year-old Sub-Lieutenant 'Johnson' who should have been in 'A' turret was recovering in the sick-bay from a surfeit of soused mackerel. The call to 'Action Stations' on the afternoon of the 31st effected an instantaneous cure. Like a bomb he was out of his bunk and into his turret. Or rather, on top of his turret, in order to get a better view of the gun-fire from the German battle cruisers, flashing a lurid orange through the murk. 'I was up there during a lull', he wrote, 'when a German ship started firing at us, and one salvo "straddled" us. We at once returned the fire. I was distinctly startled and jumped down the hole in the top of the turret like a shot rabbit!!' Prince Albert was probably as near to death as his brother had been the year before at the Front, when he returned from a tour to find his waiting chauffeur and car destroyed by a shell. Among the dreadful shapes of death which lurked and heaved all round, the Prince's ship remained miraculously unscathed. There is a whiff of disappointment in his report: 'I saw visions of the masts going over the side and funnels hurtling through the air etc. In reality none of these things happened and we are still quite sound as before.'

The Germans had inflicted even graver damage on Britain than vice versa. Nevertheless the enemy ships steamed painfully away into the fog and smoke, not to reappear as the High Seas Fleet during the War. And Prince Albert, like every sufferer from a chronic complaint, dared to hope yet again that his own enemy would never return.

The Battle of Jutland was Prince Albert's great adventure. By recovering just in time to be present he had enjoyed the minimal amount of good luck which a man needs in life. Less than three months later his enemy was back.

This time the ulcer was correctly diagnosed. He hung on for another year with intermittent pain and even more intermittent hope. Then at last his entreaties to have an operation and put an end to his semi-invalidism, were granted. His health was restored but not his naval career. It was good-bye to the sea.

Neither of Prince Albert's next assignments really established a new pattern for his life. He was to continue his war with the Royal Naval Air Service at Cranwell, (later amalgamated with the Flying Corps to form the Air Force), and to introduce himself to peace at Cambridge. But with the loss of the Navy he was still missing his *raison d'être*.

Flying was not his passion. But the squadron of 'Boys' whom he commanded caught his imagination and stimulated his later concern for youth. 'Mr Johnson' had passed away and he was now known affectionately as 'P.A.'. In fact he was the 'Officer Commanding Boys', showing a touch of his father's stern discipline towards cadets who persistently refused to keep their huts clean. A companion of his naval days, Dr Louis Greig, taught him the meaning of friendship and family life. Married with children (Greig was forty) he invited his much younger friend into his home at Cranwell. It was the smallness which delighted Prince Albert. He had found something hitherto wanting from his own existence. When hostilities ended his job at Cranwell ended too, and after 'entering' Brussels triumphantly in the entourage of King Albert, and entering Paris equally happily with his brother David, Prince Albert decided to return home, work in the Air Ministry and learn to fly. This was an act of resolution. He did not enjoy it. But one of his rewards was to go down to history as the first King of England to be a fully qualified pilot.

In the Air Ministry he also got to know and admire the race of civil servants, an important asset for a modern king. His biographer quotes his feeling words at a Civil Service dinner in 1928:

They never spare themselves but continue to serve their country until at last the sad day comes when they, like their files, must be stamped with the letters P.A. ['Put Away'] and disappear.

Ten years earlier 'P.A.' had stood for Prince Albert. Where was he to be 'put away' next, before they found him a real niche?

He did not rate Cambridge the 'dreary chore' which his brother had rated Oxford. He was much older for one thing, having gone up to Trinity College during his twenty-fourth year. He even enjoyed performing the duty of every royal generation, namely, the study of Bagehot and the *English Constitution*. His brilliant young tutor, J.R.M. Butler, instructed him in Bagehot's views about the conflict between 'mystery' and 'daylight' in the monarchy.

Above all things [wrote Bagehot] our royalty is to be reverenced, and if you begin to poke about it you cannot reverence it. . . . Its mystery is its life. We must not let in daylight upon the magic.

Prince Albert was able to reply with a family anecdote about Queen Victoria, who had a way of applying a blanket of mystery to an awkward situation that was all her own.

Sir William Harcourt had been sent for by the Queen after Mr Gladstone's resignation. Would she ask him to be her Prime Minister? The following conversation took place. The Queen: 'Good morning, Sir William Harcourt.' W.H.: 'Good morning, Ma'am.' The Queen: 'I hope you are well, Sir William Harcourt.' W.H.: 'Yes, thank you, Ma'am.' The Queen: 'I hope Lady Harcourt is well.' W.H.: 'Yes, thank you, Ma'am.' The Queen: 'Good morning, Sir William Harcourt' – whereupon he retired. It was all Gladstone's fault, who had sent Harcourt to the Queen by mistake. Harcourt in fact knew that her next Prime Minister was to be Lord Rosebery, not himself, but his hopes must have risen nonetheless, only to be dashed by the Queen's inexplicable behaviour. As for Queen Victoria, she was far too old and wise to let in any daylight on the mystery.

Prince Albert's stammer and shyness still impeded him in making many contemporary friends, apart from his cousin Lieutenant Lord Louis Mountbatten, son of the former Prince Louis of Battenberg, who was up at Christ's College. Their friendship had begun in the Grand Fleet and blossomed at Cambridge, where Lord Louis took him to Union debates. When Prince Albert bought a motor cycle his father was heard to mutter that 'only cads and bounders' rode such things. His great stand-by was still Louis Greig, with whom he played better and better tennis. His biographer emphasises his liability to despair even over games, for which he had a great natural aptitude. At one time he would break off rather than risk defeat. Greig refused to see this fine character crumbling through lack of encouragement. 'My contribution was to put steel into him,' he said. King George V added a touch of honey in June 1920 by creating him Duke of York.

He and Greig went on to win the RAF doubles that July, and indeed his tennis was henceforth to be championship class. Many can remember his mental as well as physical endurance at Wimbledon some eight years later. He was playing on a side court, but the whole vast crowd from the Centre Court moved over and swarmed round him. Literally hard pressed by the spectators as well as metaphorically by his opponent, he showed signs of strain. 'Try the other hand, Sir,' shouted a well-meaning supporter to this excellent left-handed player. Despite everything, the Duke steeled himself to finish the set in fine style.

Over the royal dukedom King George V had been deeply touched at his son's pleasure. He sent his son a letter as affectionate as any he had ever written. Nevertheless there was a sadness in the last sentence:

I hope you will always look upon me as yr. best friend & . . . you will find me ever ready to help you & give you good advice.

Unconsciously King George was echoing the words he had written in his diary when his own father died: 'he was my best friend'. How true that had been. Yet he and his son Bertie, though in many ways alike, had never become 'best friends'.

Perhaps it was partly because King George so often had only 'good advice' to offer. Bertie needed something better than that. And he was to find it somewhere else.

The summer of 1920 had acquired a lustre for him which dukedoms and royal duties could not give. There had been a sudden encounter with the remembered fairy child of his shy youth. At a children's party a sparkling little girl of five had once given a stammering boy of ten the glacé cherries off the top of her cake. She was Elizabeth Bowes-Lyon, daughter of the Earl of Strathmore. Now he met her again at a dance, still the loveliest girl in the room and the kindest. He fell in love with her. But was she as kind as he needed? It was a great sacrifice to give away cherries at five; a far greater one to surrender freedom at twenty. For if she accepted his love, it would mean exchanging the free life of ordinary humanity for the 'magic circle' of royalty. Once inside that circle and the runes were cast. You could never get out.

He proposed to her first in the following spring, his blunt father already expressing doubts about his success: 'You will be a lucky fellow if she accepts you'. She did not accept. Her mother sadly thought the affair at an end, writing to her friend Lady Airlie: 'I do hope he will find a nice wife who will make him happy. I like him so much and he is a man who will be made or marred by his wife.'

None of them had reckoned with the rejected suitor. A life of frustrations had fortunately taught him never to give up. He might despond, he might seem to despair; but perseverance was his dominant trait. For nearly two more years he pressed her to change her mind and on 13 January 1923 she did. 'Alright, Bertie', he telegraphed to his mother, who knew of the crisis. His two triumphant words were followed by a letter moving in its humility: 'I am very very happy & I can only hope that Elizabeth feels the same as I do. I know I am very lucky to have won her over at last.' He had not just won her, he had won her *over*. It had been a tug-of-war; but both were to turn out victors.

Lady Elizabeth Bowes-Lyon was the youngest but one of ten children. Her family life had been as gay and loving as the Duke's had been wanting in variety and intimacy. The family homes were the ancient Scottish castle of Glamis, 'gothic' as Otranto, and the eighteenth-century mansion of St Paul's Walden Bury in Hertfordshire. Glamis was older than the English monarchy, and the Strathmores' English home so much more beautiful than Sandringham that comparisons were impossible. As a girl she had been cut off by the war up at Glamis, where she helped roll bandages and read to the wounded who were convalescing there, but with peace the family took a house in London at 17 Bruton Street.

Lady Strathmore was a Cavendish-Bentinck, descended on the maternal side from Wellington's most brilliant brother, the Marquess Wellesley. Lady Elizabeth's father, the fourteenth Earl, was that same Lord Strathmore who towards the end of Queen Victoria's reign had warned his elder children against the court. But his youngest daughter had become linked with the court through being Princess Mary's bridesmaid in 1922, along with Princess Patricia of Connaught and Diamond Hardinge, whose courtier brother was to threaten the plans of King Edward VIII. In at first refusing the Duke of York, she was not so much afraid of the court as of 'the public life which would lie ahead of her as the King's daughter-in-law'. It may have been just because she held no high opinion of her own fitness to become the King's daughter-in-law that she triumphed so completely as the King's wife.

No match could have been more popular. The press reverenced her royal Scottish ancestry and loved her charming unaffected Scottish manners. That the King's son was marrying a commoner gave as much pleasure as if no such thing had ever happened before (Queen Victoria's daughter Princess Louise had married a commoner – though heir to a duke.) It is indeed true that the Duchess of York was to bring that fresh air and daylight into the monarchy which King Edward VIII contemplated doing through a very different agency. There was to be a moment of exquisite irony in October 1936, on the day before Mrs Simpson's decree *nisi*, when an American newspaper congratulated the Royal Family on its new marriage policy. How sensible of King Edward and the Duke of York each to select 'a lady of the people'.

Westminster Abbey was the magnificent scene of the wedding. Not one omen was bad apart from the fact that the unfortunate Richard II had been the last royal prince to be married there. The King was half in love with the bride himself, the bridegroom was handsome and the bride radiant. The sun came out and shone precisely as she entered the Abbey on that 26 April 1923, a day of April showers. There was even an attempt to bring the wedding right into the twentieth century, by having the service broadcast. But this the Chapter of Westminster vetoed, though the Dean was willing. The rotundly eloquent address was given by the then Archbishop of York, Cosmo Gordon Lang. 'The warm and generous heart of this people,' he said, 'takes you today into itself. Will you not, in response, take that heart, with all its joys and sorrows, into your own?'

This was in fact what the reserved, tongue-tied Prince had been trying to do ever since he left the Navy. Now, through the medium of the heart he had won, all successes would be doubled, all failures halved.

He had only waited for the peace to involve himself in social affairs. In 1919 he was approached by a group of social reformers. Would he give to industrial welfare what sport and the Services had long enjoyed, royal patronage? The Prince thought first of the need – those rough-and-ready cadets at Cranwell perhaps about to work in factories – and then of his stammer. Patronage he would give, but it would have to be informal. 'I'll do it provided that there's no damned red carpet.' Thus he became president of the Boys' Welfare Association, soon renamed the Industrial Welfare Society. He was a president with a difference. No spit-and-polish were applied before his visits to factories. Contrary to Bagehot's belief that only ministers, not monarchs, were able to see 'common life as in truth it is', here was a prince who wished to do that very thing. Industrial life in the Twenties included a glue factory of which the smell alone made one sick and a lift which crashed with the Duke to the bottom. He became the 'Industrial Duke'. His brothers made jokes about 'the Foreman' and he himself made jokes with his new friends. On a visit to South Wales in 1924 to play a golf match against Frank Hodges and Evan Williams – the first a workers', the second an employers' leader – he was welcomed by Union Jacks along the way interspersed with occasional red Welsh petticoats hanging on clothes lines. 'Hodges, another member of your party!' the Duke would call out as they passed one of these 'red flags'. In a significant respect 'red flags' were better for him than red carpets. They did not make him stammer.

The Duke's activities suddenly expanded in 1921 into his famous Duke of York's Camp. His idea, fertilised by colleagues, was that he, a King's son, should not merely visit the workers but invite their sons to visit him and an equal number of rich men's sons for a week's camping each summer. This experiment in symbiosis had been the Duke's own inspiration: 'Let's have a camp.' The first Camp of course had its growing pains. The press were suspicious and the campers at first bedevilled by shyness; this quickly gave way to the excitement of competitive games. 'Duke's Day', destined to be an annual event from 1921 to 1939, began uncomfortably for the Duke who arrived from Cowes in a suit and bowler – that brand of head-gear which his father considered so casual. Next year the Duke was in shorts and shirt. The Camp song, 'Under the Spreading Chestnut Tree', evoked images which the Duke hoped would be reproduced throughout the nation: an image of class harmony spreading like the tree's branches; an image of royalty inspiring no 'touching mania' but an era of the common touch. Admittedly many miles of social change and advance lay between the Duke of York's Camp and the Duke of Edinburgh's Awards. The Camps had to urge employers to send 'the right sort of boy'; for the Awards, every boy is the right sort. Nevertheless the Camps were genuine milestones. They also marked progress along a parallel path: the right sort of monarchy.

The year 1926 was to be an *annus mirabilis* for the House of Windsor. Two events took place which were radically and radiantly to change its future.

On 21 April 1926 there was born to the Yorks at 17 Bruton Street, the Duchess's old home, a daughter: Elizabeth Alexandra Mary. Christened by Dr Lang at Buckingham Palace, this new Elizabeth of York was third in line to the throne. The King, who was particular about names, had approved these without question, while noting that Bertie 'says nothing about Victoria. I hardly think that necessary.' For generations the name Victoria had been not only 'necessary' but also safe: it provided an anchorage in the past. From now on the Royal Family was to be of a different sort. The baby's father, however, was not yet thinking in such terms. 'We always wanted a child,' he wrote to his mother, 'to make our happiness complete, & now that it has at last happened, it seems so wonderful & strange.'

The second wonderful and strange event took place six months after Princess Elizabeth's birth.

On 19 October 1926 the Duke met the man who was to cure him of his stammer, though not entirely of hesitations. Lionel Logue was an Australian of impressive character and talent. He had achieved many remarkable cures through a combination of breathing exercises and encouragement. The Duke was a perfect subject for his art. So depressed had he become about any cure that only his wife's persuasiveness brought him round to making one final attempt. Within a month Logue's treatment had begun to work. Self-confidence returned as the strangling silences began to be re-placed by measured, if slow, speech. It was just in time, for the Yorks were about to embark on a world tour of the Commonwealth. Until the Duke met Logue this enterprise had seemed hazardous, the nearest approach to it having been a visit to East Africa in the winter of 1924–5.

For the young mother it was a sacrifice which is periodically required of the Royal Family. 'I felt very much leaving on Thursday,' she wrote to Queen Mary, 'and the baby was so sweet playing with the buttons on Bertie's uniform that it quite broke me up.'

The Duke was passionately eager both to serve and to try his own wings, now that a true take-off was at last possible. He had exactly ten years, though he did not know it – from 1926 to 1936 – in which to fit himself for kingship.

The Duke and Duchess shared the honours of their six months' tour equally: he through his complete naturalness and sensitive anxiety to bring pleasure to the people and honour to the crown; she through an irresistible delightfulness, which was sum-med up by the remark in Australia that she had left behind 'a continent in love with her'. In New Zealand he coined a characteristic slogan – 'Take care of the children and the country will take care of itself' – while she, with her bright eyes, managed to give the magical impression that she was smiling at every member of the vast crowds individually. One Communist was bowled over: 'Why, they're human!' His child had waved to the Duchess and – 'I'm blessed if the Duchess didn't wave back and smile right into my face. . . .'

At Canberra, where the Duke opened the session in the new Parliament House on 9 May 1927, there was a real sense of continuity and also of change. His father had opened the first Parliament of the Commonwealth government on 9 May 1901. Here was continuity. Change was no bogey to young Australia, and the Duke confidently predicted 'better things', with a meaningful glance at his own personal life:

Today marks the end of an epoch and the beginning of another, and one's thoughts turn instinctively to what the future may have in store. One's own life would hardly be worth living without its dreams of better things, and the light of a nation without such dreams of a better and larger future would be poor indeed.

This speech was a curtain-raiser, being made on the Duke's own suggestion to the crowds gathered outside Parliament House. It was broadcast to the whole of Australia. But even the miracles of science could not forecast the largeness of the 'larger future' which lay in store for the Yorks.

King George v, who had been following the tour with a keen eye for technical errors in protocol as revealed by photographs, forestalled his son's triumphal arrival in London with an admonitory note: 'We will not embrace at the station before so many people. When you kiss Mama take yr. hat off.' There were to be no hatless descents on London as yet. In thanking his hosts at the customary Guildhall banquet, the returned traveller advocated what seemed to be the unquestionably right policy for Britain, that of Commonwealth unity: 'If we hold together we shall win through.' Yet in less than fifty years even this was to be disputed.

A multitude of extra royal functions fell to the Yorks as a result of King George's severe illness of 1928–9. Fortunately for them they now had a firm base in London from which to perform them. Ever since their marriage they had been saddled with a cumbersome white elephant, White Lodge in Richmond Park. They longed for a more central and compact home. The Duchess wrung a smile out of the unpleasant situation by saying, 'It would be very nice if we could live in the Queen's Dolls' House.' Now on returning from their 1927 tour they moved to a splendid site at Hyde Park Corner, 145 Piccadilly, next door to Apsley House. In the old days Lord Rothschild had owned this house and been permitted to send his great neighbour, the Iron Duke, cases of splendid claret and magnificent hot-house grapes.

Four years later the King gave the Yorks a romantic *cottage orné* in Windsor Great Park known since the frolicsome days of George IV as the Royal Lodge. Here in 1826 the little Princess Victoria had first exchanged compliments with her bedizened 'Uncle King'; here in the 1930s the little Princesses Elizabeth and Margaret Rose gladdened the last years of their grandpapa. For at Glamis Castle on 21 August 1930 a second daughter had been born to the Yorks. This time the Duchess wanted to have an 'Anne of York', but she was not so lucky as before with her father-in-law. He took exception to 'Anne Margaret' but passed 'Margaret Rose'. Another Anne in the family had to wait for another generation.

The early Thirties might have been a busy time for the Duke of York. A new Governor-General of Canada was due to be appointed as from 1931. To the Conservative Prime Minister at Ottawa, R.B.Bennett, the Duke's name would have been acceptable. J.H.Thomas, however, Labour Secretary of State for the Dominions, vetoed a royal appointment: 'They did not want a Royalty in Canada,' he said, 'as it was too close to the USA and the Canadians pride themselves on being as democratic as the Americans.' King George v had to accept his minister's advice, despite his secretary's explosive 'I *do not believe it*. The Americans are the greatest worshippers of Royalty. . . .' So the democratic Canadians got the Ninth Earl of Bessborough instead.

In the Thirties, therefore, there dawned for the Duke a period of calm before the storm. His biographer, Sir John Wheeler-Bennett, speaks of 'six quiet years' – 1930–5. The quietude was partly induced by the slump. Like other members of the Royal Family, the Yorks made their economy cuts. Away went the Duke's stables and all his beloved hunters. He had become the best horseman as well as the best shot among his brothers, and for a reserved character with relatively few intimates, saying goodbye to his horses was like being torn from friends: 'The parting with them will be terrible,' he wrote. 'I am only doing this after careful consideration of the facts (damned hard facts).'

Planning the future of dilapidated Royal Lodge and its gardens was a compensation. The Duke of Windsor was to describe himself as no clean-fingered admirer of nature but a 'dirt gardener'. The Duke of York was a 'dirt gardener' also, and beyond that, green-fingered with a gift for landscaping and a knowledge of shrubs and trees on a par with the Duchess's beloved youngest brother, David Bowes-Lyon. One autumn the Duchess was ill and unable to accompany her husband on a visit to the famous Lochinch gardens in Scotland. On returning home, the Duke sent his hostess a letter of thanks written most expertly in the 'language of rhododendrons'. It had been 'such an Agapetum (delightful) time', he began, and his wife was 'miserable at having missed the Formosum (beautiful) days'. She was now much better, though still 'looking Microleucrum (small and white)'.

His two daughters were small and pink, still 'wonderful' but no longer 'strange'. As they grew taller they were allowed to hand round the plates in the informal atmosphere of parties at Royal Lodge. To him, it was a perfect home. He could neither imagine nor want a change. In the words of his biographer, the idea of becoming king seemed never within the bounds of possibility. Yet the paradox of those 'six quiet years' was a remarkable one. In that very year 1930 when domestic tranquillity descended on the Duke of York, the Prince of Wales met Mrs Simpson.

The brothers' relations had hitherto always been open and affectionate, the younger full of admiration, the elder protective. Gradually with the Thirties an impenetrable curtain descended.

King Edward VIII's accession in January 1936 brought no improvement to the Duke's position. The Duchess of York was naturally the first to notice her husband's isolation from his brother's new circle, and the wound it inflicted. She recognised the cause and did not like it. Mrs Simpson was no less observant, from her angle. When the denizens of The Fort first drove over to meet those at Royal Lodge in 1936, Mrs Simpson noted that whereas the Duke of York admired the King's American station-wagon, the Duchess did not take to his other American acquisition. The changes at Balmoral were particularly grievous to the Duke. 'David only told me what he had done after it was over . . .,' wrote Bertie to their mother. 'I never saw him alone for an instant. . . .' One of the minor changes was that Dr Lang was not invited to Balmoral.

The Yorks took him in at Birkhall, where the two 'entrancing' Princesses cheered him with a programme of action-songs.

November was a nightmare. On the 17th King Edward broke the news about his marriage. 'Bertie was so much taken aback by my news,' recalled the Duke of Windsor, 'that in his shy way he could not bring himself to express his innermost feelings at the time.' A few days later, however, he sent the King an affectionate letter saying that 'he [Bertie] of all people should be able to understand my feelings' and expressing confidence that the King would decide in his people's best interests. That these were not the Duke's 'innermost feelings' must have been obvious even to the insensitive King. The Duke in fact spent the next ten days trying to plead with his brother. Despairingly he wrote to Queen Mary, 'He is very difficult to see & when one does he wants to talk about other matters.' On 3 December the Yorks returned from a few days in Edinburgh. Huge posters confronted them on Euston station: 'The King's Marriage'. Again the Duke started up the weary round of attempting to establish contact. From the 4th to the evening of the 7th his telephone calls met with a stultifying series of postponements – Come on Friday – no, come on Saturday – no, come on Sunday – no, not Sunday – Monday? Perhaps Monday evening, after dinner . . . It was the Duke who said 'No' this time; 'I will come & see you at once.'

The dinner party at The Fort on the 7th was another nightmare, but at least, in the Duke's words, 'The awful & ghastly suspense of waiting was over.' On the 9th he brought Queen Mary the abdication papers to see. 'I broke down,' he wrote in his crisis diary, '& sobbed like a child.' Queen Mary's incredulous horror was conveyed in her diary by 5 exclamation marks: '. . . David's abdication of the Throne of this Empire because he wants to marry Mrs Simpson!!!!!' It was a terrible blow to the whole family, she concluded – 'particularly to poor Bertie.' Poor indeed, for his stay and support, his wife, had gone down with influenza in London. But when he returned after the signing of the Instrument, he found a large crowd outside 145 Piccadilly, 'cheering madly'. Like his father, popularity came to him as a surprise: 'I was overwhelmed.'

'*Prosit omen!*' – cheers for a good omen. Thus did the Archbishop of Canterbury write in his diary on receiving his first letter from the new King. It was a Christmas greeting and the King's handwriting, especially his signature 'George R.I.', showed no appreciable difference from that of his father. So Dr Lang welcomed the future with cheers.

The omens no doubt seemed good by Christmas. But on 13 December, when King George VI made his Accession broadcast, no one quite knew what was going to happen.

The King himself was at first utterly prostrated. His biographer speaks of 'shock', leaving him 'emotionally disturbed', followed by 'merciful numbness'. On the first evening as King while his brother was still packing, he had almost broken down at the thought. 'Dickie, this is absolutely terrible,' he cried desperately to his cousin Lord Louis Mountbatten. '. . . I'm quite unprepared for it. . . .' (That was his father's fault.) 'I've never even seen a State Paper. I'm only a Naval Officer, it's the only thing I know about.' Lord Louis had the heaven-sent answer: Bertie's own father had felt the same when Prince Eddy died and had said the same to Dickie's father, Prince Louis of Battenberg. And Prince Louis had replied: 'You have been trained to be a Naval Officer. There is no finer training for a King.'

It was a triumph of will-power that the unfortunate King George VI got through his speech on the 13th, despite an ashen face and many seemingly interminable pauses.

Now that the duties of Sovereignty have fallen to Me I declare to you My adherence to the strict principles of [long pause] constitutional government. . . .

Even Logue had not enabled him to master completely the fatal 'c' at the beginning of a word, and in this time of appalling stress the 'c' defeated him.

Apart from doubts about the new King's fibre, there was alarm over the possible effect of the Abdication on the monarchy. Almost everyone agreed then, and many would still agree now with Lord Beaverbrook's solemn pronouncement: 'Without doubt, the throne trembled.' Clement Attlee was to declare in 1945 that the Abdication was 'very unfortunate and undoubtedly affected for a time the prestige of the Monarchy'. Beaverbrook went further: 'It is an object lesson in the quick disposal of a monarch.' He envisaged the ex-King becoming a 'martyr' and the new King failing 'to command to a complete degree the loyalty and devotion of his people'.

Not one of these disagreeable things happened. The reason was plain. Without fuss the loyal majority had simply moved from King Edward, who had 'thrown up the sponge', to King George who had not. Republicans or neutrals were not going to make a fuss anyway. As A.J.P. Taylor was to say of the Abdication, 'A curious and unimportant episode in a curious and no longer important institution.' Indeed Jimmy Maxton, MP, had made much the same point at the time. When he returned to Glasgow and found no excitement among his constituents, he said: 'How very trivial an impression the whole thing has left on the minds of the masses of the nation, indicating the rightness of our view that the monarchical institution does not matter a damn.' Most people felt that this was a more correct assessment of Jimmy's views. A shopkeeper was probably the nearest to becoming a *vox populi* when he said that last week he would have died for King Edward but this week he would give his life for King George.

The date for the coronation was still 12 May 1937 – only the King had changed. Why was he crowned King George and not King Albert? Some people thought because Albert sounded too German. Shades of 1917. But it was to knit the monarchy together again by emphasising the links with King George V. And so once more there was a change of name within the Royal House.

168

Queen Elizabeth with Princess Elizabeth and Princess Margaret,
c. 1937.

ABOVE: The Royal Family and Queen Mary on the balcony of Buckingham Palace after the coronation, May, 1937.

RIGHT: King George and Queen Elizabeth in the gold state coach after the opening of Parliament in 1938. The coach was first made for George III and the panels were painted by the Florentine artist Cipriani. Princess Elizabeth, aged 12, noticed the similarity of the panels to a ceiling by the same artist at Broadlands, home of Lord and Lady Louis Mountbatten.

ABOVE: The King riding with his daughters in the grounds of
Windsor Castle on Princess Elizabeth's twelfth birthday, 21 April
1938.

LEFT: King George and President Roosevelt drive to the White
House during the King's North American tour of 1939.

LEFT: The King with General Alexander during his visit to Polish troops fighting with the Eighth Army in Italy, 1944.

BELOW: A crowd gathers in the East End as the King and Queen emerge from inspecting an air raid shelter, August 1941. After the bombing of Buckingham Palace the year before Queen Elizabeth said she could 'look the East End in the face'.

ABOVE: The King and Queen talk to a Londoner whose home has been destroyed by bombs, September 1940.

The two Princesses were evacuated 'to a house in the country' –
Windsor Castle – for the duration of the war.
TOP: Princess Elizabeth in her guide uniform sits in the grass of
Frogmore, 1942.
ABOVE: A scene from 'Old Mother Red Riding Boots', one of several
pantomimes at Windsor in which the Princesses acted.

In the Coronation Service there were other more radical changes. The King's broadcast called attention to them. 'Never has the ceremony itself had so wide a significance,' he said, 'for the Dominions are now free and equal partners with this ancient Kingdom.' In order to rub in their freedom, the Dominions had deliberately proclaimed their King on different dates ranging from 10–12 December. Now they were to bring about changes in the Service to emphasise that he was 'their' King and that he maintained their 'Gospel', of whatever communion, rather than solely the 'Protestant Reformed Religion', as in the United Kingdom. On a more mundane level, South Africa's High Commissioner resolved to wear evening dress in the procession instead of knee-breeches when carrying his country's standard. Some of his colleagues thought he would look like a waiter and should carry a tray, but the Earl Marshal said, 'We don't want to break up the Empire for the sake of a pair of trousers.'

In Westminster Abbey the great day was made by solemn pageantry and marred by the usual mistakes. A chaplain fainted, the Dean tried to put on the King's *colobium Sidonis* inside out, the Archbishop's thumb covered the printed words of the Oath, the Lord Great Chamberlain's fingers could not fasten the sword-belt, St Edward's Crown was almost placed back to front and a bishop stood on the King's robe, nearly bringing him down. 'I had to tell him to get off it pretty sharply,' noted H.M. At a pinch, King George VI could assume the 'quarterdeck' manner of King George V.

Exactly a fortnight after the coronation, on 27 May, the King effected two more changes. He accepted the resignation of Baldwin as Prime Minister, appointing Neville Chamberlain in his place; and on the very same day he settled the style and title of his eldest brother, the 'Duke of Windsor'. King George had already announced in the Accession broadcast his intention of creating the dukedom of Windsor. This was officially confirmed on the following 8 March. The Duke's style and title of 'Royal Highness' was now conferred by Letters Patent on 27 May 1937. This was because he had been *born* in lineal succession to the crown, and notwithstanding his exclusion from it by the Abdication. His wife and children, if any, were specifically excluded on the implicit ground that the children would not be in the lineal succession.

A week later, on 3 June, the Windsors were married in France.

For this deprivation of the H.R.H., which virtually made the Duchess a morganatic wife after all, the Duke never forgave those responsible. But who were they? Walter Monckton heard that *au fond* neither the King nor his ministers were averse to an H.R.H. for the Duchess, but that the Dominions vetoed it. It is also widely believed that the Royal ladies were opposed. Certain it is that when the Duke met King George at Windsor for the first time since the Abdication, in 1939, it had to be a 'stag party' – no women present. And Walter Monckton heard that it was Queen Elizabeth, not

King George, who was deeply opposed to the Duke being domiciled and working in England by 1938, as he wished.

Of course if the Duke had volunteered to live abroad, as all abdicated Continental sovereigns did, the Duchess might have been 'Highness' and no bones broken. But the Duchess could not bear to think of her husband banished from the seat of power, through her. She desperately wanted position for him; he passionately wanted honour for her. (Nicolson once heard the Duke refer to his wife as 'Her Royal Highness' in Antibes. There was a general gasp and shudder at this solecism.) The unlucky King George was forced to share the misery of their dilemma through the medium of continual embittered telephone calls, put through by the Duke of Windsor. The Duke's fluent discontent was more than a match for the King's embarrassed stammer. At last Walter Monckton managed to put a stop to the telephoning. Possibly because they had nothing else to do, the Windsors now set out in August 1937 on a round of fact-finding visits, social and economic, to Germany. Though they disliked what they found, the news of 'Windsors in Naziland' constituted yet another unacceptable face of exiled royalty.

The Third Reich presented no healthy field for amateur activity whether by the Windsors or the British Prime Minister. For Chamberlain was an amateur in foreign affairs compared with Anthony Eden, who resigned in February 1938. Hitler's lemmings were gathering pace and their precipice was less than two years ahead. In March Austria was annexed; in September Czechoslovakia was threatened – and 'defended' by Chamberlain's Munich agreement; on 15 March 1939 Hitler announced, 'Czechoslovakia has ceased to exist' – and so had all hopes of peace; a week later the heat was turned on Poland and Lithuania; in April Mussolini annexed Albania, and Chamberlain made his 'U' turn, guaranteeing four European countries; on 22 August Russia signed the Nazi-Soviet pact.

King George had always been a conciliator and now, through taking the advice of his ministers, he could be called an appeaser. Nevertheless he respected those like Eden and Duff Cooper who, in denouncing the Government, had the courage of their convictions and resigned. King George himself was almost pathetically eager to go anywhere, do anything of which Chamberlain approved, in order to sustain the fading cause of peace. To his chagrin, he was prevented from writing to any of the Axis big three, as one Head of State to another, for fear of a rebuff. But in July 1938 he and his consort had promoted the *Entente* in Paris, Queen Elizabeth gallantly catching every favourable breeze that blew with the airy grace of her crinolines. As late as March 1939 the royal pair sailed to Canada through fog and icefields, and afterwards visited the United States. They took both by storm. King George had insisted on 'no more high-hat business, the sort of thing that my father and those of his day regarded as essential', thus underlining the generation-gap between himself and King George V. As a result the message of youth and informality was conveyed no less emphatically but far less abrasively than it had been by his brother. Lord Tweedsmuir, Canada's Governor-General, called them 'most remarkable young people' and the Roosevelts both wrote of the friendly 'nice young people'.

King George VI returned home no longer feeling 'only a Naval Officer' but full of confidence in himself, and bringing back from President Roosevelt the prospect of far more substantial benefits than ever poor Chamberlain had brought from Munich. The words of Lord Hugh Cecil denouncing Lloyd George's Irish policy seemed to apply: 'Peace with honour, peace with honour; considering he has brought us so much dishonour he might have brought us a little peace.'

On 3 September 1939 at 6 pm the King broadcast to the nation: 'For the second time in the lives of the most of us we are at war. . . .' In his diary he added, '& I am no longer a midshipman in the Royal Navy'. He had come out of 'A' turret at last, to man the Round Tower of Windsor Castle.

9

Looking the people in the face

*'I'm glad we've been bombed. It makes me feel I can
look the East End in the face'*. Queen Elizabeth in 1940.

KING GEORGE VI was only forty-three on the outbreak of the Second
World War. He looked younger, though his face was often touched by
anxiety and sometimes drawn. But there were no 'deep lines' under his
eyes such as he had noticed sadly under his elder brother's at the time of
the Abdication. His wife, with her unfailing sparkle of expression and
voice, was still in her thirties, 'one of the most amazing Queens', according to
Nicolson, 'since Cleopatra'. His elder daughter had just reached her teens, his younger
daughter was not quite nine. Yet the War at a stroke changed this young man into the
father and guardian of his people. He felt his role intensely, as we shall see. And the
people sustained their tutelary family as they had sustained his father and great-
grandmother in time of war – with devotion, advice, prayers and poetry.

The poem which King George preferred to all other offerings had been composed
by Marie Louise Haskins, a typical 'New Woman' of the First World War who
supervised women workers in a factory and later became a lecturer at the London
School of Economics. She had written it when he was the same age as his elder
daughter was now. It was called 'The Gate of the Year'. She sent it to the King as a
talisman for the coming year, 1940, and he introduced it into his 1939 Christmas
broadcast. But it was just as truly, 'The Gate of the War'. As such, the King delivered
its message.

I said to the man who stood at the Gate of the Year, 'Give me a light that I may tread
safely into the unknown.' And he replied, 'Go out into the darkness, and put your hand into
the Hand of God. That shall be to you better than a light, and safer than a known way.'

The poem struck many chords in the King. He was acutely conscious of the 'darkness' and the 'unknown' into which he and the nation were stepping. Subconsciously
he welcomed this expression of his own needs and temperament, not forgetting the
perpetually hideous 'unknown' of the broadcast itself. He could never enjoy
Christmas until that terror was behind him. He was also religious, in ways profoundly
different from his brother David. His brother did not care for church services though
he sometimes enjoyed listening in solitude to the music of St George's Chapel. King
George's religion was as direct as it was unsentimental. The successive crises of the

War always stirred his religious instinct, especially D-Day. 'It was a great opportunity to call everybody to prayer,' he wrote then. 'I have wanted to do it for a long
time.'

The King's guide-line in all practical spheres was to be unity. With his passion for
friendly co-operation, inculcated by positive training in the Navy and reaction
against youthful experiences at Sandringham, he felt the War was a turning-point in
which the nation must unite or fall. Thus he chose a passage from Isaiah as his
permanent desk-memo: 'They helped every one his neighbour and every one said to
his brother, Be of good courage.' The theme was always to the fore in his public and
private thoughts: in 1940, 'this time we are all in the front line and the danger together'
and 'we shall have to stick together . . .'; in 1942, the story told by Abraham Lincoln
to unite America and now retold by King George to unite Britain, of a small boy
carrying a child up a hill who was asked whether the burden was not too heavy and
replied, 'It's not a burden, it's my brother'; in 1943, a quotation from John Buchan,
that no task can be too formidable 'if a man can *link up* with what he knows and
loves'; in 1944 to the Home Guard, 'You have found how men from all kinds of
homes . . . can work together . . . and how happy they can be with each other'; in
1945, 'I should like to see this team stay together' – and here the King meant primarily
the war-time coalition but also the whole nation, from its foundations in the people to
its apex in the crown.

The 'Phoney War' presented the country and Commonwealth with many problems of unity which the King personally could help, or already had helped, to solve.

The Commonwealth demonstrated the King's power to draw the forces of unity
together. Canadians had heard him tell them in May 1939 how 'sense of race' could
either be disruptive or, within the Commonwealth, strengthening to both English
and French cultures. Now on 10 September 1939 the Canadian races were united in
their declaration of war. But the date was significantly one week later than Britain –
independence had to be registered – whereas Australia and New Zealand unanimously
declared war on the same day. In South Africa – declaration on 6 September – the
three days' delay was occupied with bitter divisions, a narrow vote against neutrality
and a new Prime Minister – Smuts. The Irish Free State did not need to vote for
neutrality. It went without saying. Thus King George VI could see within the Commonwealth certain strains which he and still more his daughter were to help alleviate.
He was not to see – though his daughter was – a military historian, Correlli Barnett,
arguing in the Seventies that Commonwealth 'unity' was an indefensible strain on the
mother country.

With Britain and the Commonwealth at war, King George turned his attention to
allies. A monarch might always be thrown in at the eleventh hour to convert
irreconcilable foreign heads of state. Chamberlain had postponed any royal appeal to
the Axis powers until too late, and an appeal for firmness by King George to the

Vichyite Pétain was to be too late also. But the King's function as an 'emollient' was successfully exhibited when a military mission arrived from a potential ally, Turkey, to obtain guns. There were no available guns but His Majesty's tactful handling of a disgruntled envoy restored friendship. An Anglo-Turkish treaty was signed.

If only the Duke of Windsor had been as responsive as General Mehmet Orbay. Here it was domestic unity which had to be considered. The Windsors had been caught by the declaration of war at Antibes. Unlike Napoleon I, who had begun his Hundred Days with a triumphant dash from Antibes to the Tuileries, the Windsors were not to enter any English palace. Brought home in his destroyer *Kelly* to Portsmouth by Lord Louis Mountbatten, they were posted back to France, where the Duke served on General Gamelin's staff until France fell. They were then rescued from Lisbon by Walter Monckton and eventually deposited together in the Bahamas, of which he remained Governor for the duration.

The situation in Lisbon, until Monckton arrived, had been melodramatic. There was a secret Nazi plot to install the Windsors as puppet King and Queen after the 'invasion' of Britain. Unaware of such hidden lunacy, the Duke was half persuaded by open Falangist propaganda that once he reached the Bahamas Churchill would have him assassinated. It took all Monckton's arts to fly his charges out of Lisbon. The Battle of Britain, with its multiple risks and rumours, would have been no place for a couple who still attracted, willy nilly, the lurid attentions of the enemy propaganda machine.

Meanwhile in December 1939 King George followed the example of his father, his elder brother and his twenty-year-old self in visiting his troops in France. Introduced also to the Maginot Line, he compared it to 'an underground battleship'. Alas, this French battleship was about to be boarded by a pirate horde.

The Gate of the War – a war of action at last – was suddenly wide open in May 1940. Churchill seemingly had unlocked it early in April by laying a minefield in Norwegian home waters, hoping to prevent German trade with Scandinavia. At least when Canning pre-empted Napoleon's strike at the Danish fleet in 1807 he had not jeered, 'Boney has missed the coach'; but this was precisely how Chamberlain chose to rejoice: 'Hitler has missed the bus.' Within a month the man who had 'missed the bus' was in control of Norway, while the man who had accused him of losing it was fighting for his life in the House of Commons. A prominent Conservative, Leo Amery, lashed him with Cromwell's memorable words, 'In the name of God, go!' Next day, on a vote of confidence, his majority had sunk from around 200 to an incredible 81. Two days later, on 10 May, France, Belgium and Holland were invaded. Hitler's panzers were in, Chamberlain was out.

Quotations from Cromwell were not likely to appeal to the King. Indeed an outraged sense of unity and fairness led him to see Chamberlain's defeat as the beginning of political disruption. Beyond that, Chamberlain had endeared himself to the King.

He belonged to the ministerial type who clears his own mind by taking the monarch into his confidence. The King was to write: 'When he was Prime Minister he really did tell me what was in his mind & what he hoped to do. I was able to confide in him, & . . . have our talks.' With his dislike of sudden upheavals King George had not been able to conceive of having 'our talks' with Churchill. Lord Halifax, another appeaser, he knew. His wish was for Halifax as Chamberlain's successor.

'Chamberlain wanted Halifax. Labour wanted Halifax. Sinclair [Liberal] wanted Halifax. The Lords wanted Halifax. The King wanted Halifax. And Halifax wanted Halifax.' All but the last three words in this chant by Lord Beaverbrook were true. Lord Halifax himself did not want to be a premier in the Lords, and the King's suggestion to Chamberlain that Halifax should sit in the Commons with his peerage in temporary abeyance fell on stony ground. 'Then I knew', wrote King George, 'that there was only one person whom I could send for to form a Government who had the confidence of the country & that was Winston.'

The stage now became Churchill's. Already 'Winston' in the King's diary, he was soon to be a trusted friend. Together they enjoyed self-service during their weekly luncheons at the Palace in order to avoid the presence of third parties. The King's biographer found in his diary for the new year, 1941, a revealing entry: 'I could not have a better PM.' It might so easily have been, 'the best Prime Minister I've got.'

But before the new year dawned, dark but not hopeless, the King had fearful experiences to go through, many of them unprecedented for a king as for most of his civilian subjects. The first repercussion of the 'Shooting War' to affect him, however, was not unlike his great-grandmother's experience in the 1840s. Queen Victoria had given asylum in Buckingham Palace to Louis Philippe's daughter-in-law Victoire, Duchess of Nemours, after a Paris revolution. Poor Victoire had 'lost all her clothes to the mobs'. A century later King George was sheltering Queen Wilhelmina of the Netherlands in Buckingham Palace who similarly 'had brought no clothes with her'.

From the end of May until well into June King George was meticulously logging the evacuation of Dunkirk. This was 'Operation Dynamo', to be followed by 'Torch' (North Africa) and 'Husky' (Sicily) and to reach its climax in 'Utah', 'Omaha', 'Mulberry', 'Neptune' and 'Overlord' (D-Day). 'Operation Dynamo' left the King in the only possible state for him and his people – patriotic defiance. 'Personally I feel happier now that we have no allies to be polite to & to pamper.' From now on the King and Queen faced Germany's proposed 'Operation Sea Lion' (invasion) with what might be called their own private operations, 'Evacuation' and 'Stay Put'. Queen Mary was reluctantly evacuated to her niece the Duchess of Beaufort's home at Badminton, where she spent her days pruning trees, giving lifts to soldiers on leave and learning about the countryside. Her lady-in-waiting, Lady Cynthia Colville, soon realised that this widow of the 'Norfolk squire' was no country-woman. It took a war to teach her the difference between barley and oats.

At Madresfield, where a haven had once been prepared for King George III against a Napoleonic invasion scare, a refuge was again made ready in darkest secrecy for the Royal Family. It was never used. Nor did King George and Queen Elizabeth ever suffer the agonised self-questioning of other British parents who had to decide for or against evacuation of their children to the New World. Queen Elizabeth settled that matter: 'The children could not go without me, and I could not possibly leave the King.' She told Harold Nicolson, 'I should die if I had to leave.' But Windsor Castle had to be, and was, something of an open prison for the young princesses. As their father was to say on VE-Day, after launching them into the crowds in the Mall, 'Poor darlings, they have never had any fun yet.'

Halfway through August the Battle of Britain was in full swing, but not until 7 September did London receive its first storm of fire. From the East End Goering directed his air force to the West End on 9 September, when a bomb fell on the garden side of Buckingham Palace and next day exploded, smashing much glass. On the 12th the King and Queen almost met their fate. The sirens wailed as usual. Suddenly through the swish of heavy rain they heard a plane zooming overhead. A stick of bombs was dropped over the Palace by a daring Luftwaffe pilot who had flown straight up the Mall beneath the ceiling of cloud. Two bombs fell in the Quadrangle directly outside the King's study. Another wrecked the Chapel and the rest plunged into the garden. Daring the pilot certainly was, but the Nazis' *coup* against the crown was to prove in its way as much a boomerang as Japan's 'Pearl Harbor'. The Dominions and even America – the latter still resolutely neutral – were shocked, while bombed-out Londoners felt that here too were a man and wife living beside the rubble, waiting for the next near-miss.

The shock and nervous reaction – waiting, listening, glancing out of the window – affected the King painfully for days. Nevertheless he and the Queen continued their visits to raid victims, he in naval uniform, she in flowery hat and pretty shoes stepping over the debris of splintered wood and glass. The George Cross, mainly for civilians, was his own idea. 'Thank God for a good king,' someone shouted from a bomb-site, and the King called back, 'Thank God for a good people.' He felt to the depths of his being a new unity with his people. Nobody was 'immune' from the Luftwaffe, he wrote; 'I'm glad we've been bombed,' added the Queen. 'It makes me feel I can look the East End in the face.'

Soon they had to look shattered Coventry in the face also – all that was left of its ancient features. 'Poor Coventry . . .,' the King lamented; 'just like Ypres after the last war.' Though Buckingham Palace was heavily guarded by professionals against possible paratroopers, King George, Queen Elizabeth and the Household set up a miniature Home Guard of their own. There was much rifle and revolver practice in the garden, Queen Elizabeth announcing that she would fight to the last ditch, unlike the kings and queens of Europe. 'I shall not go down like the others.'

On 30 January 1941 occurred one of many momentous interviews conducted that month in England. Harry Hopkins, President Roosevelt's personal representative had

OPPOSITE: King George presents the African Medal to 'She Elephant', the Queen Mother Ndlovukazi, during his visit to Swaziland in the South African tour of 1947.

ABOVE: The King initiates his daughter into the paperwork of monarchy. He had intended to give her full and careful instruction, such as he himself had sorely missed, but death cut him short at fifty-six.

RIGHT: Princess Elizabeth at Buckingham Palace after her marriage to Prince Philip in November 1947.

BELOW: The King and Queen pose with General Smuts on arrival at the top of Table Mountain, Cape Town, during their South African tour. The King handed back President Kruger's bible to Smuts; it had been captured by the British during the Boer War.

Prince Philip is met by Lord and Lady Mountbatten on his arrival to take up a naval appointment in Malta, 1949. They were his uncle and aunt.

Princess Elizabeth with the one-month-old Prince Charles,
December 1948. The King dispensed with the presence of a Minister
at his birth.

A family group at Sandringham in 1951. From left to right, standing:
The Duke of Kent, Princess Margaret, Princess Alexandra, Princess
Marina, the Duke of Gloucester, Princess Elizabeth, Prince Philip,
the Duchess of Gloucester. Seated: Queen Mary, King George,
Princess Anne, Prince Charles, Queen Elizabeth. In the foreground:
Prince Richard of Gloucester, Prince Michael of Kent, Prince
William of Gloucester.

A cartoon on the death of George VI which appeared in
the Sydney *Daily Mirror*. It was entitled 'The Gate of the
Years' and accompanied by the lines by Minnie Haskins
which the King had made famous in his Christmas
broadcast of 1939.

flown in to complete negotiations for vast new American aid to beleaguered Britain. The Destroyer–Bases exchange had been made the previous September. 'Cheap and nasty,' Churchill was to mutter of the fifty ancient US destroyers and, when Hopkins overheard and looked startled, he repeated firmly, 'Cheap for us and nasty for the enemy.' 'Lend-Lease' followed on 10 January 1941. And on 30 January King George and Queen Elizabeth received Hopkins at Buckingham Palace. The Queen's conversation moved Hopkins deeply:

The Queen told me that she found it extremely difficult to find words to express her feeling towards the people of Britain in these days. She thought their actions were magnificent and that victory in the long run was sure, but that the one thing that counted was the morale and determination of the great mass of the British people.

Equally impressed was Hopkins by the King:

The King discussed the navy and the fleet at some length and showed an intimate knowledge of all the high ranking officers of the Navy, and for that matter, of the Army and Air Force.

The King was familiar with important despatches and had read Hopkins' recent despatch to the Foreign Office. Most significant of all, the King was eager to expand his extremely fruitful private correspondence with President Roosevelt.

This dated from the visit during spring 1939 to the Roosevelts' home, Hyde Park. Friendship had sprung up between the two heads of state and their wives. (Mrs Eleanor Roosevelt was to stay at the Palace in 1942.) Hopkins now urged H.M. 'whenever he was of a mind', to send personal notes to the President, because 'that was one of the ways to keep our two countries closely related during these trying times'.

As 1941 wore on the times became more 'trying' still. December was to be the month of Japanese triumphs: the *Prince of Wales* and the *Repulse* were both sunk a few days after the American fleet had been destroyed at Pearl Harbor. If this latter catastrophe finally brought the United States into the War, King George's relationship with Roosevelt had assisted the President's previous hard and delicate work to that end.

The escape of the German battleships from the British blockade on 12 February 1942 ensured that the 'trying times' should continue, to be worsened three days later by the fall of Singapore and rendered still more 'trying' for the loyal and faithful King by a Commons' attack on Churchill's handling of the war. 'Can we stick together in the face of all this adversity?' the King wrote in his diary. 'We must somehow.' Not that he overlooked Churchill's arrogance towards the House: 'nobody will stand for that sort of treatment in this country'. It was with profound relief, however, that he heard of the Government's reconstruction and consequent political victory. The adverse minority had included one vote for his brother, the Duke of Gloucester, to be Commander-in-Chief!

OPPOSITE: Queen Elizabeth the Queen Mother and her daughters stand veiled as the coffin of George VI is carried from the train at King's Cross Station. On the coffin are laid the imperial crown and the Queen Mother's wreath. The King, like his father, had died at Sandringham and his body was brought to lie in state in Westminster Hall before the funeral at Windsor.

Less than six months after Churchill's political victory there were Allied victories in North Africa, Russia and Asia. The slow tide had begun to turn. But there was one signal defeat during August which later was to bring undeserved trouble upon the Royal Family. The Dieppe Raid of 19 August 1942 had resulted in severe losses to the Canadians, who had made their own plans for the landing. Nevertheless the overall responsibility rested with the Chief of Combined Operations, Lord Louis Mountbatten, and Lord Beaverbrook claimed to believe with increasing obduracy that Mountbatten and others had deliberately planned the expedition's failure to discredit his, Beaverbrook's propaganda for an immediate 'Second Front'. That, coupled with Mountbatten's refusal of Beaverbrook's offer to help him deal with the Chiefs of Staffs' Committee, produced recurrent hostility towards Mountbatten, which was to have its repercussions on the latter's relatives. As we shall see, the effect of Beaverbrook's hostility was not negligible.

The death of the King's gallant young brother Prince George, Duke of Kent in an air crash, was a tragic personal blow. Like Queen Victoria after the death of her cousin Princess Mary Adelaide of Teck, King George VI made his own will. A joyous family event was Princess Elizabeth's attainment of the age of eighteen. There had been moves to have her made Princess of Wales, but the King, with his insistence on correctness, convinced the Cabinet that this title belonged exclusively to a Prince of Wales's wife.

That autumn the King was allowed to fly to North Africa as 'General Lyon' (the Queen's maiden name). He inspected the troops for a gruelling fortnight, afterwards writing words which echoed Queen Victoria's during the Crimea: 'I feel I have done some good. . . .' *The Times* went much further, calling the monarchy a main safeguard of democracy within the constitution, as well as a continuous repository of knowledge, surpassing any individual statesman.

To be the repository of Churchill's plans was one of King George's compensations for insufficient personal activity. It was therefore not unamusing that when D-Day was at last approaching there were some sharp rivalries between King and Prime Minister as to whether both, one or neither should hearten the invasion force by sailing on board the Admiral's flag-ship. 'W. [Winston] cannot say no if he goes himself,' wrote King George in his diary on 30 May 1944, '& I don't want to have to tell him he cannot. So?' But to the King's hopeful 'So?' his private secretary, Sir Alan Lascelles, urged an emphatic 'No'. After prolonged arguments the resolute Lascelles dissuaded the King, who in turn dissuaded Churchill. 'I must defer,' Churchill conceded, 'to Your Majesty's wishes & indeed, commands.' There was to be no overlord for 'Operation Overlord'. Had things gone the other way it is theoretically possible that on Monday 6 June 1944 the same fatality could have put Anthony Eden into 10 Downing Street and Princess Elizabeth on to the throne.

As it was, those two splendid romantics, Churchill with his 'V' sign and King George with remote centuries of sovereigns behind him who had indeed led their men into battle, were there on VE Day, 8 May 1945, the King to stand on the Palace balcony with the united Royal Family. King George had not pushed his case like his elder brother in 1915, with any such words as, 'What does it matter if I am killed? I have two daughters.' He was a man of sensitivity and common sense. Moreover, he knew in his heart that the traditional balcony overlooking the Mall was a far better place for a modern king than the bridge of a destroyer.

From the Mall to the polling-booths: from unity to division. That was King George's feeling when the war-time Coalition broke up on 23 May 1945. 'Country before Party has been its watchword,' recorded the King. 'But now what?' It was not that he wanted to keep Labour out. Like most people, he probably expected Churchill to win. Coalitions, however, have always made the monarch's constitutional path smoother and been correspondingly popular. Nevertheless King George recognised the force of the demand put forward by Labour's National Executive for a new Parliament. The Parliament which was ending had been the longest in the history of the United Kingdom: from 26 November 1935 to 15 June 1945, extending over all three reigns of the House of Windsor. The answer to the King's 'now what?' was an overwhelming Labour victory.

He was quite within his rights in expressing 'personally' to Churchill his profound regret, especially for the loss of friendship and 'our talks'. Labour's Foreign Secretary, however, Ernest Bevin, was able to supply at least the latter. 'Bevin is very good & tells me everything that is going on,' he was to write that Christmas. King George had in fact played a valuable though small part in Prime Minister Attlee's appointment of Bevin.

King George has since been accused on both sides of the Atlantic of overstepping his constitutional rights by virtually 'demanding' that Bevin should fill this key post. These malicious rumours have been scotched both by the King's biographer and later historians. What happened was this. Attlee told King George he was thinking of sending Bevin to the Treasury and Hugh Dalton to the Foreign Office. 'His Majesty begged him to think carefully about this,' recorded Lascelles immediately after Attlee's audience, 'and suggested that Mr Bevin would be a better choice.' That evening the King wrote in his diary, 'He said he would,' probably meaning that Attlee had said he *would think carefully about it*. (The royal diary read, however, as if Attlee had said he *would do it*.) Next day several politicians, according to later claims, gave Attlee the same advice as the King. Attlee then changed his own mind, finally swayed by the thought that if he sent Bevin to the Treasury there would be trouble on the home front, where Morrison was in charge. 'Ernie and Herbert didn't get on together. . . .' Attlee put the record straight in 1959: 'I naturally took into account the King's view, which was very sound; but it was not a decisive factor in my arrival at my decision.'

One last question. How did the King reach his conclusion? He rated foreign affairs as of the first importance and rightly judged Bevin the biggest man available. Beyond that, he found Bevin's personality warm and Dalton's strangely antipathetic, considering he was the son of George v's devoted tutor, the Reverend. Dalton junior admitted he was anti-court, more pro-Russian than Bevin – no recommendation to H.M. – and would have been more 'unforgiving' towards Germany. The King's view was as Attlee said 'very sound'.

Encounters between King George and Attlee were not always easy. Each was rendered silent by shyness. One recalls the King's own description of John Winant, a former American ambassador, and his wife as 'two silent people'. With H.M. that made three; except that there was always Queen Elizabeth to make a lively fourth. But when Attlee came to the Palace the King and he handled their silences alone.

Added to the physical pause there was hesitation in the King's mind about Labour's policy. In principle he had favoured social advances for the people ever since his 'Industrial Welfare' days. Unlike his father, he was genuinely liberal. But he feared the Labour machine might run away with him and the country. As before, his cousin Dickie Mountbatten gave him confidence. 'You are now the old campaigner,' Mountbatten said, 'on whom a new and partly inexperienced Government will lean for advice and guidance.' One of the experienced Labour ministers, Herbert Morrison, did indeed pay tribute to the King's helpfulness: how 'calmly and willingly' he accepted ministers of very different outlook from their predecessors; how 'fair' he was; how 'assiduous' in reading their documents, even to the extent of sometimes holding a 'friendly contest of knowledge' and tripping them up on detail. Here was a lighter function for monarchy – to keep ministers on their toes.

Notwithstanding these pleasantries, there were all too many post-war political and economic crises to keep the King also on tiptoe, and the War itself had affected him more than he at first realised – 'I feel burned out'. History seemed to be repeating itself. The Parliament Bill of 1911 had dislocated King George v's first pre-war years. Eventually in the interests of Home Rule the Lords' powers of hold-up were cut to three sessions. Now in the interests of Steel Nationalisation a new Parliament Bill cut the Lords' powers by another third, after worrying King George VI almost to death during his first post-war years. For he took things hard. That was the difference between him and Attlee. 'He was rather the worrying type, you know,' said Attlee after his death. 'I'm not a worrier.' Sudden glooms were indeed apt to descend upon the King. For instance, when conferring the CH on Vita Sackville-West (Mrs Harold Nicolson) in 1948, he learnt that her ancestral home, Knole, had gone to the National Trust. He raised his hands in despair, reported Vita's son Nigel. 'Everything is going nowadays. Before long, I shall also have to go.'

Nevertheless the restless, changing times brought their rewards. The year 1947 was remarkable for appearing to preserve a balance of strength, however precarious, throughout his beloved Commonwealth. The Mountbattens' historic 'passage to India' took place this year. Thanks to the incomparable touch of India's last Viceroy and his wife, complete agreement was reached on how to bury the British Raj with honour. Its requiem was sung in perfect harmony from the viceregal palace itself – a typically British procedure – while India and Pakistan were reborn as Dominions. The King was no longer 'George Rex *Imperator*'. Burma left the Commonwealth in 1947 – the first country to secede since America. But the South African tour of the Royal Family during the same year seemed to restore the balance. The beauty of the country, the sunshine, the size and enthusiasm of the crowds despite the known strength of republicanism, above all the experience of travelling everywhere with a beloved family – all four together – gave the King intense joy. It was equalled only by his exhaustion. This latter he could cope with, but the knowledge that Britain was suffering an appalling fuel crisis commensurate with a savage northern winter made him want to fly home and share his people's sufferings as in 1940. Sensible Mr Attlee, however, said it would only create panic.

If anyone could have purged South Africa of republicanism (and worse evils) the Royal Family would have done so. Indeed the great Smuts thought they *had* done so. Their 'sheer humanness', he said, had brought the touch of healing South Africa craved. (Smuts lost his seat next year, a sad commentary upon optimism in South Africa.) King George at the Guildhall was glad to acknowledge South Africa's 'full measure of manhood'. Decisions about her future 'must be her own'. He hoped none-theless for racial 'adjustment' involving millions of coloured people – 'above all, African'. Yet if he mildly criticised, he also warmed the Union with his affection, speaking at Pretoria of 'the secret of its great attraction' which he and the Queen had 'plumbed'. Queen Elizabeth played her inimitable part. When a veteran of the Boer War half apologised for his inability to forgive England's conquest, the Queen replied, 'I understand that perfectly. We feel very much the same in Scotland.' For Princess Elizabeth came a moving opportunity to tell the whole Commonwealth, South Africa especially, that princesses were human beings too and felt 'very much the same' on their birthdays as other girls, though in her case with a peculiarly solemn dedication to service.

She broadcast her message on 21 April 1947, her twenty-first birthday. Before she was three months older her engagement was announced to Lieutenant Philip Mountbatten, RN, in November they were married and a year later (November 1948) Prince Charles was born – truly another *annus mirabilis* for King George and Queen Elizabeth, containing as it did their own twenty-fifth wedding anniversary.

The sun shone far more strongly and continuously on the Silver Wedding celebrations of 26 April 1948 than it had on the showers-and-shine of their wedding day. After a traditional Thanksgiving Service in St Paul's and a spectacularly extended motorcade through twenty miles of cheering Londoners, both husband and wife broadcast – so rooted had the idea of the family become in their people's imagination. 'I make no secret of the fact,' said the King, speaking of popular goodwill and his own burden, 'that there have been times when it would have been almost *too* heavy but for the strength and comfort which I have always found in my home.' They all knew what he meant; some may have remembered the broadcast words of another King who could not shoulder the burden without the woman he loved at his side – and gone on to think that what had seemed a catastrophe to the throne had turned out a blessing. Even 'Chips' Channon, once so frank a partisan of the Windsors that in 1940 he had credited the new royal pair with no impressiveness, no 'thrill', none of 'the divinity that doth hedge a king' – now, in 1948, 'Chips' was writing of the State Opening of Parliament, 'It was like a Grand Slam in Hearts.'

'We were dumbfounded over our reception', wrote the King to his mother. 'It spurs us on to further efforts.' Like his father, he was genuinely surprised to be popular.

The King recapitulated his year during the Christmas broadcast:

In the course of it I have had three vivid personal experiences . . . all of them in their different ways have made a deep impression on me. In April I celebrated my Silver Wedding; then in November, I welcomed my first grandchild . . .

And the third experience? Sadly, he was following his father's trail of exactly twenty years earlier –

and, finally, I have been obliged to submit, for reasons of health to a spell of temporary inactivity.

He summed up the three personal events – anniversary, birth, illness – with a human touch:

All these are events which may have happened to many of you.

The King's illness, a thrombosis, was in its way as desperate as his father's illness of 1928, but whereas the father was an extraordinarily bad patient, the son was stoical, co-operative, grateful and interested in his treatment. Scheduled tours had to be cancelled and amputation of the right leg was narrowly avoided. In March 1949 he underwent a right lumbar sympathectomy, stoically insisting beforehand, 'I am not in the least worried.' Like his father, he fought back to health after a year's invalidism, but King George had only two years more in which to enjoy the results of his fortitude, instead of his father's seven. Even these last two years were interrupted by a severe operation in September 1951 which his friends and family knew was for lung cancer. And over all hung the threat of another thrombosis.

His postponed tour to Australia and New Zealand had to be postponed once more. But in fact he was giving up more than tours; he was a living sacrifice to duty. As Churchill was to say after he died, 'He walked with Death and made Death his friend.'

Meanwhile the Commonwealth of 1949 had become like a mountain range in springtime, when the seeming solidity is broken by the thunder of avalanches, now near, as in Ireland, now distant and incalculable in their effect as in India. Eire proclaimed herself a republic on Easter Monday 1949 – a date indissolubly linked to the 1916 Easter Rising of King George v's first tumultuous decade. King George VI was to ask the Irish Foreign Minister jocularly, 'What does this legislation of yours make *me* in Ireland, an undesirable alien?' Shades again of 1917 and the House of Windsor's birth.

On the fate of India depended the future of the Commonwealth. The once 'brightest jewel' in Queen Victoria's crown now hung poised like the Maltese cross in the Imperial Crown of 1930, either to be jolted and jarred until it fell out altogether and rolled away, or to shine anew in an ingenious modern setting. For 26 January 1950 was to be the date when India would declare herself a republic. Post-war India no longer wished to owe allegiance to the crown. Yet the India of Nehru and the Mountbattens' friendship did not want to quit the Commonwealth either. Could a formula be found to solve such a constitutional conundrum? It seemed impossible that allegiance to the crown, enunciated in the Statute of Westminster as the essential Commonwealth link, should be broken, yet the breaker remain inside. Nevertheless it had to be done. If the case of India were to establish that republics and the Commonwealth were incompatible, it was the Commonwealth which would go down. No one doubted that to be a republic in the post-war climate would make complete independence feel more independent still. The fashion would be catching and the departure of India only the first of many farewells.

So the impossible was accomplished. Words were told what they had to mean, as in *Alice*, and being words, they obeyed. A combined operation was mounted by Attlee, a special Cabinet committee, a Commonwealth Conference of Prime Ministers and the King's private secretary. Slowly every pocket of resistance was cleared – precedent, protocol, logic – all driven out by that time-honoured quartet: necessity, invention, accommodation and compromise. King George VI would be acknowledged as 'Head of the Commonwealth' by all members including India; but 'allegiance' to the crown was no longer a prerequisite of membership. From being the essential link, the crown would become 'a symbol of association'. Mr Attlee had wondered how H.M. would take this pill. If it had been King George V there would assuredly have been much angry 'chaffing' and references to the medicine as 'damned muck'. But King George VI, in his biographer's words, had 'an agile mind' and was no Bourbon. 'He knew how to learn and how to forget, and he never confused the substance with the shadow.'

Under stress of the Korean War and economic crisis, King George decided in 1951 to involve himself in the consciously enlivening Festival of Britain. On seeing plans for the Festival Hall itself, he told Morrison that it deserved the title 'Royal'. Morrison grasped the offer enthusiastically: 'Its success is assured.' The King did not tell Morrison his opinion of that major exhibit, the 'Skylon': an unfortunate symbol for Britain's economy, he thought, since 'it had no visible means of support'.

The crown itself was a symbol. But its 'means of support' were amply visible in popular concern over the King's health and sympathy with his family. 'The incessant worries & crises through which we have to live got me down properly,' he wrote in 1951. Probably the return of a Conservative government [Churchill's] with a respectable majority, instead of Attlee's hazardous one, reduced the worries of that autumn. Christmas came with a family party at Sandringham. His beloved Lilibet and Philip were here before setting out on the postponed Commonwealth tour; and he had Prince Charles, as always 'too sweet stumping about the room', two-year-old Princess Anne, Princess Margaret to play to him, sing and make him laugh, and of course his wife who, as he had once told Princess Elizabeth, was in his eyes 'the most marvellous person in the World'.

On 31 January 1952 he stood on the tarmac waving good-bye to his daughter and son-in-law. A cold wind blew and he was 'hatless', as the journalists noted, using the word which had become memorable in 1936. But a 'hatless' King Edward VIII landing on the runway had symbolised a carefree being without encumbrances, whereas King George VI seemed careworn, touching and vulnerable.

After 'Keepers' Day' on 5 February in the frosty, sunlit fields of Sandringham the King could not ask for more happiness. He died from heart failure in the early hours of 6 February 1952.

Death had crept up on him during sleep, so that in his end, as in his youth and manhood, events had taken him unawares. His marriage was the great exception; and this in fact epitomised his inherent will to conquer. No king faced more frustrations, more misfortunes. He nevertheless carved from this cross-grained material a rich and comely life, at the core of which was family solidarity unknown to the Royal House for centuries. He had intellectual curiosity, dry humour, kindliness and good sense; he had the qualities of resilience and concentration which go with athletic talent; so transparent was his goodness that if he had been a medieval monarch, born to the same poignant circumstances, they would have made him a saint. The sudden gusts of fury or depression were no more than the measure of his trials.

Abdication had compelled him to consolidate the monarchy rather than to modernise it. But other events forced changes upon him. Still young himself, he was nearer to the people than a king had ever been. To his daughter he handed on a nation ready to welcome the imaginative touch of extreme youth. To the people he bequeathed, in her, the 'brightest jewel in his crown'.

OPPOSITE: Queen Elizabeth with Princess Elizabeth and Princess Margaret in the grounds of Windsor Castle.

5

QUEEN ELIZABETH II
AND
PRINCE PHILIP

OPPOSITE: King George VI at Buckingham Palace.

IO

A young gleaming champion

'We thank God for the gift He has bestowed upon us, and vow ourselves anew to the sacred causes and wise and kindly way of life of which your Majesty is the young, gleaming champion.' Churchill toasting the Queen, 1955.

'CHARMING little creature! I do hope they don't work her too hard.' The words were spoken by Lord Pethwick-Lawrence in St George's Chapel at Windsor. We were sitting waiting for the funeral of King George VI to begin. Subdued and sad, we occasionally spoke in low voices while the organ played. Suddenly the organ stopped and there was dead silence. Except for Pethwick-Lawrence. The old gentleman was rather deaf and had not noticed the silence. At the sight of the royal catafalque and the slim, almost childlike figure of the Queen – for we were high up among the grey traceries and she looked very small – he said loudly what most of us were thinking. Added to that, he had been an ardent supporter of the suffragettes in youth and there was a special poignancy in being ruled over by a woman. Her loneliness and the black clothes made us feel deeply protective. This young Sovereign was part of 'us'; and 'they' must be prevented from driving her too hard.

Over a century ago people had felt solicitous in the same way for little Victoria, Queen at eighteen. But in her case the feeling had been romantic. No one really expected her to overwork. Her great-great-granddaughter, on the contrary, had just lost a father, as everyone knew, from stress and strain. The *Lancet* was to write, 'As doctors we should have special reason to welcome an assurance that . . . Her Majesty's health and vitality will be protected from her hereditary sense of duty.' And old Queen Mary said later that year, after her granddaughter had paid a particularly successful visit to Edinburgh, 'I only hope that they will not kill the poor little girl with overwork.' All these concerned voices were assuming that Queen Elizabeth II would carry on the tradition of her family – extreme conscientiousness and dutifulness for which the House of Windsor was already famous. They assumed a continuity of type and attitude. In this they were to be proved right. There were others, however, whose wishful thoughts hovered over the prospect of a totally different era embodied in a new young queen and consort.

'Let us hope that there will now be a clean-out, a clean sweep,' Channon noted in his diary three days after King George VI's death. Apparently forgetful of the 'Grand Slam in Hearts' which he had justly attributed to the reigning pair only a few years earlier, he now wrote about the late King much as a poet had once described the month of November – 'No sun – no moon . . . November.' To Channon it had been a reign of Novembers – 'no wit, no learning, no humour . . . no vices . . .' But at last Channon was again rapturously happy. 'I rejoice in the new reign and welcome it. We shall be the new Elizabethans.' A month or so later he felt the House of Windsor's rejuvenation had somehow breathed life into the whole Government and nation. 'There is a new festival spirit about. A young queen; an old Prime Minister [Churchill] and a brave buoyant Butler budget. Has he put us [Conservatives] in for a generation?' The sobering answer lay as usual in history. Socialist Hugh Dalton had sensed precisely the same festive spirit about the Labour victory of 1945: 'We are in for the next twenty years,' he prophesied. A week, we know, is a long time in politics.

This is not the place to probe into the psychology of the 'New Elizabethans'. There was indeed a gallant and pathetic attempt to make the British people pull themselves up by their own bootstraps – with the indispensable aid of the Queen's golden chains and silken chords. The new Queen had a name to conjure with. She was in fact called after her mother – 'the most marvellous person in the World', as her father had said – but her name nevertheless linked her with Gloriana, Elizabeth I. By one of those happy coincidences the two Elizabeths had ascended the throne at the same age – twenty-five. Not since Queen Victoria had Britain acclaimed a young sovereign. With Edward VII in his sixtieth year and his three successors in their forties, Queen Elizabeth II did indeed excite hopes centred on youth – her own youth and the youth of the nation wishfully regenerated; become chivalrous as Sir Walter Raleigh, bold as Sir Francis Drake; a match for America's wealth through a new race of 'Merchant Adventurers', and for Russia's armadas through a revival of – what? Possibly there were day-dreams about small English privateers, working their magic once more on the oceans of the world. Essentially the vision was of private adventurers, both in public and private life. Away with the old stagnation. No more economic 'stop-go'; no more moral or mental hang-ups.

It took the country some years to realise that there were no short cuts to Utopia. The impresarios could bill a star-cast for 'The New Elizabethans', but the stage would remain empty.

As for the Queen, she was not averse to clean sweeps, but her idea of the operation had a rhythm and object all its own. 'We live in an age of growing self indulgence, of hardening materialism, and of falling moral standards,' she had told her young fellow-mothers and wives in 1949. 'Some of the very principles on which the family, and therefore the health of the nation, is founded are in danger.' Divorce, separation, broken homes were responsible for 'some of the darkest evils in our society today'. Yet a fear of being labelled 'priggish' or 'intolerant' was preventing more and more of us from daring to disapprove of what we knew to be wrong.

Who could say whether this was a new broom or a return to the oldest standards of domestic economy?

The idea of a clean sweep, as a matter of fact, had first come to Elizabeth at the age of three. Her grandmother's lady-in-waiting, Lady Airlie, gave her a housemaid's set for Christmas, including the usual dustpan-and-brush. Lady Airlie noticed the 'resultant passion for housework' that swept over the nursery of 145 Piccadilly. The Princess's tastes were indeed as orderly as her father's and grandfather's and, translated into feminine terms, domestic. Her absorbing love for ponies may well have illustrated what psychiatrists see in girls as an incipient devotion to babies. In any case, stables have long been the place for small girls to perform a 'clean-out' and 'clean sweep', without becoming in any way slaveys. The Princess's addiction to tidiness was said sometimes to have been a burden to herself and a joke to her sister. At night, instead of throwing her shoes under one chair and her clothes on another, she would arrange them meticulously more than once before going to sleep. Her sister and governess laughed her out of the habit. She stored a box with neatly rolled ribbons saved from chocolate boxes and pieces of smooth folded coloured paper. Nothing was wasted. Not only did she keep an accurate list of her own presents received at Christmas, but one for her sister also. As Princess Margaret's elder by four years, her sense of responsibility was always alert. If Margaret called out 'Wait for me!' as they scampered between Byron's statue and the railings of Hamilton Gardens, Elizabeth would always wait. When it was small London evacuees during the War who shouted 'Wai-i-t, Lilibet!' she would still wait. Her style was to give a gentle lead in the old, tried ways; never to outstrip, or to disappear from sight along new, unblazed trails.

She was sensitive to atmosphere; but the absolute trust and security in her own childhood home prevented her from feeling more than a passing shadow from her parents' ordeals. 'Who *is* she?' Princess Elizabeth asked her governess in 1936 after Mrs Simpson paid a visit to Royal Lodge. The governess detected unmistakable suspicion. Fortunately Mrs Simpson noticed only how well scrubbed the children were, how blonde, how good mannered. When the time came, Princess Elizabeth wrote 'Abdication Day' at the top of a note; her sister had just learnt to write 'York' and was annoyed both at this wasted labour and at now being Margaret 'of *nothing*'.

The coronation of her father and mother was an opportunity for Princess Elizabeth to show her seriousness and aptitude for a great occasion. Like her great-great-grandmother Queen Victoria at eighteen – Princess Elizabeth was eleven – she kept a diary of the day, but for her parents to read. Victoria had not dreamed of showing her diaries to 'Mama' once she was Queen and no longer in parental thrall. Such a condition – thralldom – then or ever would have been unthinkable to Princess Elizabeth. Queen Victoria had been awakened at 4 a.m. by the noise in the Park; she rose feeling 'strong and well'. Princess Elizabeth, when woken at 5 a.m., felt rather chilly but jumped out of bed at once, and obediently wrapping herself like her beloved nursemaid 'Bobo' (Margaret Macdonald) in an eiderdown, watched the scene from their window. The next responsibility was for her six-year-old sister: 'She is very young for a coronation, isn't she?' But the sprightly Margaret behaved perfectly, except for an occasional loud whirring of the pages of her prayer book. Their grandmother Queen Mary sat with them. Though they did not know it, this was a change in royal protocol. Hitherto dowager queens had absented themselves from a young queen's triumph. But Queen Mary wished to mark her solidarity with the new reigning family; more than anyone, she had visualised the strain which David was shifting on to Bertie's shoulders, saying, 'The person who needs most sympathy is my second son. He is the one who is making the sacrifice.' In sixteen years' time Queen Elizabeth the Queen Mother would be at her own daughter's coronation, providing a handbag for the occupation of five-year-old Prince Charles.

During the two years between the coronation and the Second World War, Princess Elizabeth went steadily forward in an aura of happiness from which only normal experiences were missing. Neither she nor her sister ever went to school. It is doubtful whether the King would have consented to pitchfork his treasures into that maelstrom even if their mother had wanted it: 'I've never heard of a King going to a hospital before,' he had protested when this strange place was at first suggested for his operation. 'A Princess going to school' would have sounded even odder. The Queen had certainly spent a short period at a girls' school in London, but the experiment did not make a deep or glowing impression. Today not only would the advance in medicine necessitate a king going to hospital, but a princess has also gone to boarding-school (Benenden). Moreover in the 1930s when the young Princesses did venture outside the Palace gates on to a thrilling bus or tube, they were almost immediately recognised and mobbed. In the end the governess would telephone for a royal Daimler to rescue them from the gathering crowd. Today, again, things have changed, thanks to three main factors: the foresight of Queen Elizabeth II and Prince Philip; the co-operation of the press; and a saner attitude in the public.

One unavoidable element in the cloistered nature of their lives was Buckingham Palace itself. So much did the children miss the neighbourly layout of 145 Piccadilly, with its nursery quarters always within sight of what went on downstairs, that they dreamed at first of an underground passage between the Palace and Hyde Park Corner, along which they could escape back 'home'. There would be visitors to No. 145, such as Archbishop Lang, Mr Baldwin and Mr Macdonald at whom the Princesses could peer down the well of the staircase. One day Princess Elizabeth conversationally remarked to Macdonald that she had seen a picture of him in *Punch* leading a flock of geese. He gave, according to the Princess's governess, 'a wan smile'.

Buckingham Palace seemed both cheerless and vast, all the suites – State, King's, Queen's, secretarial, kitchens, offices, nurseries – being measureless caverns worthy of Kubla Khan, separated by interminable corridors. 'People here need bicycles,' was Princess Elizabeth's verdict. In the next generation there were indeed to be toy tricycles and pedal-cars lined up behind the great pillars of the Marble Hall, after bed-time. Guests of the owners' parents were pleased to think that those wide open spaces had at last become a positive advantage. Within the confines of the Palace the Princesses were given a taste of life with children of their own age – dancing, singing-games, Girl Guides and Brownies. Patricia, elder daughter of Lord Mountbatten, was invited to become patrol leader and created the Kingfisher Patrol at Buckingham Palace. There was not much variety on which their minds rather than their legs could be stretched, except for grown-ups ranging from a nanny ('Alah') to the Provost of Eton, who was soon to teach the young Elizabeth history.

Fortunately the sisters themselves were as unlike as possible, so that they could strike sparks out of one another. Princess Margaret mischievous, vivacious, 'outrageously amusing' according to Lady Airlie, '*espiègle*' according to Queen Mary, and spoilt by her father as an irresistible '*enfant terrible*'; Princess Elizabeth her father's constant companion out of doors, good at riding, bad at knitting, gay without being a fire-cracker and at war with no one, not even herself. When she was presented for confirmation it was again Lady Airlie who saw the thing they were all looking for: 'there was about her that indescribable something which Queen Victoria had.'

Then came the Blitz and the young family, complete with 'Alah', 'Bobo', 'Crawfie' and corgis were swept off to Windsor. 'Who is this Hitler, spoiling everything?' demanded Princess Margaret, much as her grandmother Queen Mary had voted 'this fellow Hitler' to be a most ghastly bore. Life could be cold in the Castle in winter, especially when descending to the dungeons during an air-raid, and nasty things had to be endured in summer, like washing up camping saucepans afloat with grease and taking cover from 'doodle-bugs'.

The children's lively talent for acting burst forth in plays and pantomimes. You could go right back through the House of Windsor and into the House of Hanover and still find excellent mimics. Now they performed in the Waterloo Chamber where old Queen Victoria had once occupied a post in advance of the front row, fanning herself and ringing her little golden bell to make the curtain rise. The great portraits painted for King George IV by Sir Thomas Lawrence, including the King himself, his family and family heroes like Wellington, had all been removed from their frames and stored in safety. This gave a chance for both Princess Margaret and her father to sharpen their wit. Princess Margaret had the empty frames filled up with pantomime posters of Mother Goose, Prince Charming and the Ugly Sisters; 'How do you like my ancestors?' the King would ask his guests. He dissolved in tears when his daughters acted a Christmas play; their expertise as Prince Charming and Cinderella took his breath away.

Meanwhile the real Prince Charming had taken the boards once or twice, only to vanish again. Princess Elizabeth was eight when she first saw Prince Philip of Greece, a yellow-haired, blue-eyed third cousin five years older than herself. They had met again briefly at the coronation when she was eleven. Philip had spent a disagreeable year in Germany at Kurt Hahn's famous progressive school, Salem. Not that the school was disagreeable; it was the advent of Hitler that year which put his back up. Danes do not like militarism; and Philip was a Dane on his father's side. His grandmother, Princess Victoria of Hesse, was a granddaughter of Queen Victoria who had married Prince Louis of Battenberg. The Battenbergs' eldest child was another Alice, born at Windsor and, thanks to Queen Victoria's hierarchical arrangements, in the same bed in which her mother also had been born. For each birth Queen Victoria installed herself like a high priestess at the bedside uncannily aware, it seemed, that this particular Victoria and that particular Alice were to carry on her line. In due course Princess Alice married Prince Andrew of Greece. She gave birth to her last child and only son, Philip, on 10 June 1921. Meanwhile the Battenbergs' youngest child, Prince Louis ('Dickie') had been born on 25 June 1900 at Frogmore House in Windsor Park. One of Queen Victoria's last pleasures was to insist on this birthplace and to become the child's godmother. 'Uncle Dickie' would be to Philip's generation what 'Uncle Leopold' had been to little Victoria's. He was a midshipman in the Royal Navy when 1917 arrived and all the names were changed.

Twenty-two years later, his nephew was beginning his own naval career at Dartmouth. That July Dartmouth was the scene of a family gathering, almost 'reunion' if one can be reunited with a place. King George VI was revisiting the haunts of 'P.A.' for the first time, accompanied by the Queen, his daughters, his naval ADC Dickie Mountbatten and Dickie's naval nephew Philip. Though now eighteen, Philip kindly played trains with Margaret on the floor and jumped over the tennis net for Elizabeth. Some of this has been called 'bumptious'; but bumptious or not, that energetic boy certainly amused his two third cousins. His life had been far from sheltered, and at this date the distance between him and his thirteen-year-old cousin was probably something in the region of light-years.

Born in Corfu but more familiar with Paris than anywhere else until he was sent to Cheam, his first English boarding-school, Philip became entirely anglicised. He had the usual obsession with games and more than the usual talent, especially in high-jump and high-diving, which seem in retrospect to suit his rightly ambitious temperament. Kurt Hahn's new scholastic venture at Gordonstoun in the highlands of Scotland was clearly the perfect setting in which a boy of Philip's character might wrestle with nature, man and himself for the next four years. By the time he was ready for Dartmouth, Hahn had discovered in him all the typical instincts of youth in extreme forms: he was funnier, sharper, more impetuous, more daring and responsive than most; a perfectionist, an all-outer; yet alive with human sympathies. 'He has the greatest sense of service', wrote Hahn, 'of all the boys in the school.' All the same, when Hahn finally summed up his best as 'outstanding' and his second best as 'not good enough', one can take it that the schoolmaster was right – and also that young Philip was perfectly well satisfied with these priorities. Second best did not interest him. His 'best' included becoming head boy of Gordonstoun and winning the school prize for the best all-rounder. At Dartmouth he was to win the King's Dirk. The 'best' of life also was his during the holidays, when he would whirl around Europe, wherever his father's multiple family happened to hold out welcoming hands; or stay in England with his mother's family, the Mountbattens.

The sophistication of a much-travelled boy was rapidly deepened by experiences aboard ship in war-time. He fought in engagements off Libya and Crete, and in the Battle of Cape Matapan where he was mentioned in despatches. When in 1942 his cousin Elizabeth was created an honorary colonel (Grenadier Guards) Philip was a naval lieutenant; when in 1944 Elizabeth became a Councillor of State, Philip was second in command of a destroyer – she always pinned to the honorary ladder, he leaping up the active ladder with ever-increasing brilliance.

Harold Nicolson, introduced at Buckingham Palace, gave a brief flash of her at this period (1944): 'Princess Elizabeth is a clear, nice girl. I talked to her about the Grenadiers.' It was not till the beginning of 1945 that King George at last agreed to his daughter doing her National Service. A new name and character then emerged, Second-Lieutenant Elizabeth Windsor, of the Auxiliary Transport Service, No. 1 Mechanical Transport Training Centre; an expert driver and able to do repairs and change a wheel, unlike most girls of her age or indeed any age. Soon everyone rejoiced to know how deft she was with a spanner as opposed to a knitting needle. Popular enthusiasm finally subscribed to a legend of her careering about in her heavy army vehicle with the sirens wailing, the guns maybe blazing away and she alone at the wheel. Actually, to be alone at the wheel was not what this rather remote spirit required; her real need was to meet her contemporaries, not hand-picked but just as they came. This she did in the A T S.

Princess Elizabeth's longing to play an active part in the war-effort can probably be traced to the influence of young officers on leave. Like her uncle the Duke of Windsor before her, she saw no reason why 'all my friends' should serve but not the heir to the throne. 'I ought to do as other girls of my age do.' Among her friends were Philip and his first cousin David Mountbatten, third Marquess of Milford Haven, later to be his best man. Philip had been spending odd days of leave at Windsor ever since 1941 when Elizabeth was fifteen – quite old enough to fall in love with someone who looked and talked as he did, and whom all her family liked.

However, Queen Mary seems to have traced the romantic moment to Windsor in July 1946. Queen Mary enjoyed putting her friend Lady Airlie into the picture from time to time. Thus Lady Airlie had heard of Philip, on holidays from Gordonstoun, as 'intelligent . . . plenty of common sense' and 'very handsome' with the good looks of both the Danish and Mountbatten side of the family; and at the beginning of 1946, as having been Princess Elizabeth's choice for at least a year and a half. When speaking to his biographer Basil Boothroyd many years later, Prince Philip confirmed that 1946 was the date. 'I suppose I began to think about it seriously,' he told Boothroyd's tape-recorder, 'oh, let me think now, when I got back in "forty-six" and went to Balmoral. It was probably then that we, that it became, you know, that we began to think about it seriously, and even talk about it.' But her parents thought nineteen too young for an engagement. 'They want her to see more of the world before committing herself,' explained Queen Mary, 'and to see more men.' Lady Airlie objected that she herself had fallen in love at nineteen and it lasted for ever. 'Yes, it does sometimes happen,' agreed her friend, 'and Elizabeth seems to be that kind of girl. She would always know her own mind. There's something very steadfast and determined in her – like her father.'

Nevertheless her determined father insisted on another sixteen months of growing-up and more knowledge of the world, in the shape of South Africa. She arrived home with her family on 5 May 1947, thin as a shadow but glowing like the sun.

Prince Philip was still trying to conclude certain plans concerning his own name and nationality which the coming of war had interrupted.

Philip was a prince of Greece, theroretically in succession to the Greek kingdom, if and when Greece was a kingdom. He had no surname. His father Prince Andrew, however, died in 1944 with the unfulfilled wish that his only son should take British nationality. Prince Andrew's reason had been simple: namely, that his son should be able to continue his career in the Royal Navy. (Commissioned rank in the Navy was not open to foreigners in peacetime.) Naturalisation as the means to a naval career was also the wish of Philip himself and of Lord Mountbatten, his guardian since the death of his elder uncle Lord Milford-Haven in 1938. However the War, plus the possible bad effect on Greek politics of a royal prince renouncing his nationality, combined to postpone Prince Philip's naturalisation. The entry of Greece into the War on the Allied side meant that Greek nationals were assured of their commissions for the duration. Greek politics again held up Prince Philip's case after the War, but at last, early in 1947, his family were able to proceed with his naturalisation. On 28 February 1947 it was announced that he had become a British subject.

As in 1917 the problem was again a name. King George VI immediately offered his young cousin the title of 'H R H Prince Philip'; but Philip himself preferred to drop his former titles, becoming plain Lieutenant Philip – what? A surname had to be found. There being no Greek surnames, it would have been possible to go back to Denmark for, say, Oldenburg, translated as Oldcastle. But somehow Philip Oldcastle did not sound right. The Labour Home Secretary, Chuter Ede, then performed a service similar to Lord Stamfordham's in 1917: he came up with an admirable suggestion, the surname of Prince Philip's mother's family, Mountbatten.

There were those who, knowing neither the chronology nor the facts, were later to point the finger of scorn and criticism at the royal marriage of Elizabeth and Philip. They declared that Princess Elizabeth was marrying a foreigner; that Prince Philip's naturalisation had a single, self-inflating object – to facilitate his marriage to the heir. It was all rubbish. And to increase the irony, it emerged in 1972 that the naturalisation of Prince Philip had never in fact been necessary. He was a British subject all along. As a result of the case, 'Attorney-General *v*. Prince Ernest Augustus of

Hanover', all descendants of the Electress Sophia are British subjects by virtue of the Act of 1705 passed in the reign of Queen Anne.

The engagement was announced on 10 July 1947. Harold Nicolson went to the Buckingham Palace garden party on that day self-consciously wearing his top-hat. He emerged from the marquee where he had eaten some chocolate cake to report: 'Everybody is straining to see the bridal pair – irreverently and shamelessly straining.' The wedding day was fixed for 20 November. It was all perfectly traditional. Indeed the scarlet and gold, the trappings and trumpets, seemed more traditional than ever against the fiercely resistant austerity of a post-war world. The bride's veil was off her face, according to royal custom. In the wintry sunshine her wedding-dress shone with flowers of pearl, visible to all through the large windows of the time-honoured Glass Coach. People were glad to feel that little had changed since the days of Queen Victoria, though when Princes Elizabeth's dress came eventually to rest in the London Museum, it proved to be several sizes larger than her great-great-grandmother's, much freer in design and not quite so durable in material. Twenty-five years later the silk in places had begun to fray.

Wedding presents had poured in, afterwards to be exhibited for charity in St James's Palace. Seeing them so soon after the War, when normal household equipment was grey in colour and feeble in texture, one's eyes were dazzled by the sumptuous froth of lace, linen and wool, fluffy as omelets, thick as cream. Among them was Mahatma Gandhi's gift, which, according to Lady Airlie, caused Queen Mary so much pained surprise. He appeared to have sent them a loin-cloth, made by himself. 'What a horrible thing', exlaimed Queen Mary, coming to a halt before the little offering. 'I don't think it's horrible,' interjected Philip, who overheard. 'Gandhi is a wonderful man; a very great man.' No comment from Queen Mary. But in fact she was mistaken on all counts. Mahatma Gandhi, enchanted by the news of the engagement, had summoned the Viceroy to bestow his blessing, though sorry that he could give no wedding-present, since he had no possessions. 'You can spin,' replied Lord Mountbatten, 'and have it made into something.' So Gandhi's spinning wheel whirred and a table-mat was crochetted on his own design. The Queen keeps it among her special treasures.

Queen Mary was generally the first to champion Philip's new ideas and attitudes. At least one member of the Royal Family had taken leave to wonder whether Philip's education at a 'crank' school would prove useful or baleful to him as Princess Elizabeth's husband. 'Useful,' replied Queen Mary. 'The world has changed,' she added in telling this anecdote to Lady Airlie, '. . . and it will change still more.'

There was one other change which the foolish chose to interpret as a royal attempt at putting the 'uppish' Philip in his place. On 6 November, a fortnight before the wedding-day, King George had written to his mother Queen Mary that he was giving the Garter to Lilibet on the 11th and to Philip on the 19th; Philip would also be created a Royal Highness, Baron Greenwich, Earl of Merioneth and Duke of Edinburgh. 'It is a great deal to give a man all at once,' added the King, 'but I know Philip understands his new responsibilities on his marriage to Lilibet.'

In the light of Queen Elizabeth II's action ten years later, when she created the Duke of Edinburgh a Prince of the United Kingdom, it has been suggested that King George VI deliberately withheld from his son-in-law the title of Prince in order to assist him towards a more reasonable degree of self-conceit. The whole story is flagrantly untrue. The King, as we have seen had already offered Philip the title 'Prince' earlier that year. If he had really wished to cut Philip down to size why should he top up the glittering pile of his peerage with an H. R. H.? The H. R. H. without 'Prince'' was certainly an anomaly; but the idea of King George slighting his adored Lilibet's husband, a man he always greatly liked, makes no sense whatever. It should be treated as another of those 'show-off' fables connected with Prince Philip's youth, and relegated to the appropriate limbo.

A letter reached Princess Elizabeth on her honeymoon. It was from her father:

Our family, us four, the 'royal family' must remain together with additions of course at suitable moments!! I have watched you grow up all these years with pride under the skilful direction of Mummy, who as you know is the most marvellous person in the World in my eyes, & I can I know, always count on you, & now Philip, to help us in our work.

Touchingly her father confessed to the relief he felt now that she admitted the long wait before the engagement and wedding had been for the best. He had not been without fears that she would think him hard-hearted. Nor did he conceal from her the 'great blank' left in his life nor his natural ambivalence towards the successful suitor. 'I can see that you are sublimely happy with Philip which is right but don't forget us. . . .' Nevertheless the overriding message of his letter was 'our work'. *Us four* had become us *five*, five hearts united in duty and work; perhaps after all 'Chips' Channon was wrong and the royal suit had been spades.

A disturbed honeymoon was quickly followed by public duties. The disturbance was caused by ardent sightseers, who succeeded in driving the young couple out of 'Broadlands', the Hampshire estate lent to them by Lord Mountbatten, and into the fastnesses of Scotland. This first misadventure with peeping Toms no doubt confirmed the young husband in his view that one of his functions was to protect his wife from people who had not read their Bagehot. 'Poking about' the monarchy, whether with lorgnettes or modern lenses, has always provoked a sharp reaction. When Disraeli turned his quizzing-glass on Queen Victoria at the Prince of Wales's wedding, the Widow at Windsor had to wither him herself. Princess Elizabeth was lucky in having a husband to wither Dizzies and quizzes for her.

A charming and conscientious princess will always find her knight errant. Princess Elizabeth's dedicatory broadcast from South Africa had gone straight to the heart of a young war-hero, 'Boy' Browning. 'It is my vocation to serve that young woman,' he said to himself – and joined her staff. Prince Philip's private secretary, Michael Parker, described the husband's role in vivid language. Rather than a medieval knight errant, he saw Prince Philip as 'a kind of super Chief of Staff' who gives his wife 'the complete lowdown on absolutely anything'. What about their Paris visit in May 1948? Was it all right for her to do as the French did and go to the races on the Sabbath? Certainly; and the Lord's Day Observance people, whose skirmishes with royalty dated back a hundred years, must again be driven off territory that was not their own. Later Prince Philip's Sunday polo, watched by the Queen, was to become as much a battle-ground as a game.

This was his semi-public vocation. In private life he had four years, as it turned out, in which to become 'the master in the house'. Those words, quoted from Prince Albert when he was lamenting his position as mere husband but not master in Queen Victoria's palaces, illustrates Prince Philip's happier state. Whereas Victoria became queen first and wife afterwards, with Elizabeth II it was the other way round. From the human angle, this was vastly preferable. 'Within the house, and whatever we did, it was together,' Philip told Boothroyd. 'I suppose I naturally filled the principal position.' It was not until after his wife's accession that the Consort would need to grapple with a whole set of new problems, including a life of his own.

Meanwhile behind the changes in nation and Commonwealth, a steady volume of affection was building up for the new family in Clarence House. An entertaining example is given by Robert Menzies. This statesman, about to be Prime Minister of Australia for the second time, happened to be in London with his family on the night when Prince Charles was born at Buckingham Palace. Swept up by popular fervour, the Menzies family rushed to the bulletin on the Palace gates, joining with excited Londoners, all strangers, in clapping one another on the back and shouting 'most lustily and senselessly' for 'Philip' and 'Grandfather'.

Despite the basic affection, Princess Elizabeth had to accustom herself to inaccurate paragraphs in the press about the ruinous cost of their decorations and the criminal waste of cubic feet; these were the bubbles which at least showed that the stream was moving. While the bubbles were pricked with one hand the stagnant waters had to be stirred with the other. Up till 1951 the Princess had been forbidden to make long-distance flights. That year, however, Prince Philip used an already tight schedule to deliver an ultimatum. Either they must fly or a projected Canadian tour must be cancelled. So another 'first' was notched up: the first time the heir to the throne had flown the Atlantic. Times change, as everyone kept saying. Early in 1952 they flew off again. While in Kenya they heard that the greatest and saddest change for them had come about.

'Princess Elizabeth is flying back from Kenya. She became Queen while perched in a tree in Africa, watching the rhinoceroses come down to the pool to drink.' The combined effect of dead-pan and drama in this extract from Nicolson's diary was a good deal nearer to the truth than many other contemporary accounts. Deeply tragic though it was to know that her father had died while she was so far away, she was not prostrated by the news as some sentimentalists have imagined. She had carried with her a sealed envelope containing messages to both Houses of Parliament the year before, in case the blow fell while she was in Canada. Now her first thought was to get home and carry on.

Nor was her secretary, Martin Charteris, the broken reed that one lachrymose legend represents. Instead of groaning, 'My poor dear lady', and asking a local journalist to save him the anguish of breaking the news to Michael Parker by doing it for him, he himself telephoned to Parker immediately. Then he held the first press conference regarding 'the Lady we must now call Queen'. In Kenya no one was overcome; all were stimulated. The royal party touched down at Heathrow airport only a week after they had taken off.

Perhaps this is the moment to say a word about the House of Windsor at the hands of writers. Our Royal Family have been dissected with a freedom that was conceded only to cartoonists during the last century. On the whole that is an advantage. Nevertheless there are still a good many synthetic character sketches and third-hand judgments going the rounds from typewriter to typewriter. The more royalty can speak for themselves the better. Boothroyd's tape-recorder, for instance, has given a freshness to his picture of Prince Philip which effectively destroys the stale old clichés about 'show-offs' and 'bumptiousness'. Here is someone who can be critical and caustic. But at any rate he knows it, and has all the graces of self-awareness. It was a pity that Queen Victoria's aptitude for self-criticism was never mentioned by her contemporaries. She went down to history as a complacent old lady. That has not been the fate of her descendants. Only recently another record was broken when her great-great-great-granddaughter told inquisitors on television that she was sorry for something she had said to reporters at Kiev. Princess Anne's grandmother once said gloomily, 'We are not supposed to be human.' Today it is they themselves who have given the royal 'we' a human edge.

Queen Elizabeth II was proclaimed in her capital on 8 February 1952. The form of words used there and elsewhere in the Commonwealth produced several surprises. 'By the Grace of God, Queen of this Realm and of all Her other Realms and Territories, Head of the Commonwealth, Defender of the Faith . . .' So it ran in London. Australia, New Zealand, Pakistan and Ceylon all swore allegiance in the new phrase 'Head of the Commonwealth', while Pandit Nehru, as was to be expected, merely sent a welcoming message from India to the 'Head'. But Canada and South Africa, strangely, ignored the new title 'Head of the Commonwealth', and adopted the old-fashioned formula ending with 'Supreme Liege Lady in and over Canada', 'Sovereign in and over the Union of South Africa . . .' Yet these two countries had been keenest of all on their independence.

Two facts stood out: first, the once proud title of 'Dominion status' was giving place to the new status of 'Member' or 'Realm'; second, there was no uniformity in the Commonwealth, not even among the 'old' countries. The debasement of the name 'Dominion' was significant in itself. The old title had been intended to emphasise the independent states' 'dominion' over themselves; but now in this touchy new world it began to sound like British dominion 'over palm and pine', over South Africa and Canada. As for the mysterious relationship between the young Queen and the republics, this still gave pleasant opportunities for speculation. Churchill confined himself to resonant generalities about the republics' 'proud and respectful association' with the crown; but Professor Mansergh was probably nearer the mark when he spoke of England's 'satisfaction' that, as a result of republican infusion, the Commonwealth 'had become still more difficult for foreigners to understand'. Whether it would in time become too difficult for natives to work, was not a question one asked as the coronation drew near.

The many changes in the monarchy which took place after the Queen's accession have frequently been noted. There was Prince Philip's modernisation of the Palace. His introduction of labour-saving schemes made people think he must be studying biographies of Prince Albert. This was not the case. Prince Philip had none of his ancestor's thoroughgoing, conscientious gloom. He made improvements because he liked them, without dwelling too lugubriously on the previous state of affairs. Changes in family life and upbringing were all being prepared: school for Prince Charles like other children, and a children's hospital for Princess Anne when she needed to have her tonsils out, instead of the unit brought into the Palace, as in the past. Adult life was going to be infinitely more mobile, with the Prince's helicopter landing in the Palace garden and even the Queen Mother in due course 'chopping' to and from her granddaughter's school, her own racing stables and her public assignments. Royal speeches depended more on humour, wit and irony for getting off the ground, and less on straight moral uplift. It was a far cry from King George V, who would often remind his sons that his public speeches never contained jokes. One remembers old Queen Victoria telling her children that she never smiled for a state portrait.

All this and far more has been noticed in great detail. But one change not altogether welcome to the young family which happened early on and lingered awkwardly for many years is rarely mentioned, despite its considerable interest. It was the name again.

Nothing could have been more popular, we have seen, than the Royal Family's change of name in 1917 from Coburg to Windsor. Windsor it would remain – until the moment when there was a queen regnant instead of a king. Like every woman in the land a queen of England receives her husband's name when she marries. No doubt she still continues to reign under the name of her father: Queen Anne was the last Stuart, Queen Victoria the last Hanoverian. But when Queen Victoria died the House of Hanover came to an end and her heir, having inherited his father's name like every other legitimate child, initiated the House of Coburg. A comparable moment had arrived again. Queen Elizabeth II ascended the throne as the last sovereign of the House of Windsor, the first of the Family of Mountbatten. Her son Charles and her daughter Anne were Mountbattens. When Charles succeeded he would inaugurate the House of Mountbatten.

This in fact was the legal position for two months of British history. From 6 February to 9 April 1952 the surname of the Royal Family was Mountbatten; but on that date, 9 April, the normal course of history was changed. The *London Gazette* announced:

The Queen today declared in Council Her Will and Pleasure that She and Her Children shall be styled and known as the House and Family of Windsor, and that Her descendants, other than female descendants who marry, and their descendants shall bear the name of Windsor.

Though the Queen did not explicitly renounce the surname of Mountbatten for herself and her descendants, this was the effect of her declaration.

According to ancient usage, such declarations are always the sovereign's 'Pleasure' as well as 'Will'. It is highly improbable, however, that the *London Gazette* of 9 April 1952 gave the young Queen any pleasure whatsoever. Why should she be pleased to banish her husband's name from the pedigree of England? She had made an intensely romantic love-match; she had adopted the old formula of wives towards husbands – to 'love, honour and obey. . . .' This had caused some controversy when she married, as it was to cause some more when her daughter used it at her own wedding. 'I'm an old-fashioned girl,' said Princess Anne engagingly in explanation. In that sense, Elizabeth II was surely 'an old-fashioned queen'. But if it was not the Queen's 'Pleasure', what was it?

The answer is twofold. First, it was everybody's pleasure to preserve the dynastic name of Windsor, not only for one more reign but for ever. There had been something both traumatic and blessed in the birth of that dynasty. With the world of the Fifties so unstable, there was every reason to maintain a name which had acquired a noble patina from the Queen's father and grandfather. After all, names could be whimsical. Suppose King Charles III were to be succeeded by a daughter who married a man called Bunbury or Buggins? Ladies did such things, as witness Lady Sarah Lennox, George III's goddess, or Lady Cecilia Gore, afterwards the Duke of Sussex's wife. The House of Windsor had rightly come to stay.

But the second stage was altogether indefensible. There was no need to go so much further and sweep away the father's name. We are told that the Queen agreed only under pressure. In the *Law Journal* of 18 March 1960, Edward S. Iwi, the brilliant constitutional lawyer, wrote: 'This [the Family of Mountbatten] continued for only

OPPOSITE: Conversation Piece at the Royal Lodge, Windsor, by James Gunn, 1950.

The scene inside the Abbey at the coronation of
Queen Elizabeth II, 1953, as the Archbishop of
Canterbury hands the orb to the Queen.

OPPOSITE: The Queen and Prince Philip after the coronation,
photographed by Cecil Beaton.

ABOVE: The Queen leaves No. 10 Downing Street after dinner with Sir Winston Churchill before his retirement in 1955. He was her first Prime Minister.

The Queen with Prince Charles and Princess Anne in the early fifties: (left) at Balmoral Castle; (right) out for a drive in Windsor Great Park.

LEFT: Chief Oba Adenji-Adele II, President of Lagos Town Council, escorts the Queen to her car after reading an address of welcome during her Nigerian tour of 1956.

ABOVE: The Queen pictured at her desk in Sandringham after her first televised Christmas Day speech in 1957.

RIGHT: Princess Margaret with Antony Armstrong-Jones, now Lord Snowdon, before their marriage in 1960.

TOP: The Queen and Prince Philip ride elephants to the Balua Ghat during their visit to India in February 1961.

ABOVE: Prince Philip was presented with a sun hat when the Queen attended a durbar of Northern Region chiefs at Tamale, during the royal tour of Ghana, November 1961. It was mainly due to the Queen's own determination that she went to Ghana. Fears for her safety at Accra dissolved in a great triumph.

ABOVE: The Queen Mother on her way to Prince Andrew's third
birthday party in 1963.

TOP: A cartoon drawn by Wally Fawkes during the Shakespeare
Festival of 1964 was the first cartoon to be published of Queen
Elizabeth II.

two months because, it is said, as a result of great pressure by Sir Winston Churchill a change was made.' Certainly there was a stiff press campaign in favour of the Family of Windsor as against the Family of Mountbatten, not least in Lord Beaverbrook's *Daily Express*. The name Mountbatten, as we have seen, had ceased to chime sweetly in Lord Beaverbrook's ears ever since 1941 and 1942. Lord Mountbatten's negotiation of independence for India five years later did nothing to mellow this imperial crusader towards the bearers of that name. In the words of Dermot Morrah, Arundel Herald of Arms Extraordinary, this ruling of April 1952 'did less than justice' to Her Majesty's husband, 'as the progenitor of the dynasty to come'.

Fortunately there was to be plenty of time during a long and happy reign for the promulgation of further changes, by which the father's rights, so to speak, should be restored. Meanwhile as early as September 1952, the Queen was able to raise her husband's name to the highest position in the land after her own. On 30 September the *London Gazette* announced:

The Queen has been graciously pleased by Warrant bearing date the 18th instant to declare and ordain that His Royal Highness Philip Duke of Edinburgh . . . shall henceforth upon all occasions . . . except where otherwise provided by Act of Parliament have, hold and enjoy Place, Pre-eminence and Precedence next to her Majesty.

This time the Queen must have been in truth 'graciously pleased', for the warrant ensured that her husband would be the first, after the Archbishop of Canterbury, to swear fealty to her at the coronation. Her sudden radiance at the Opening of Parliament on 4 November was noted by many peers and one of them reported his impression to Harold Nicolson. 'Gerry [Wellington] told me how struck he was by the Queen's astonishing radiance at the opening of Parliament this morning – her lovely teeth, hair and eyes, and that amazing quality of skin. Then add the wonderful voice and the romance, and you have a deeply moving effect.'

Coronation day arrived on 2 June 1953 without bringing with it 'Queen's weather'. No one was crass enough to see an ill omen in the rain. Indeed popular superstition was all channelled in the opposite direction, joyously awaiting a reign of pure euphoria. We were all to be Hillarys, Hunts and Tensings, the news of whose Everest climb arrived on coronation day.

The Queen had characteristically insisted on prolonged and careful rehearsals, so that the day was not marred by accidents. The Commonwealth Conference of December 1952 had at last reached agreement on the Queen's style and titles: in addition to each territorial designation (e.g. 'Elizabeth the Second, Queen of Ceylon') there was to be a common element – Queen of Her other Realms and Territories and Head of the Commonwealth'. Then there were the areas which tradition looked after: the huge gilded and painted coach of George III, the eight Windsor greys, the coachmen in their neat white wigs, the coronation robe woven by Nationalist

OPPOSITE: The Queen takes the salute at the march past of the Guards outside Buckingham Palace during the ceremony of Trooping the Colour in June, 1965. Prince Philip rides at her left and other members of the Royal Family watch from the balcony.

Chinese silk-worms on two British looms. Among the busy diarists, Harold Nicolson appreciated the remakable change of a televised coronation service and the joke of an ambulance for horses bringing up the rear of the royal procession. 'Chips' Channon noticed only people: the Queen 'quite perfect', Prince Philip 'like a medieval knight', Winston smiling and strutting, the Garter Knights 'clumsy', the new Archbishop's voice not as sonorous as that of 'wicked old Lang' and – something new and modern indeed at a coronation – a gentleman in a blue lounge-suit, the socialist Aneurin Bevan 'as unsuitable as possible'. However, the thirteen duchesses in the front row of the peeresses' block more than made up to 'Chips' for the single lounge-suit. The Duchess of Devonshire was said to be wearing the eighteenth-century robes of Duchess Georgiana, and all their lovely arms looked like swans' necks as they curved upwards to put on their strawberry-leaved coronets and shout 'God Save the Queen!'

Three days before the coronation, Malcolm MacEwen gave the Queen a send-off in the Communist *Daily Worker* with the reflection that she was at the end rather than the beginning of her pilgrimage:

It seems to be as certain as anything can be that the trend against monarchy which has completely outlived its usefulness as an institution, will continue.

Some years later it was the *Daily Worker* which had 'outlived its usefulness' and changed into a somewhat faint *Morning Star*.

On the evening of coronation day a lady-in-waiting, Lady Cynthia Colville, having watched the ceremony from the Queen's own box in the Abbey, finished up with a gin-and-orange on the house in a Shoreditch pub. This Shoreditch where she still did social work was much less poor than the one she had known in the past, 'but equally loyal to the Queen, and as loyal as the gorgeous throng in the Abbey'.

Why were they so loyal? King Edward VII had been held in respect. But no trace of the veneration bestowed on his mother brushed off on him. His son, King George V, no more expected to be venerated than to levitate. Yet two generations later a touch of the old magic had undoubtedly filtered back. And this, despite the fact that the House of Windsor was now closer to the people, more sensible, more 'of this world' and further from the world of faery, than any of their ancestors.

In every age a coronation has had two aspects: the people's submission to the Sovereign and the Sovereign's dedication to the people. Rule and service. But both aspects have not always weighed equally in the mind of the individual who was being crowned. It was possible to regard the symbolic holy oil on the forehead more as a badge of power than of service. With the House of Windsor it has been the other way round. Queen Elizabeth II was noticeably serious at her coronation, in contrast, say, to King George IV who behaved with more gallantry than decorum, or King William IV who wanted to get on with the job of kingship without any coronation at all.

A YOUNG GLEAMING CHAMPION

The old Sir Winston Churchill saw her as 'the young, gleaming champion' of a wise and kindly way of life. To Queen Elizabeth II her coronation was the shouldering of an awesome burden for which she would need all available help, human and divine; to George IV it had been the start of a great spree. Queen Elizabeth's subjects realised the extent of her self-dedication and, awestruck themselves, felt anew the magic of monarchy which enabled this girl to undertake such things.

I I

A family on the throne

A family on a throne is an interesting idea also. It brings down the pride of sovereignty to the level of petty life. Walter Bagehot, 1867.

THIS story is palpably unfinished. It can be only a mid-term report. Any tracing of patterns in the reign of Queen Elizabeth II must be tentative, since even her Silver Jubilee is still several years ahead. With this proviso it is safe to say that the threads of the Fifties continually crossed and snapped, that the Sixties began to produce a smooth bright weave, while the Seventies are alive with possibilities and a style in monarchy which is both novel and sophisticated.

The disappointments of the Fifties were due to three main causes. First, the public euphoria was founded on nothing but hopes and was bound to collapse when the new reign ceased to be new; the 'new Elizabethans' quickly became old grousers, especially the press. Second, events were unlucky: the Queen's first decade included Suez in the Old World and an unwelcoming spirit in the New. Third, the Royal Family personally faced some bad patches. To cope with them, there was a shy young Queen and a brashly brilliant Consort, who had already decided in his own mind that monarchy must make a crash-landing into a new age. It did; but a certain amount of landing-gear was buckled in the course of duty.

The death of Queen Mary in 1953 introduced the first faint doubts: 'There has not been a word of criticism of the grand old lady,' wrote Channon, implying that criticism of others would soon be forthcoming. 'Her appearance was formidable, her manner – well, it was like talking to St Paul's cathedral. . . . The world is poorer.' She had indeed given a protective venerability to the House of Windsor which her death removed.

Not long afterwards the love-story of Princess Margaret and Group Captain Peter Townsend seemed to confirm the impression that royalty was slipping. The couple of decades which had elapsed between the Simpson and the Townsend divorces had made the situation that much more complex for the Royal Family. In the Thirties, a vast majority of the people were against the monarch becoming involved, however indirectly, in the modern trend towards divorce. Despite first appearances to the contrary, the Abdication divided the country scarcely at all. By the Fifties, however, public opinion on divorce reflected the great increase in its occurrence. Opinion was more divided. This made it harder for the Queen (apart from the personal distress which would afflict any family in similar circumstances) to adhere to her principles enunciated in 1949, that divorce caused some of 'the darkest evils in our society today'. Yet it was essential that the pre-Abdication atmosphere should not be re-created.

We do not know – nor is it our business to 'poke about' – exactly how the tensions were relieved, though Randolph Churchill has hinted at the answer. 'Archbishop, you may put your books away,' Princess Margaret is supposed to have said with finality, 'I have made up my mind.' Princess Margaret herself issued a moving statement of what was in her mind:

> I would like it to be known that I have decided not to marry Group Captain Townsend I have been aware that, subject to my renouncing my rights of succession, it might have been possible for me to contract a civil marriage. But mindful of the Church's teaching that Christian marriage is indissoluble, and conscious of my duty to the Commonwealth, I have resolved to put these considerations before others.

Nevertheless there were more people in 1956 than in 1936 or 1949 who still thought, notwithstanding the solution, that members of the Royal Family should be free in a changing world to marry the men or women they loved – particularly when they possessed the delightful traits of a Townsend. It was therefore particularly ungracious of some journals towards the buffeted Family to welcome the engagement of Princess Margaret to Antony Armstrong-Jones (Lord Snowdon) with remarks about his preference for Pimlico over Belgravia. The same voices which called for more democracy were later to make snide references to the manufacture of plebeian sausages by the family of Mark Phillips.

The Queen's children were not entirely immune from unwanted attentions during the Fifties. In 1957 Princes Charles began going to a London day-school, Hill House; and soon the inhabitants of Kensington and Chelsea became aware that among the crocodile of small boys lifting their chestnut-brown caps to courteous motorists who let them by on the pedestrian crossings was the heir to the throne. The Queen and Prince Philip, hoping to keep the interest in their son down to this casual level, had made an unprecedented appeal to the press for cooperation when he started school, so that he might 'enjoy this in the same way as other children'. However, when eight-year-old Charles followed his father to Cheam in Berkshire, the press stories came thick and fast: 67 stories, it was said, for the 88 days of his first term. No doubt the distance of Gordonstoun from London – four hundred odd miles as opposed to Eton's twenty – partly explains why Charles also followed his father to his Scottish public school. If the earlier schooling experiments had their ups and downs like other royal activities of the Fifties, at least they laid the foundations of success for younger members of the Family.

We have now seen the Royal Family involved at the periphery in lighter or graver skirmishes with the press. It was not to be expected that in a carping and disillusioned mood born of extravagant expectations, the public should allow the central couple themselves to go scot-free.

The Suez crisis of November 1956 caught the monarchy in the spray of its anger. The Queen was at Goodwood races when Parliament reassembled and it became necessary for her to sign a Forces' call-up. Should she return to London for the signing? She was advised not to. But afterwards there were remarks about the contrast between Goodwood and Suez. At times of alarm all institutions are apt to get the rough edge of the nation's tongue. People were as much irritated by the thought of the Suez Canal flowing through Lady Eden's drawing-room at No. 10, as by the news that it was not flowing through the Queen's box at Goodwood.

The resignation of Sir Anthony Eden on 9 January 1957 and the method of appointment of a new Prime Minister led to further murmurings. It was not the Conservative practice to elect their leader until 1970. Therefore the Queen's Prerogative of choosing the Prime Minister had a peculiar significance in 1957. In making her choice she would also in effect choose the Tories' party leader. During the earlier change from Churchill to Eden there had been virtually no party involvement, since Eden was the only candidate. But two years later the situation was very different. There were strong rival Tory candidates, Harold Macmillan and R.A.('Rab') Butler. Each had his political following. How was she to select one of them without getting involved in Conservative party politics? This was the cause of Labour party uneasiness, though the Queen's actual performance in the circumstances of the time could meet with nothing but approval.

Having sent for two elder statesmen, Lord Salisbury and Winston Churchill, she learnt from the former the views of the Conservative Cabinet. She then slept on their advice and the result was Harold Macmillan. (There is no truth in the legend that the Queen deliberately postponed her decision in order to emphasise the Royal Prerogative.) This result had been obtained by Cabinet vote. Election by the Cabinet was the solution which King George IV had urged during the Canning versus Wellington crisis of 1827; but it was felt to constrict the Sovereign's constitutional choice and was refused. After 1957 it was again felt that this method did not enable the Sovereign to take deep enough soundings. As we shall see, the methods were changed twice more.

With the advent of Harold Macmillan it might be thought that the Queen's life would become more tranquil. Certainly from his angle the strength of a Prime Minister in a monarchy was well exemplified. Writing of her 'kindness and consideration', he added, 'I had seen her not infrequently yet this was the beginning of a quite different relationship. The Prime Minister is above all the Queen's first Minister. His supreme loyalty is to her.' With some politicians (and perhaps the majority of soldiers) service to country is still mediated by the Queen. This is how Disraeli used to speak of Queen Victoria. A man of Macmillan's historical imagination could never have achieved that special relationship with a president.

Part of the Queen's magic for Macmillan consisted in worldly talents of a high order. She read like lightning and remembered what she read. He told her, for instance, in February 1957 that the Government might not last more than six weeks. 'She smilingly reminded me of this', he wrote, 'at an audience six years later.' Then there was her well-informed mind. On presenting her in February with his Cabinet changes he wrote: 'She is astonishingly well informed on every detail.' Harold Wilson's first visits to the Queen in 1964 were no doubt routine; very soon, however, they had become for him not only a pleasure but an essential part of his prime ministerial duties. She was a voracious reader of all state documents – 'and if she quoted one I hadn't yet read, I felt like a schoolboy who hadn't done his homework.' The Queen knew that Macmillan came as much to receive encouragement and sympathy as to exchange facts. 'She particularly liked the decision on the F.O. [Selwyn Lloyd],' he recorded in February. And when in October Peter Thorney-croft, Nigel Birch and Enoch Powell resigned, to be replaced by Derek Amory and Reginald Maudling, Macmillan wrote, 'The Queen was very sympathetic.' But whether Her Majesty was sympathetic because Thorneycroft had written the Prime Minister a 'contemptuous' letter of resignation [Macmillan's word] or because she 'particularly liked' the new man is not revealed.

It is probable that the function of a queen regnant in a modern monarchy varies slightly from that of a king. A 'female sovereign', as the Victorians used to say, has greater powers of sympathy and encouragement. Yet with all these blossoming gifts, 1957 was not altogether a good year for Queen Elizabeth II.

The Duke of Edinburgh had been on a long Commonwealth tour, beginning in autumn 1956 and lasting until the following spring. His work was important, for it included studies of Antarctica, Darwin's Galápagos Islands and the problems of conservation, as well as being an intellectual treat for a man of bounding energies. It may be likened to the self-supplied activities of an earlier consort, Prince Albert, especially his absorption in the Great Exhibition and Horticultural Gardens, the latter of which Queen Victoria came to regard with jealous loathing. There is not a spark of evidence that Queen Elizabeth begrudged the time her husband spent on his Commonwealth tour or his interest in wildlife, but rumours circulated nonetheless that there was a rift. It was true that the Duke had been absent during the Suez after-math and no doubt the Queen missed his advice. (For who can doubt that the Consort, though constitutionally 'only a husband' in the narrowest sense, was humanly all and more that a husband should be – support, adviser, heartener, confidant?) The Queen's secretary, Sir Michael Adeane, denied the rumours with all the incisiveness of a 'First' in History: 'It is quite untrue that there is any rift between the Queen and the Duke of Edinburgh.' The idea that the voyage to Antarctica symbolised a frozen relationship was a fabrication; more symbolic was the Duke's favourite photograph, taken in the Galápagos Islands, of two iguanas with their arms round one another.

On his return the Duke made some pointed but controlled remarks on the subject to the usual Guildhall audience. 'The journey was completed,' he said ironically, 'against every expectation, to the day of our original estimate – perhaps unfortunately as it turned out.' (Some journalists had professed to see lack of ardour in his failure to fly home ahead of schedule.) He went on to talk of his long separation from wife and children. As a sailor four months away from home 'meant nothing at all'. Now it meant much. But there were some things in life worth a sacrifice. 'I believe that the British Commonwealth is one of those things and I, for one, am prepared to sacrifice a good deal if, by doing so, I can advance its well-being by even a small degree.'

The Commonwealth was, and would remain, the ideal to which Queen Elizabeth II gave herself and her energies without stint. To signalise her agreement with her husband's ideal, which was the same as her own, she created him a Prince of the United Kingdom. Perhaps it was a fortunate chance that the lawyers had left out that title ten years earlier. For something big was needed at this moment.

Prince Philip has been described as hurt by the attacks on his private life. Like King George V in 1917, he was probably more enraged than hurt. 'Those bloody lies,' he is said to have stormed at a journalist, 'that you people print to make money. These lies about how I'm never with my wife.' For there are modern ways of 'poking about' royalty which Bagehot had not dreamed of. They are ways which Prince Philip does not tolerate for his family or himself: 'If photographers poke a long lens through a keyhole into my private life,' he says, 'then I am bloody nasty.'

Meanwhile, if the lens was barred the pens were still at work; and indeed the monarchy does and must expect to be fairly criticised. This time the pens began scratching at the Queen.

By the summer of 1957 magazines and newspapers (and now not only Beaverbrooks)' discovered that the 'wonderful voice' in which the Queen had opened her first Parliament was not so perfect after all. Among a variety of critics, Lord Altrincham (John Grigg) attacked her whole style, writing in his *National Review* that her 'personality' was that of a 'priggish schoolgirl', her entourage 'conventional upper class' and her reading voice 'a pain in the neck'. Others bandied about nouns like 'boredom' and 'fatuity', adjectives like 'frumpish' and 'dowdy'.

The remarks about her voice were unjust, since the Queen's voice strongly resembles her mother's and lyrical praise has always been accorded to the way the Queen Mother speaks. But a faceless voice is never the easiest method of projecting a personality. Moreover the Queen, unlike her grandfather George V, was not a natural broadcaster. There is no doubt that the criticisms – whether fair or unfair – bore some fair fruits.

Within four months (Christmas 1957) Nicolson was listening to the Queen's voice while on a Caribbean cruise: 'She came across quite clear and with a vigour unknown in pre-Altrincham days.' The shining blue eyes which Nicolson described as her greatest beauty, were at last seen on British television. Incidentally, her experiences in this new medium were described to dinner-guests soon afterwards with a wit and self-mockery which delighted her listeners as much as the Christmas TV message itself. Like most new performers in those early days, she had not expected to be made up as a clown, with blobs of yellow paint on cheekbones, forehead and the tip of her nose. A large family luncheon at Sandringham was laced with icy draughts, due to the outside walls having been pierced by BBC cables. The Queen shivered with cold as well as nerves. Gradually she noticed that an uneasy silence had fallen on her family. Aware of her shivers they were assuming that poor little Lilibet would break down completely in front of millions of viewers. The result was not a break-down but the beginning of a new style in royal impact and immediacy.

Mention of the Queen's dinner-guests leads on to another innovation which was introduced in order to get the Fifties moving. Towards the end of that decade the Queen and Prince Philip cancelled the age-old spectacle of 'Presentation Parties' for improbable debutantes at Buckingham Palace, having meanwhile introduced in-formal luncheons and dinners for their meritorious elders. On one of these occasions the Queen said to the great conductor Barbirolli,

'Sir John, you have been in the public eye for many years. You must have received some adverse criticism? How do you react?'

'Ma'am, I do nothing about it. Long ago I made up my mind not even to notice it. It has no effect whatever.'

'I wonder if that can really be possible . . .'

In telling this story to a fellow-conductor, Barbirolli commented: 'I realised then that it was not my Sovereign speaking to me but an injured colleague.'

These new-style parties were popular, especially with the middle classes from which the guests were mainly drawn; everyone was pleased that the Queen wanted to get to know him or her, and they all congratulated themselves that it would be of benefit to H.M. to do so. Prince Philip was a gay host, always with that touch of astringency which prevented guests from basking in his smile. They as well as he had to be alert. Both the Queen and Prince Philip have a naturally relaxed line in throw-away humour. When Churchill handed in his resignation as Prime Minister in 1955, the Queen offered him a peerage in words which clearly amused him. 'Would you like a dukedom or anything like that?'

Indeed ever since the House of Windsor got into its stride, visitors to the Sovereign have been struck by Palace informality rather than pomp. Walter Monkton was amazed by the absence of solemnity when King George VI bestowed on him the first knighthood of the reign: 'Well, Walter, we did not manage that very well,' said the King at the end, 'but neither of us had done it before!' Lord Gage was playing golf one day at Windsor when a message came that King George wanted to see him. 'I'll just go and change,' he said. 'No, come as you are,' replied the King's secretary. So Lord Gage found himself kneeling down to receive the KCVO in his plus-fours.

It was with equal surprise that Harold Wilson in 1964 was appointed Prime

Minister by Queen Elizabeth II without the expected formality. 'Strangely to me and contrary to all I had understood about the procedure,' he wrote in his memoirs, 'there was no formal kissing of hands. . . . It was taken as read.' Incidentally the Labour leader had arrived in a short black coat instead of the 'morning coat and striped pants' he found he required. 'It turned out,' he was happy to relate, 'that no constitutional issue was raised.'

Harold Wilson's experiences at the Palace belong to the Sixties when Labour won its first election for thirteen years. With the Sixties, as has been said, the monarchy left the doldrums for a more rapid current. But there were still some moments when the winds seemed to be blowing in all directions or none, especially in the Commonwealth.

'Royal progresses', as little Princess Victoria had discovered over a century ago, have their disadvantages. Royalty could be worn out and all sorts of errors committed which at times seemed to cancel the good done. In the twentieth century, the country expected young mothers like the Duchess of York and now Queen Elizabeth II to be parted from their children for months on end. The small figures of Anne aged three and Charles, five, were lined up on the deck as *Britannia* sailed into Tobruk to greet her at the end of her first Commonwealth tour. Good things had been achieved, to make the sacrifice bearable. One day the Queen, after watching some exhilarating African ceremonies, remarked to Prince Philip: 'I feel like an African Queen.' 'You are an African Queen,' he replied. 'The Queen of Australia' was vociferously cheered as she landed at Sydney; on leaving that key realm she was able to define the crown's place in the Commonwealth with exactitude and without exaggeration:

The Crown is a human link between all peoples who owe allegiance to me – an allegiance of mutual love and respect and never of compulsion. . . .

Queen Elizabeth II, be it noted, did not in 1954 make the mistake of some enthusiast' and describe the crown as 'the *only possible* link' between the Commonwealth peoples, but correctly as '*a* human link'. Moreover she emphasised the voluntary nature of the union – what England had once tried in vain to establish with Ireland, 'A Union of Hearts'.

It was therefore all the more to be regretted when things went wrong and Commonwealth hearts were accidentally riled instead of being warmed: when no coloured person was invited to a certain Bermudan dinner or one was put under arrest for throwing down his jacket in a misunderstood 'Raleigh' gesture. Three years later there were protests in Nigeria because the Queen visited Ibadan University without the students having been previously consulted. A more violent repetition of the same thing was to occur in Scotland in the Seventies. It all went to show that on sensitive subjects like race or students' rights, the royal impact could inadvertently create irritation rather than unity. In areas where irritations already abounded, anything might happen. The North American tours were cases in point.

Separatism in Canada was one of the forces which Elizabeth II had to contend with in the Sixties. A glamorous and devoted young Queen could not fail to win Canadian hearts, whether their tongues spoke French or English. But by the time of her second visit (1957) there were criticisms despite strenuous efforts to please; for instance, her very first television appearance was made in Canada but it was said that she saw too many official types and not enough ordinary people. Fashion writers were 'miffed' by lack of detail. Who could make anything of 'a flowered afternoon dress with matching accessories'? As for Prince Philip wearing 'a white tie and decorations' – 'and nothing else?' hissed a female journalist. More important, a minor 'separatist' scene caused by young Québecois heralded a fiercer future. 'After plastering stickers all over town,' reported the *Ottawa Citizen*, 'the youths stormed the royal limousine, tossed an object at the Queen's feet and thrust another into her husband's hand.' The objects were not bombs, but petitions to have a new hotel in Montreal named after its French founder instead of after Queen Elizabeth.

Her journey continued into the United States, where success, on the contrary, was instantaneous. Forgotten were British insults to Mrs Simpson, forgotten even was King George III. The British Ambassador at Washington, Harold Caccia, told Macmillan after the Queen's visit: 'She has buried George III for good and all.' Caccia proved to be right. When she visited Chicago in 1959 Mayor Dick Daley said to her, 'Your Majesty, Chicago is yours.' Only a generation earlier Mayor Bill Thompson had threatened to punch the King's nose.

Just before and after this Canadian visit, the Queen had begun to show a vigour and stoutness over Commonwealth and foreign affairs which surprised even her own entourage. It was here that her imagination played most creatively over the scene, rather than over domestic reforms. And with good reason, since the monarchy must always keep clear of party controversy.

She had proposed Windsor instead of Buckingham Palace for the Commonwealth Conference banquet of 1957. This gave a family atmosphere to the proceedings and was voted a 'happy suggestion' on the part of H.M. In the following year she gave a state dinner at Windsor to the German Chancellor, Konrad Adenauer, and Queen Juliana of the Netherlands: 'The Germans thoroughly enjoyed themselves,' wrote Macmillan. 'The old Chancellor sat between the two Queens, and flirted with both.' Queen Elizabeth II's state visit to West Germany was an even more significant follow-up. For the first time since two world wars, she boldly drew attention to the Royal Family's German ancestry. Nineteen-seventeen was wiped out. She had put paid at last to the debt of honour which her family had been forced to incur, through no wish of their own, to their historic past.

By 1959 it was time to try Canada again. The visit was a heroic, jam-packed, exhausting exercise in determined democracy, made by a Queen who had just become pregnant for the third time. She saw every sort of Canadian – from trade unionists to musicians, from the proprietress of a Newfoundland fishing fleet to a 'new Canadian' from Central Europe. As she left Lansdowne Park in Ottawa an over-enthusiastic spectator 'leaped more than 10 feet over the grandstand railing'. He was taken to hospital with a compound fracture of the right leg.

Home again, the Queen kept up her record of successes. For the 'Swinging Sixties' had begun, and it was time to swing into battle again for her name and her clan.

Eleven days before the birth of Prince Andrew on 19 February 1960, Queen Elizabeth II made it clear that her implied renunciation of the name Mountbatten in 1952 was now in turn abandoned. She declared in Council on 8 February:

... while I and my children shall continue to be styled and known as the House and Family of Windsor, my descendants, other than descendants enjoying the style, title or attributes of Royal Highness and the titular dignity of Prince or Princess, and female descendants who marry and their descendants shall bear the name Mountbatten-Windsor.

And to make sure that this new declaration was not taken to apply merely to future generations, the Queen issued an explanatory statement:

The Queen has always wanted, without changing the name of the Royal House established by her grandfather, to associate the name of her husband with *her own and his descendants*. The Queen has had this in mind for a long time and it is close to her heart.

Note that all the Queen's descendants (see my italics above) including her children, were to bear the name Mountbatten-Windsor. This, as we shall see, was not universally understood.

All in the same month of February 1960 the Queen was to reintroduce the name of Mountbatten and also to welcome a new name into the family, that of Antony Armstrong-Jones, later created Earl of Snowdon. Princess Margaret married him in Westminster Abbey that July. A photographer, designer and film-director, Lord Snowdon was to bring not only a new name but a new variety of interests into the House of Windsor.

The 'Mountbatten-Windsor' declaration had been the Queen's first important act of the Sixties. There were some sceptics, however, who maintained that H. M.'s declaration would in fact make no difference to the coming child (Prince Andrew) nor to any of her children, born or unborn, since princes and princesses had no surnames. The new name of Mountbatten-Windsor, they argued, would come into play only with the third generation from the Sovereign.

Such a view was untenable, and indeed it was to be dramatically refuted. The majority of constitutional lawyers and experts, headed by Edward Iwi, have always held that though the Queen's children did not include their surname as part of their usual signature, they all possessed a 'hidden' or 'latent' surname, which they would transmit to their descendants and use on special occasions.

The first special occasion arose thirteen years later, to prove this school of thought abundantly right. (Sadly, Iwi himself did not live to witness the victory.) On her wedding-day, 14 November 1973, the only daughter of Queen Elizabeth and Prince Philip signed her name in the Abbey register, 'Anne Mountbatten-Windsor'. It was photographed and published on the 15th in the *Daily Express* and is reproduced in this book. There can be no doubt that when the time comes, the signature of 'Charles Mountbatten-Windsor' will bring intense satisfaction to all concerned.

The Queen had thus won her battle of Bosworth in this War of the Names. Mention of the *Daily Express* calls to mind the fact that peace was soon to be signed in other combat areas also, where the family had for long been under assault. The early Sixties saw a petering out of Lord Beaverbrook's hostility towards Lord Mountbatten. Labour leaders like James Callaghan and Conservatives like Harold Macmillan had already protested against what they regarded – though Beaverbrook did not – as the *Express* newspapers' vendetta. There came a day when Roy Thompson, a fellow press-lord, quietly brought the unsuspecting Beaverbrook and Mountbatten together, at a large dinner-party in Claridges. As the two moved away from the table after dinner, it happened that they converged at the same moment on the exit. Beaverbrook stood back. Mountbatten picked up his limp hand.

'Max, for the affection which you used to bear Edwina in the old days,' he said, 'I must shake you by the hand and wish you well.' (Edwina Mountbatten, by a tragic coincidence, had died in Borneo on 20 February 1960, the very day after Prince Andrew's birth.) Never the man to remain unmoved by such a gesture, Beaverbrook gradually called off his troops.

Another curious anomaly, not unlike Philip's lack of the title 'Prince' from 1947 to 1957, was finally removed in the Sixties.

Prince Charles had been created Prince of Wales in 1968 and invested at Caernarvon Castle a year later.

> *The splendour falls on castle walls,*
> *The snowy summits old in story . . .*

In 1967 he and his sister were both due to appear in yet another place 'old in story', the House of Lords. For the first time the Queen was to open Parliament in the presence of her two elder children as well as her husband. Where was Prince Philip to sit?

Hitherto he had occupied a chair of state on the Queen's left hand, *outside the canopy*, expressly reserved by the Act of 1539 for the children of the Sovereign. Now Princess Anne would occupy this seat while Prince Charles would sit on his mother's right, also outside the canopy. There was only one place for Prince Philip – his rightful place on the Consort's throne. The anomaly had consisted in a prince consort (like Prince Albert or Prince Philip) sitting outside the canopy on a chair, while a queen consort (like Queen Alexandra, Queen Mary or Queen Elizabeth) sat beneath the canopy on a throne. By 1967 circumstances had brought the anomaly to a head – circumstances being the advent of the royal children. The Consort's throne, a few inches lower than the Sovereign's, was duly brought from Lord Cholmondeley's home at Houghton Hall, where it was traditionally stored, and placed under the canopy beside H. M. Queen Elizabeth II. At last the Consort had been restored to his rights in every sense; in each case, be it noted, because of the advent of children. The truth was, however, that his own dynamic contribution to the effectiveness and poise of the Royal Family entitled him to every honour which the country could justly bestow.

For the work, meanwhile, of the House of Windsor in the Commonwealth had achieved dramatic proportions.

Having triumphantly brought back the 'Mountbatten' into the family, the Queen was determined to do her utmost to keep Ghana in the Commonwealth. All Africa was in ferment during the Sixties. It was while on the voyage home from his 'Wind of Change' speeches in Ghana and South Africa, that Macmillan found time to deal with the 'Queen's Affair' of 8 February 1960. Macmillan has described how Dr Verwoerd's policy of Apartheid finally lost South Africa her place in the Commonwealth. It was fortunate that King George VI's happy vision of the Union was not marred by these events, but that it fell to his more equable daughter to face a squalid South African future. But she did her best to avert it. At the Commonwealth Conference of May 1960 she again invited delegates, including the South Africans, to Windsor, dined them in the Waterloo Chamber, showed them the State Apartments, stayed with them till midnight – indeed Macmillan, though full of admiration, was 'very tired' by his young Sovereign's inexhaustible hospitality. Having already ceased to be a monarchy that autumn, South Africa left the Commonwealth in the following March. Ironically, Macmillan had congratulated South Africa in 1960 on 'the Golden Wedding of the Union' (1910–60); next year the marriage had irretrievably broken down and there was divorce.

It was therefore all the more urgent that Ghana, for different reasons, should not go the same way. Ghana was a republic, headed by Kwame Nkrumah. The Queen had first met the exotic Nkrumah at the 1957 Commonwealth Conference. Now he was President of something very like a police-state, thought to be wooed by the Kremlin. At the same time he had not been won. High hopes as well as deep fears were attached to the prospect of a visit by the Queen.

The fears centred on her personal safety. She was due to fly out on 9 November 1961. Throughout September and October various members of the Cabinet like Lord Home, and ex-members like Churchill and Eden, expressed their anxiety, while

Nkrumah did his best to make their fears seem justified. He arrested Opposition leaders and colleagues, including Sir Stafford Cripps's son-in-law, Dr Joseph Appiah, and was himself threatened with reprisals. Even if the Queen personally escaped all attacks, might she not stop a bullet intended for her host? But thanks to the unwavering support of her secretaries, Adeane and Charteris, and to Macmillan's conviction, backed up by the majority of Conservatives and Labour, that cancellation of the visit would amount to kicking out Ghana – thanks above all to the Royal Family's calm resolution, the packing went on.

'How silly I should look if I was scared to visit Ghana,' she said, 'and then Krushchev went a few weeks later and had a good reception.'

Suddenly, on 4 November, only five days before the Queen's departure date, there was literally a bombshell. A violent explosion in Nkrumah's capital rocked more than Accra. Doubts that had been subsiding burst out again with redoubled force. Still the Queen refused to be panicked, and this time she was chivalrously assisted by Duncan Sandys, the Commonwealth Secretary. In the words of the *Annual Register* (quoted approvingly by Macmillan) his plan was to 'try it out on the dog':

Mr Sandys, flying out to Ghana . . . and bravely assuming the role of the dog, drove with stately deliberation accompanied by President Nkrumah, along the royal route in accordance with the projected royal timetable. He emerged to tell the tale.

Good marks for Dog Sandys.

Nevertheless there was mounting dismay in Parliament and a possibility, however remote, that a terrified House would vote against the royal visit. Macmillan would then offer his resignation, the Queen would refuse to accept it, he would reiterate his advice that she should fly into the jaws of death and she would do so – while Macmillan himself remained behind to be impeached if not beheaded.

At this eleventh hour the House in fact did not divide, Hugh Gaitskell having declared Labour's faith in Her Majesty's message and admiration for her courage. The visit was a wild success. Though Nkrumah has since gone, Ghana still acknowledges the Queen as Head of the Commonwealth. And it is probable that President John F. Kennedy afterwards went ahead with Ghana's Volta Dam (a hitherto doubtful project) partly out of respect for the Queen's firmness of purpose.

Queen Elizabeth II has not often been compared with her tough forebear. But Macmillan's comparison, written into his diary for 13 November 1961, is both apt and moving:

The Queen has been absolutely determined all through. She is grateful for MPs' and Press concern about her safety, but she is impatient of the attitude towards her to treat her as a *woman*, and a film star or mascot. She has indeed 'the heart and stomach of a man'.

After Ghana, it was not to be expected that the Queen would flinch from what Australia or Canada had in store. As Macmillan had added in his diary: 'She has great faith in the work she can do for the Commonwealth especially.'

While Australia, according to the eminent historian J.D.B.Miller, showed no general tendency to republicanism, royalty had to watch its step there. In June 1963 Menzies proposed, amid loud dissent, that the unit for the new Australian decimal currency should be called a 'royal'. The country eventually settled for a dollar.

The Queen's fourth visit to Canada was planned for October 1964. But as early as February there were reports of violent separatism and threats to the Queen's life. Dr Marcel Chaput, a French separatist leader, declared that some people 'are resolved to let her know brutally she is not welcome in Quebec or French Canada'. Asked whether Quebec could be another Dallas (John F. Kennedy had been assassinated at Dallas in 1963) Dr Chaput replied, 'It could.' French-language papers like *Le Devoir* condemned the Queen's proposed visit as propaganda against French rights and demanded its cancellation. Royalists began to lose heart, predicting an insulting welcome of drawn blinds and silent streets. In England that September the *Mirror* came out with flaring headlines: 'THE QUEEN – MURDER PLOT PROBE – We'll kill her on royal tour says Canadian killer gang.' Even *The Times* considered submitting to blackmail rather than risking a bomb. But the Prime Minister (now Sir Alec Douglas-Home) and as usual the Queen herself refused to be intimidated. As a result, the visit hovered between heaven and hell for her and Prince Philip; while for the people, in the words of the *Canadian Annual Review*, it was a 'tragedy'.

The Queen took off from Heathrow 'serene and smiling' under sunny autumn skies, but 60 m.p.h. gusts were expected on the day of her arrival – and worse than that. While Britons 'offered a silent prayer' for her safety, the loyalists of Prince Edward's Island were shocked to see – or rather, not see – their Queen received within a steel enclosure topped with barbed wire. Why should the Islanders suffer for the sins of a few 'crack-pots' in Quebec? they asked indignantly. But the British *Sunday Telegraph* had spoken of Cuba-trained Quebec terrorists resolved to 'kill a Canadian member of the Queen's entourage', and Canadian police were taking no chances. On Saturday 10 October Quebec was indeed a scene of terror – but terror created by the authorities.

The royal route itself was 'calm and cold', what with massed guards, hideous yellow barricades and spectators turning their backs or holding up posters reading 'Elizabeth Chez Vous (Go Home)' or 'Chômage' – a French word meaning Un-employment, which suggested that Queen Elizabeth instead of receiving *homage* in Quebec, would find herself out of a job. But away from the route, demonstrators were manhandled and innocent passers-by beaten up by police with long 'nightsticks'. The day became known as *le samedi de la matraque* – 'the Saturday of the cudgel'. Some people blamed the 'yellow press' for exaggerating the separatism; others said it was the yellow barriers of the Federal government; others again said the separatists had been made martyrs; while the backlash from English-speaking Canada provoked further bitter post-mortems. 'Canada has walked to the edge of the crisis,' lamented the *Globe and Mail*. If civil war had been avoided, a split seemed certain nonetheless.

Queen Elizabeth II returns from her coronation in the gold state
coach, 1953.

OPPOSITE: The Queen and Prince Philip walk in procession to open Parliament in 1958. Lord Home bears the Cap of Maintenance and Lord Montgomery carries the Sword of State.

The Duke and Duchess of Windsor attended their first public ceremony in the company of the Queen when they were present at the unveiling at Marlborough House of a plaque in 1967 commemorating the centenary of Queen Mary's birth.

Prince Charles with friends at Timbertop, the bushland annexe of
Geelong Grammar School, Australia, where he went in February
1966.

TOP: This photograph of Prince Philip and Princess Anne barbecuing sausages comes from the film *Royal Family*, made for television in 1969. In a very successful break with tradition the film attempted to look behind the mystique of the monarchy to the home life of the Queen's family.

ABOVE: Smiling gallantly, the Queen passes a drinking student during her visit to Stirling University in 1972, when students demonstrated against the cost of her visit.

ABOVE: The Queen and Prince Philip kneel for the Archbishop of Canterbury's blessing at the end of the Service of Thanksgiving in Westminster Abbey on occasion of their Silver Wedding.

LEFT: The Queen accepts a posy from a girl in the crowd during the walkabout in the Barbican, as part of the Silver Wedding festivities.

ABOVE: A large family group taken in 1972 to mark the Silver Wedding. Back row, standing, left to right: the Earl of Snowdon, the Duke of Kent, Prince William of Kent, the Duke of Edinburgh, the Earl of St Andrews, the Prince of Wales, Prince Andrew, Hon. Angus Ogilvy and (extreme right) his son, James Ogilvy. Seated on chairs, left to right: Princess Margaret, the Duchess of Kent holding Lord Nicholas Windsor, Queen Elizabeth The Queen Mother, Queen Elizabeth II, Princess Anne, Marina Ogilvy, and her mother, Princess Alexandra. Seated on floor, left to right: Lady Sarah Armstrong-Jones, Viscount Linley, Prince Edward, Lady Helen Windsor.

RIGHT: An informal picture of the Queen and Prince Philip taken for the Silver Wedding.

The Queen with Prime Ministers and delegates of the Commonwealth countries in Ottawa, 1973. An informal television picture of the Queen moving about among her ministers was shown during her Christmas message, 1973. Front row, left to right: General Gowon (Nigeria), Lee Kuan Yew (Singapore), Mrs Sirimavo Bandaranaike (Sri Lanka), Julius Nyerere (Tanzania), The Queen, Pierre Trudeau (Canada), Duke of Edinburgh, Errol Barrow (Barbados), Dom Mintoff (Malta). Second row, left to right: John Christophides (foreign minister, Cyprus), Mujibur Rahman (Bangladesh), Swaran Singh (foreign minister, India), Edward Heath (Britain), Sir Ramgoolam (Mauritius), Fiame Mata'afa (Western Samoa), Prince Dlamini (Swaziland), S. Ramphal (minister of justice, Guyana), Mainza Chona (vice-president, Zambia), Brigadier N. Y. Ashley-Lassen (chief of defence staff, Ghana), Lynden Pindling (Bahamas). Third row, left to right: Dr Siaka Stevens (Sierra Leone), Chief Leabua Jonathan (Lesotho), Norman Kirk (New Zealand), Gough Whitlam (Australia), Daniel Arap Moi (vice-president, Kenya), Michael Manley (Jamaica), Ratu Sir Kamisese Mara (Fiji), Paul Etiang (foreign minister, Uganda), Prince Tu'ipelehake (Tonga), Khir Johari (minister without portfolio, Malaysia), Sir Seretse Khama (Botswana), Andrew Camara (vice-president, The Gambia), Francis Prevatt (minister of petroleum and mines, Trinidad and Tobago), J. B. Msonthi (minister of education, Malawi).

ABOVE: Lieutenant Mark Phillips pats Princess Anne's horse, Doublet, after the Princess received her prizes for winning the Combined Championship in the Hickstead show-jumping arena in July 1973.

RIGHT: A portrait of Princess Margaret by Bryan Organ, 1970. Its style has been described as 'a lonely flirtation with the present' in contrast to the 'fixed formula' for royal portraiture handed down from the past.

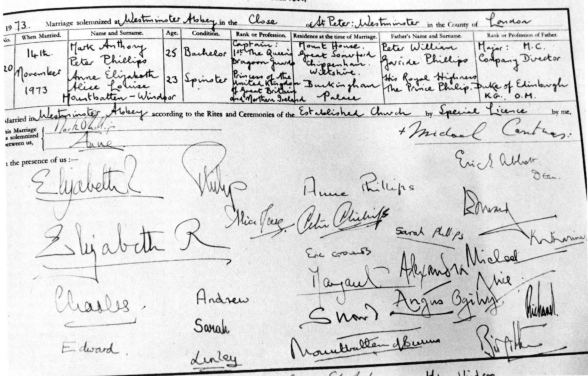

TOP: The marriage certificate of Princess Anne and Captain Mark
Phillips showing the use of the surname Mountbatten-Windsor.
Some people had not realised that the Queen intended this surname
to be borne by all her children, as well as by remoter descendants.
ABOVE: Princess Anne curtsies to the Queen before processing down
the aisle after the signing of the register.

A family group at Balmoral, 1972.

Far from uniting Canada, the French felt the monarchy was being exploited by the British to dominate them. The Queen's speech to the Legislature on the 10th had spoken of 'le centenaire de notre confédération'. South Africa's 'Fifty-Years' had ended in divorce. Was Canada's 'centenary' going the same way?

On the contrary, five years later Prince Philip was in Canada again, making the rough places plain and saying the things that had to be said. For instance:

I think it is complete misconception to imagine that the monarchy exists in the interests of the monarch. It doesn't. It exists in the interest of the people.

And how did Prince Philip prove this? By opting for a popular monarchy or none at all:

I think the important thing about it is that if at any stage people feel it has no further part to play, then for goodness sake let's end the thing on amicable terms without having a row about it.

Then came the Seventies. In 1973 the striking effects of this *détente* were suddenly visible. Pierre Trudeau, the French-Canadian Prime Minister, invited Queen Elizabeth II to visit Ottawa for the Commonwealth Conference that year. Who could have believed it? It now seemed possible that the 'Queen of Canada' would help Canadians to think globally rather than prove a divisive influence. This was certainly the Queen's own view, for during an earlier tour in June she had answered the *Toronto Star* which demanded a Canadian head of state. She was Queen of *all* Canadians, she replied, not just of 'one or two ancestral strains'. To the people of Toronto she presented a dual-purpose monarchy:

It is not only a link between Commonwealth nations, but between Canadian citizens of every national origin and ancestry.

The Queen and Prince Philip did indeed meet immigrants from Poland, Germany, Hongkong, Portugal, Greece, India, Yugoslavia, Italy. 'This is your monarch?' asked an Italian reporter on the *Montreal Star* of Elvira Gatto who spoke no English. Elvira replied, 'Of course!' At an open-air gathering the Queen spoke to Tjitske from the Netherlands married to Mr Cicione from Italy. Mrs Tjitske Cicione was ecstatic. 'The Queen isn't hard to talk to at all.' Prince Philip she found 'plain' – meaning candid and straightforward. 'Frankly this tour keeps getting better at each stop,' wrote the formerly despondent *Globe and Mail*.

Regard the crown as an idea, the Queen had said, a unifying idea, not as a person. She was echoing her father and grandfather. No doubt some Canadians of non-British stock disliked the idea. Others, however, liked it as a counter-weight to Americanisation and were prepared to translate the idea into a person. 'Prince Charles for Governor-General!' And this at a time when Uganda had changed the name of Prince Charles Drive into 25th January 1971 Road.

OPPOSITE: Princess Anne and Captain Mark Phillips at Buckingham Palace after their wedding in November 1973.

As for Australia in 1972, she had been carried dancing and singing into the twentieth century by Gough Whitlam, the Labour victor of a general election. Did this mean he would carry Australia out of the monarchical system into the growing group of republics? The High Commissioner thought so; and certainly the new Prime Minister favoured the abolition of Australian appeals to the Privy Council and seemed to favour a new flag and new national anthem. But providing 'Waltzing Matilda' was not tripped up or impeded, he expected the Queen of Australia to remain. Even the alert Mrs Margaret Whitlam, who had at first been surprised to receive a royal Christmas card addressed merely to 'The Prime Minister' – 'No name. Just a title . . .' – was perfectly happy when she heard this was not a 'slap of reproof to the Whitlams' but the Sovereign's universal practice. 'I find that interesting,' commented Mrs Whitlam, 'understandable and most satisfactory!'

That the Queen herself found her relations with the Commonwealth 'most satisfactory' and worth sacrifices, is obvious. For the first time she has attended a Commonwealth Conference overseas. With the march of colonial nations to independence, she presided in August 1973 over a family gathering of thirty-two realms – exactly half of them republics or possessing their own monarchs, the other half monarchies owing allegiance to her. It had been suggested that to save her from undue exhaustion she should meet privately only those premiers whom she did not already know. The Head of the Commonwealth insisted on meeting all thirty-two individually.

How much it had meant to her was shown by the content of her television message for the following Christmas. At this religious festival, she chose two subjects to illustrate her role as Queen: her daughter's wedding in London and the Commonwealth Conference in Ottawa. The televised picture of the Queen and her husband moving among the throng in Ottawa's Rideau Hall lingers in the memory. 'What better bargain?' asked a Canadian journalist. 'Maybe an Indian chief one day, but not yet.' For there were contrasts and congruences in the Rideau Hall which even a laughing Minihaha or Waltzing Matilda could not have brought into focus. On the small screen at Christmas 1973 a figure moved to and fro whose smile and voice we could see and hear responding with perfect naturalness to the shining brown faces in white robes and the amiable pink ones in black coats. Yet at the same time this charming, relaxed woman of forty-seven was the august embodiment of a monarchy a thousand years old.

If the Rideau Hall was a high-water mark of the early Seventies, there were other changing currents for the monarchy to note.

In June 1970 Queen Elizabeth II appointed the first Conservative Prime Minister in history who had been *elected* as leader by his party. Hitherto the Sovereign had waited upon the oracular utterances of a few wise men before exercising her prerogative. Their deliberations had caused a leader to 'emerge' without endangering the royal prerogative, for no one knew who had emerged until the Queen actually summoned him to be Prime Minister. But if all three main parties, Labour, Liberal and now Conservative, elected their leaders, what scope had the Queen?

The answer is, first, that neither the Queen's position nor that of the Conservative party had seemed quite satisfactory even in the old days of 1963. Macmillan, suddenly ejected from the premiership by a 'stroke of fate' in the shape of a prostate operation, had no obvious successor. Having been asked by H. M. for his advice, he 'sounded' and 'consulted' various Conservative bodies, some representative, others exclusive. Finally Cabinet opinion split 10 : 4 : 3 : 2 – ten for Home, four for Maudling, three for Butler and two for Hogg. The Queen was thereupon advised by Macmillan to summon the man with the greatest overall support. She did so and Home became Prime Minister. Considerable anger, however, over the result was expressed at the time by Iain Macleod in a pungent article against the Tory 'Magic Circle' which had brought the result about. Two years later when a new Tory leader was required, there were no 'soundings' or 'consultations' but Edward Heath was democratically elected. And in 1973 Harold Macmillan, who had published his memoirs for the critical period, 1963, was accused by Humphrey Berkeley of having contrived a 'dubious episode', and by Enoch Powell of having 'deprived the Queen of the exercise of her principal prerogative', by giving her 'crucial information' which was not accurate.

These grave charges were founded on a last-minute twist in the selection drama of 1963. Some seven members of Macmillan's Cabinet (including all the defeated candidates except Butler) decided to support Butler against Home. Macmillan ignored his colleagues' 'organised revolt' as being 'distasteful and rather eighteenth century'. Had he instead informed the Queen that Butler was now running Home close, she might have felt bound to reopen her enquiries. We are told that the papers on this emotive subject now lie awaiting a day of judgment, Macmillan's, as he says in his autobiography, in the Royal Archives, Powell's in his bank. There we may safely leave them. A second problem with more of a future is the Queen's prerogative.

Can she any longer, in the circumstances of modern party organisation, effectively choose her Prime Minister? The answer is yes. In a case, for instance, of minority government, coalition, or an exceptionally even balance of the parties. A striking revival in Liberal fortunes, introducing a three-party system, could hardly fail to throw additional responsibility upon the Queen, as was clearly seen in the aftermath of Mr Heath's appeal to the country in February 1974.

Her political prerogative has been eroded but not removed. There is no need to take the extreme line of Evelyn Waugh in the Fifties, who declined to vote because he would thereby choose Her Majesty's Prime Minister for her.

A family on the throne costs money. So of course does a president on a tiger skin or in a rocking-chair. But monarchy's finances have always been the legitimate subject of controversy, especially in a democracy. *'What does she do with it?'* asked the anonymous pamphleteer called 'Solomon Temple' about Queen Victoria's Civil List. The pamphleteer got no answer. A hundred years later William Hamilton, MP for West Fife, asked the same question about her descendants' finances. Hamilton was luckier than Solomon. He got an answer from a Select Committee on the Civil List, 1971–2, on which he himself sat. After evidence on the Queen's increasing work and expenses, the report recommended a rise in the Queen's allowance from £475,000 to £980,000, with various increases for her family. Figures apart, Douglas Houghton and the Labour members unsuccessfully advocated a Department of the Crown for handling the royal finances.

The whole crisis had blown up at the end of the Sixties, when the Labour government as well as the monarchy were in financial trouble. In December 1968 the national crisis provoked a spate of rumours: that the Chancellor of the Exchequer and the Prime Minister had resigned and the Queen had abdicated. In November 1969 Prince Philip, in answering questions, told American listeners on the radio that the Royal Family would 'go into the red next year'. That was quite true. While not mentioning abdication, he did add that 'we may have to move into smaller premises'. This was jocular, or so Harold Wilson thought. On the other hand, English Kings have vacated unwieldy premises before now, recently Osborne House. At the time of writing it is reported that Sandringham, the favourite 'Big House' of King George v, will be reduced in size.

Meanwhile people reacted strongly to the royal balance-sheet, the Conservative opposition regarding the situation with 'the utmost gravity'. Lord Shinwell, a venerable left-winger from Scotland declared: 'If we want a monarchy we ought to pay them properly. We can't have them going around in rags.' Many agreed with the Shinwell point of view. Other less venerable leftists, however, like Richard Crossman in an article entitled 'The Royal Tax-Avoiders', have since attacked our age-old tradition of a relatively tax-free monarchy. He was particularly shocked by a Sovereign who dared (in time of inflation) to ask for more. 'One has to admire her truly regal cheek.' In reply one outraged monarchist sent 10p each to Crossman and Hamilton, calculating that this was the exact cost per annum of the monarchy to the individual taxpayer. But the cloak of one Raleigh will not dry up all the puddles. The problem has to be tackled at the philosophical rather than the pragmatic level. By asking, for instance, what is taxation for? If the answer is, to promote equality by redistributing wealth, the question follows, is that what the monarchy is for? Clearly not. 'Don't say the monarchy is fair,' argued one royalist, 'it's fun.'

Attempts to treat the House of Windsor like any other wealthy house, requiring them to pay death duties and surtax, have foundered on one rock. The Royal Family is not like other families. It is unique. The Queen is expected to perform a literally incomparable function, and the hive no more wish her to become a worker-bee than they themselves seriously want to be queens. Now and again, it is true, the very young may fancy a taste of the royal jelly. After the royal wedding of 1973, for example, the charming bridesmaid, daughter of Princess Margaret, seemed to hold out dazzling prospects to a pair of schoolboys, both of whom wished to marry her. And we are told that one third of the population dreams about the Queen. Perhaps like Mr Gladstone some of them dream that she asks them to 'breakfast'. Normally, however, people want to look up not sideways. They bow, they curtsy, the royal bread is not for them; only the mist. Nor is the mist as dust in their eyes. It is the light atmosphere in which they can see reflected an idealised version of some personal oasis, whether it is a home or a family or place of work.

Yet the image of a desert mirage fails totally in one respect. For the desert light cannot prevent the delightful vision from dissolving just as we draw near, whereas it is the royal light itself which must help to bring national ideals closer to us, into our homes, on to the screen, so to speak, of fifty million minds in Britain and five hundred and fifty million all over the world – the television audience for her daughter's wedding. In the royal radiance we are entitled to dream that unity will drive out dissension, compassion melt coldness, fairness put injustice to shame. This is the royal message and the royal hope. Only someone so uncommitted will be heard abroad. She is the Christian voice of Britain. The Pope alone possesses a magnetism as powerful as hers, to make hundreds of millions of eyes look inside an abbey church and listen to what is said there.

The Queen is queen of all – no more of the noble families who used to furnish the entourage of her ancestors' courts than of the Ugandan Asians who arrived yesterday. Today the royal entourage itself makes this point: some key posts are held by men from the fast-moving Commonwealth, instead of, as in the past, their going exclusively to those brought up under immemorial elms where the church clock stood for ever at ten to three.

Nevertheless, as long as there is poverty, an articulate minority will protest against individuals who spend lavishly, as also against institutions such as the church, the government or the monarchy. They have every right to advocate a simpler style of living in changing times, even to ask why the Pope still has a tiara, or the Jewel House in the Tower of London an Imperial Indian crown – but no emperor to wear it. Why does not the Church sell all its plate and give it to the poor? Why do cities spend money on street decorations? William Hamilton MP has found our Princess 'pricey'. Others find MPs 'pricey'.

The students of Ibadan, Laval in Canada, and Stirling, chose to hang their protest against authority and the system on the peg of a royal visit – though not all needed the infantile comforter of a bottle in the mouth before they could look H. M. in the eye and shout 'Queen out!' One of the girl students at Stirling justified the demo because 'most students feel that the Queen is a symbol of the class exploitation that exists in our society'. Bel Mooney, however, a journalist, attributed the outburst mainly to the students' psychological frustrations, caused by the 'sterile emptiness' of a brand new campus which looked more like 'a sanatorium in the hills' than a true university. With this Prince Philip, who in his time has had some sharp things to say about universities, might well sympathise.

Abuse of the Queen as scapegoat is another matter.

In a sense it is right that the Sovereign should focus grievances. Long ago a golden bough sheltered a priest-king who became the scapegoat for his people. The Queen and Prince Philip are well aware of this mythological feeling which dies hard. They have learnt to smile and wave back at demonstrators, whether they are anti-Common Market and chanting 'Sieg Heil!' at Covent Garden, or anti-Portugal at the Royal Academy. In such situations television shows them to splendid advantage.

They are nonetheless human. We choose that the state should be symbolised by a person, not by a bundle of lictors' rods. Citizens can bawl out a government policy. But in abusing H.M. or H.R.H. demonstrators insult humanity not ideas.

On a less serious level, the representative or symbolic nature of our Royal Family will always run them into shoals. People expect *their* Sovereign to represent *their* ideas. The League against Cruel Sports are aggrieved because the Queen does not side with them against the country's farmers and sportsmen: 'The Queen,' they once said, 'is our greatest enemy.' Today she does not hunt and seldom shoots, so she has relinquished her place of dishonour to her husband and daughter.

Not bred up to hunting, Prince Philip is an ardent sportsman with gun as well as camera. Why he does not see any contradiction between shooting and conservation he explains in his book, *Wildlife Crisis*. The argument is pragmatic: he has found from experience that 'many amateur naturalists come into it through shooting, stalking or fishing'; far from being indifferent to the environment, they care for it deeply. Not so the city-dwellers. They may not kill foxes but they poison their fellows with fumes.

Princess Anne has recently drawn the fire once directed so hotly against both her parents. Asked why she, a keen horsewoman, did not hunt, she uttered two gloomy words: 'Blood sport.' With the arrival of Mark Phillips, however, the two words lost their black magic. She went hunting with him and the League said: 'She just doesn't care a damn for public opinion.' Despite the League's counter-activities in the way of organising opinion polls and planting spies in the Palace, most people would probably take a neutral view: 'It's up to her.' *The Times* spoke for the press in saying 'that neither majority nor minority is entitled to interfere with the legitimate pursuits of others', while John Gordon of the *Sunday Express*, though he personally did not like fox hunting or grouse massacres, liked even less 'interfering busybodies who try to tell other people how to live their lives'. Princess Anne herself might have put it even more simply: 'Get off my dress.' She has long been admired as a princess with a style for the times. On her wedding day the television cameras showed her to the millions from the outside, looking up at a princess on a balcony. On Christmas Day the camera for the first time put the balcony on television from behind. Princess Anne's family were all for her returning to the balcony once more with her husband, in response to the clamouring crowds. 'All right,' she agreed. Then, to someone standing on her train, 'Oick, get off my dress.'

There was something irresistibly funny and endearing about this peep behind the scenes. In the Fifties before youth had got its head, Prince Philip defended the young generation against ignorant attacks. Today his daughter epitomises modern youth, with its cutting edge and uncompromising honesty. Her sharp competitiveness in an equestrian event or an argument is balanced by youth's compassion. One moment she will be shedding tears over a handicapped child, the next tearing strips off journalists. A group of cameramen suddenly appeared in the stable where she was working in slacks and sweater with long, loose hair. They just wanted one picture, not to be pests. 'You *are* pests,' she said promptly. As guest-of-honour at a press dinner she had the 'regal cheek', as Crossman would say, to call them 'touchy'. Whether the media are flattering or hostile makes no difference. She is not seduced by success or cowed by criticism. In 1971, having won the Individual European Three-Day Event, she gained four separate nominations as sports personality and sportswoman of the year. This did not mean she became the media's slave. Her ideal is to lead a natural life. And for a princess that means to give public service; to receive her public rewards (the 'rewards' include press interviews) for her successes; and to defend her private rights. 'Get off my dress.'

Queen Elizabeth II has not had to fight for her place in the sun. Certainly not to the extent of her father as a boy or of her husband or even of her children at boarding school, with nothing between them and the cool world except one detective apiece. No one has ever stood on the Queen's dress. If they did, her gentleness would prevent her shooing them off. But a thousand swords would leap from their scabbards to do it for her. A few alterations in the wording render Shakespeare's famous lines so apt that the small operation must be performed:

> *Her life is gentle, and the elements*
> *So mix in her that Nature might stand up*
> *And say to all the world 'This is a queen!'*

Nevertheless that great actor-statesman, Harold Macmillan, who knew her well, saw in the young Elizabeth more than a mixture of goodness and gentleness, kindness and courtesy. At the time of the Ghana adventure he was amazed, as we have seen, by her firmness in rejecting the conventional role of 'a *woman*'. She had 'the heart and stomach of a man', no less than her formidable predecessor Elizabeth I when addressing the fleet at Tilbury. If we ourselves are not 'new Elizabethans', at least there is something of that breed in the Queen.

Macmillan's next words were even more relevant:

If she were pressed too hard, and if Government and people here are determined to restrict her activity (including taking reasonably acceptable risks) I think she might be tempted to throw in her hand.

We have seen how the youthful House of Windsor, as represented by Prince Edward and Prince Albert, battered itself sick against George v and his government in an effort to reach the danger zones of the First World War. Prince Albert alone fully succeeded, at the battle of Jutland. Today the physical restrictions have been relaxed. Prince Albert's daughter got to Ghana and Prince Albert's eldest grandson has jumped from a parachute into the sea and piloted a supersonic jet solo.

But cotton-woolling is not the only enemy of a modern monarchy. An insipid, purely symbolic or ornamental role is even more soul-destroying. In the latter half of this century we are amazingly fortunate in having bred up a remarkable Royal Family. Each of them, taken individually, would make a mark in ordinary life. Prince Philip could have risen to the top of a highly competitive profession, the Navy, like his uncle Lord Mountbatten; he is among the best natural speakers in the country. Princess Anne's victory in 1971 was not just a flash in the pan: in 1973 she won the Combined Championship at Hickstead. As for Prince Charles, he is the miracle come true of which Bagehot despaired: a Prince of Wales who, despite his not coming to the throne in early youth – Bagehot's sole recipe for success – is not a 'pleasure-loving lounger' but high spirited, not a wastrel but a graduate with an excellent record at Cambridge. His talents range through mimicry, to an introduction to the *Goon Show Scripts*, to history. His foreword to John Brooke's *King George III* is a model of persuasiveness and good sense. A professional naval officer like his father, grandfather and two great-grandfathers before him, he has served on board HMS *Minerva* in the West Indies and HMS *Jupiter* in the Far East.

What is to happen to all this family talent? Boredom is a worse fate than Willie Hamilton. The Royal Family are more likely to abdicate from frustration than from blue books. A cut in the Civil List would not be the unkindest cut of all. Reduction to a tourist attraction would be that. 'She does *not* enjoy "society",' wrote Macmillan of Elizabeth II in 1961. 'She likes her horses. But she loves her duty and means to be a Queen and not a puppet.' At least royal dukes who go to the trouble of taking their seats in the House of Lords should be allowed to speak from the crossbenches. After all, King Edward VII as Prince of Wales voted twice with the minority in favour of the Deceased Wife's Sister's Bill; his mama could not bear to see good royal widowers going to waste. If Prince Philip cares to speak on the environment, let him. If Prince Charles has ideas on education or, in due course, Prince Richard on architecture, let them be heard from the crossbenches too.*

These are the problems of success. There have been times in the past when no one was felt to be stepping on a royal dress or pulling at royal coat-tails for the simple reason that their wearers were standing still. The House of Windsor is moving. Whence and whither must be the theme of an epilogue to this story.

* Since this book went into production Prince Charles has made his impressive and wholly successful maiden speech.

Epilogue

Silver wedding, white wedding

A whisper of mystery turns all eyes to the throne.
Benjamin Robert Haydon, 1821.
*A princely marriage is the brilliant addition of a universal fact, and as
such it rivets mankind.* Walter Bagehot, 1867.

A DAY of sunshine, sudden black storms and again clear skies marked the
Silver Wedding of Queen Elizabeth II and Prince Philip on Monday
20 November 1972. A few republicans like William Hamilton insisted
on treating the affair as of purely family concern. To everyone's surprise,
however, he congratulated the royal pair as individuals and hoped he
would be there for their diamond wedding. ('We don't,' shouted Conservatives
from the parliamentary benches opposite.) His tribute had considerable significance.

True republicanism is formed of sterner stuff. Moreover, republicanism thrives
where a Royal Family has glaring faults, a condition not unknown abroad. The personalities of the Queen and her husband make the task of the MP for West Fife extraordinarily difficult. In today's climate, the person has become as important as the
office. The decline in the monarchical principle and the rise in the Queen's popularity
have combined to bring this about. For this latter development the Queen deserves
praise without stint.

Others had their grumble at the Silver Wedding on principle. All anniversaries
look backward, they argued, and are therefore to be avoided. This revolt against the
past, against the repetition involved in ceremony and the continuity which every
pageant glorifies, is characteristic of our times. Everything must be new, original,
ad hoc. An instant president can offer '*œufs* Lucullus' and '*bœuf* Wellington' to a visiting foreign dignitary just as well as a monarch and that, they believe, is all a Head
of State is for. The queue of VIPs from every quarter of the globe waiting for their
invitation to Windsor answers that point. No one can conceive that the end of the
British monarchy, with its immense historical prestige and present glamour, would
leave untouched the procession of foreign dignitaries to this island, not to mention
tourists.

The people of this country in their millions did indeed celebrate the Silver
Wedding both as a private affair and as a national occasion. And that is how it
will be treated here: first, a moment for the Royal Family; second, a milestone at
which to review the House.

SILVER WEDDING, WHITE WEDDING

The present poet laureate, John Betjeman, struck the first note of naturalness. It was literally nature on the hills and seas which bound this family to their country-loving people and to one another:

> Queen of the open air, the rocks and heather,
> Twenty-five years ago who would have known
> You and your Sailor Prince would build together
> Such family affection for the throne?
> For all your humour, calm and selfless living,
> Your subjects join me in today's thanksgiving.

Who would now remember that twenty years ago the then poet laureate, John Masefield, had seen this open-air girl 'as a symbol of a Power Eterne'? For most people today that vision of transcendental authority would smack too much of 'divine right'. The Queen herself, in fact, focused the day's religious thanksgiving on God-in-the-family rather than God-on-the-throne. This in itself is one of the Royal Family's adaptations to a changing world.

A social worker was visiting a divorced 'classroom mother' in her home when the Silver Wedding came on television. 'Well, they stuck it out, didn't they?' said the worker to the girl, arguing that family life could be happy. 'Yes, but you don't know what went on behind the scenes,' replied the girl. 'They might have been rowing all the time.' Here is the kind of cynicism which the Royal Family is out to soften. It is an uphill task. Despite the Queen's greatly increased influence since she came to the throne, divorces also have greatly increased during her reign. It was a sign of the times that when she invited a hundred couples who had been married on the same day as herself to share her Thanksgiving Service in Westminster Abbey, one man applied for tickets who had been parted from his wife for two years. He calmly brought his sister instead.

There were orchids in the Abbey of the same kind as Princess Elizabeth had carried at her wedding. But the pulpits were deeply embowered in silver-leaved shrubs which had not been necessary in such quantities before. For now they concealed intense television activity. It was television which enabled the Dean to begin the first prayer with the words, 'We are here in Westminster Abbey, *or in our homes*, to join together in thanksgiving. . . .' Television created the sharing which the Queen wanted, and which was responsible for the relaxed, family atmosphere of the service. She and Prince Philip entered the sacrarium smiling at one another; Prince Charles and Princess Anne exchanged comments; Sarah Armstrong-Jones wore no hat; the Queen hung her hand-bag on a carved lion's head when she knelt. The last prayer of all was for 'the families of this and every land.'

The Queen's subsequent Guildhall speech was the most effective of her life. We saw her driving to Guildhall from the Abbey drawn by four Windsor greys with a

Sovereign's escort of Household Cavalry in breastplates and plumed helmets. We saw her reach Temple Bar and Child's Bank at No. 1 Fleet Street, whence City fathers emerged (tycoons, Hamilton called them) to present her with the Pearl Sword. (George IV's favourite, Lady Jersey, had been a Child heiress.) Down came the rain and we saw the smiling Queen Mother disappear inside the bubble of a deep transparent umbrella – one more record for the historians of fashion.

The granddaughter of the King who never made jokes in speeches began her *tour de force* with digs at her own catch-phrases, so often mocked in the past by others:

I think everyone will concede that today, of all occasions, I should begin my speech with 'My husband and I'.

Professionally flawless as regards timing and manner, this sally provoked a burst of astonished laughter and long rounds of applause which showed how far Queen and people had moved towards each other in twenty-five years. The laughter which greeted her subsequent sallies was a foregone conclusion: the dig at the royal 'we' – 'We, and by that I mean both of us . . .'; the bishop whose opinion of sin was as simple as hers of family life: he was against it, 'I am for it.' The lightheartedness continued when the Royal Family did their first 'walkabout' at the Barbican, among hundreds of ordinary people.

Small girls were waiting with their posies to offer, small boys with nothing as yet but curiosity balanced by a huge detachment. 'Would you like to be a prince?' the BBC man asked one boy from Hackney. 'No. Too much bovver.' But nothing was too much bother for the Royal Family when they arrived. 'Look up to your right,' suggested a man with a camera to Prince Charles. 'Are you the girls who sit on the boss's knee?' Prince Charles asked a group of enraptured typists. Prince Philip had something characteristic to say of marriage. 'How long have you been married?' he asked one couple. 'Eleven years.' 'The first twelve are the worst,' he reassured them. 'After that it's all downhill.'

This first 'walkabout' overran its schedule and lasted nearly an hour. It was immensely popular. 'Walkabouts' had already been tried in the Commonwealth with encouraging results. Today every city in Britain which receives a visit from the Queen and Prince Philip to open a new building or centre enjoys its royal 'walkabout'. The coverage from the provincial press is always animated and full. But the national press, for whatever reason, is more conservative. They still use the Queen in the old way, choosing to picture her inspecting a line of faceless paladins forming a Guard of Honour instead of shaking hands afterwards with the corporal's wife. This new stride forward to a popular, democratic monarchy is thus only partially exploited by the very forces who advocate it most warmly – the press. Many people

268

are still unaware of how much more energy the Queen now expends in so often meeting ordinary people – hearing regional voices, seeing belted coats, ungloved hands, 30-denier stockings, plastic shopping-bags and nylon headscarves. In Bagehot's words, the monarchy has begun to see life 'as it really is'. Gone are the days when young Princess Elizabeth had to apologize to her parents for a lady-in-waiting who bicycled under the Palace windows wearing a headscarf instead of a hat.

Mention of Bagehot and bicycles leads us to one of the crown's abstract problems. How is the 'magic' to be preserved when 'daylight' creeps in? An *Observer* journalist said at the time of the Silver Wedding: 'The older-fashioned may have their fears of a bicycling – even perhaps a speeding – Royal Family.' But those who are not old-fashioned may still see little magic in cycles or in being booked. Anyway, is the royal magic really necessary? Is it in danger? Can it be preserved? Those are the questions.

That the most potent magic or mystique has diminished is universally agreed. We may turn up the recent memoirs of two clever court ladies: Lady Cynthia Colville and Lady Airlie. 'Although the "mystique of the Crown" is not so deeply felt as in earlier reigns,' writes the former, 'the Queen is as widely loved and respected as any of her predecessors.' The latter says: 'The new setting for Monarchy is far less brilliant than that of my youth, but in many ways it is more interesting.' Prince Philip himself posed the monarchical question in a most 'interesting' way. Referring to changes in style and function since the last reign and correctly implying that he had had much to do with them, he wondered whether the remaining great occasions (State Openings of Parliament, the Queen's Birthday Parades, Royal Weddings) are a drag on the new style. Did they make people feel that 'nothing had changed inside'? Looking at it the other way round, he asked his interlocutor, Basil Boothroyd, 'Did greater personal knowledge of the Sovereign mean less mystery . . . ?'

The answer to the whole question of magic versus daylight can only be a platitudinous compromise. Both are necessary to a modern monarchy but in changing proportions. The monarchy, like all other great institutions, reflects changes in national life. Many different things have contributed to diminution in the magic and mystery of the crown, including a less robust taste for pomp; the need for economies; a Royal Family which wants to do more and so becomes more visible; a far more inquisitive, ubiquitous and efficient press; television; and a more literate population which needs information rather than 'fundungus' – Prince Philip's word for pointless trappings.

Nineteenth-century illiteracy used to work both ways. To people who lived in unbelievable squalor, Queen Victoria seemed more mysterious than the Almighty, and her Castle and its Waterloo Chamber more unapproachable than His house. At least they could get inside a church. At the same time, illiteracy fostered a jolly, familiar approach to the Sovereign which has completely gone. The deaths of Queen Victoria and King Edward VII each produced popular couplets:

Dust to dust, ashes to ashes,
Into her tomb the old Queen dashes.

Greatest sorrow England ever had
When death took away our dear Dad.

The passing of illiteracy means that this spontaneous feeling can never be recaptured.

But other more up-to-date ways of experiencing a direct relationship with the Sovereign have been discovered and are being cultivated. The 'walkabouts' have been mentioned. They are star turns and will no doubt be developed. *On* the balcony, *behind* the balcony, *beneath* the balcony. We have now seen the Royal Family in the first two positions; the third may yet be realised if the Queen descends to earth and chats up the crowd behind the gilt-topped railings of the Palace forecourt.

The greatest burst of daylight was the *Royal Family* film. At the time it seemed wildly daring. Looking back, it was just one more necessary step on the way to achieving a modern monarchy. We were not told anything we did not know already, but things we had read about became real. There really were dogs every-where; the Queen really was a professional at the wheel of her car, or on a horse; Prince Philip really could cook; and Prince Charles really possessed a 'cello with one of whose strings Prince Edward (also said to be musical) had a confrontation.

As for the mystique, there are three points to be made. First, remoteness cannot be equated with magic. There is a law of diminishing returns. Queen Victoria's interminable seclusion was a mistake not a mystery. Queen Elizabeth's magic has increased since she came out of her shell. Second, it is in human nature to admire. TV stars, pop singers and footballers are all idols for a day, but the Queen has the magic of a lifetime and her family the *cachet* of ten centuries. Third, there are right and wrong kinds of magic. The wrong kinds – superstition, belief in 'divine right' and royal 'touching', adulation and sycophancy – died or are dying. The right kinds can always be improved.

Some people felt that what might be called the 'daylight' of the situation centring on the Duke and Duchess of Windsor was allowed to tarnish the magic of the Royal Family. It was plain as day that for many years their return to England could cause only hurt and embarrassment. But for ever? A magic touch was looked for, to bring the folk-hero back to his native land. The Queen did indeed invite them to the unveiling of Queen Mary's memorial at Marlborough House and she and Prince Philip called on them in Paris. Nevertheless, after the Duke's death, the Commons' Amendment on 5 June 1972, by which the Duchess of Windsor was personally named in their official condolence, was a measure of their continuing disappointment.

SILVER WEDDING, WHITE WEDDING

Things like these cannot be clearly understood until the Archives are opened. But there are other ways of increasing the magic which lie close at hand.

It is often said that our Royal House has shown no interest in art since King George IV. King George V's remark on Mrs Asquith's publication of her memoirs is famous: 'People who write books ought to be shut up!' (But it must be remembered that the King's ire was mainly directed against Mrs Asquith's publication of private letters from Lord Stamfordham.) When John Piper finished his watercolours of Windsor, King George VI's comment is said to have been, 'What wretched weather you had.' We are told that King George V never learnt to spell words like *mausoleum* or *academy*. (One hopes he did not have to use those words too often.) He tried to abolish the 'King's Musick' and Sir Edward Elgar saved it only by telling Stamfordham that 'the last shred of connection of the Court to Art' would be effaced.

Nevertheless the House of Windsor's inartistic beginnings have been exaggerated. It is bad luck on King George V that, while coins are accepted as an art-form, stamps are despised as a mere hobby. His Royal Philatelic Collection at Buckingham Palace, now world-famous and worth millions, was the result of exceptional expertise. He eventually collected exclusively from Great Britain and the Empire because he loved them. His special affection for Mauritius inspired him to buy many great rarities from this 'difficult' collectors' colony. His memory and flair enabled him to recognise and judge individual specimens, his particular interest lying in the technicalities of lithographic transfers, stereo-printing, the plating of the setting of surcharges, and retouched stamps. If this was not art, neither was it philistinism. It belonged to a valuable link-world of research, appreciation and collection. His wife Queen Mary was acclaimed as a Museum Director *manquée*.

Incidentally, Dr Roy Strong, Director of the Victoria and Albert Museum and formerly of the National Portrait Gallery, has castigated our present 'endless vulgar commemorative stamps' with the Queen's profile, 'shrunk to minute size' and 'tucked into a corner'. What would King George V have said?

Prince Philip has ruefully described himself as 'an uncultured polo-playing clot' – at least that is how he says artists think of him. In fact, it is mainly he who has brought about a change towards more art in the House of Windsor, as indeed he has been responsible for most of the changes in 'style'. He paints with talent if not yet with self-confidence. At Balmoral he hung some scenes from Antarctica by Edward Seago, turning out surplus portraits of Queen Victoria's children. No sacred calves. The Queen and Prince Philip buy a number of contemporary paintings each year, the Queen liking both empty landscapes and stark realism – 'Demoliton', 'Slag Formations', 'Renishaw Ironworks'.

Royal portraiture is a challenge in itself. Arguments have usually been about peripheral points, such as whether James Gunn should paint the Queen unsmiling, to which some people objected, or 'grinning' and showing all her teeth, as Gunn put it. 'Now, Mr Gunn,' said the Queen at her next sitting, 'with teeth or without?' Pietro Annigoni's two portraits have certainly reached forward somewhat. In the first, the Queen seems to be stepping out towards her destiny, and the feeling Annigoni tried for was 'being close to the people yet very much alone'. In his second, a stern red Queen rises like a phoenix from some reflected furnace, against a pinkly glowing sky. 'Is it dawn or sunset, Mr Annigoni?' the present writer asked the painter unforgivably. 'Dawn of course,' he snapped, seeing the point at once. 'The upper sky is quite a different blue at sunset.'

The formula for royal portraiture, says Dr Strong, has hardly changed since Van Dyck painted Charles I and his family. 'Bryan Organ's portraits of Princess Margaret represent a lonely flirtation with the present.' Nevertheless we must hope that all the arts, including royal portraiture, will enter 'the present' during this reign with this new royal generation. There is ample artistic talent, ranging from music to architecture and design, with a strong latent gift for the dramatic arts. Not that royal intervention in the arts has ever been without its risks. When Prince Albert dared to design new headgear for the Army, *Punch* wrote that 'it gave the wearer a certain air of low comedy'. Nor should it be counted against her that the Queen does not choose reading as her recreation. Her need for the open air is an unspoken commentary on the hours she spends each morning on state documents. Rather should we remember the opening of the Queen's Gallery in 1962, with its wonderful Gainsborough portraits commissioned by George III. 'Come friendly bombs and fall on Slough,' wrote John Betjeman, inviting the Germans to clean up certain eyesores in that town. The bombs which fell on Buckingham Palace were not friendly; but having seen her old Chapel destroyed, it was an act of fine friendship towards the nation which inspired Queen Elizabeth II to build on the ruins a royal gallery for the public.

The British nation may not yet have had its love affair with art, as it has with sport. But the patronage of art is a 'natural' for a Royal House that wishes to maintain its magic. After all, two worthless moral characters, Louis XIV and George IV, are mirrored by Versailles and Brighton Pavilion rather than by other less agreeable looking-glasses. How much more magical can be the House of Windsor, with its incomparable opportunity to crown goodness with beauty.

The conflict between daylight and magic is undoubtedly the main challenge to contemporary monarchy.

Of course there are spheres where the sovereign can play a vital part without invoking either of these categories. Concern for suffering is a case in point. Harold Wilson pays a heart-felt tribute to the way our Royal Family immediately hurried to the disaster scene at Aberfan. The Queen's sympathetic practicality always stands out. When opening a magnificent new opera house, her first observation was that there were no lifts for the handicapped.

SILVER WEDDING, WHITE WEDDING

Notwithstanding these and other important activities, the Royal House of Windsor must achieve its future through a right balance between naturalness and glamour. There can be no better instance than the wedding of Princess Anne.

The last Princess Anne to marry became Queen Anne. The bride was a great gambler, her husband, Prince George of Denmark, a hard drinker. She was married off with no choice because a peer had been ogling her. At her wedding the streets flowed with wine. Times have changed.

In a vivid memorandum to the Civil List Committee of 1971, Sir Michael (now Lord) Adeane, the Queen's former private secretary, listed some changes in the present reign; more mobility and more informality leading to more work. Something has already been said about the 'flying Monarchy' of our day, and Princess Anne seems to prefer flying over the jumps. But the second change, towards informality, was written large all over her wedding.

To begin with it was not a state but a family occasion. This pleased everyone, except some of those who had been invited to previous state weddings and were not invited to this. As a family event, there would be a shade more privacy than otherwise. Indeed one might say that the Queen has had to fight for her place in the shade, rather than her place in the sun. Privacy has been the boon which she and Prince Philip have won for their two younger children. It was a pleasure to see Andrew and Edward at the wedding, of whom so little is known; and a pleasure also to think that so little is known of them.

Again, however, the innovation of children's privacy brings its perils. Secluded royal children have always been targets for rumour in the press. Princess Victoria at Kensington Palace, Princess Margaret at Windsor during the War, and then Prince Andrew – crippled, deaf and dumb, handicapped! If certain foreign periodicals cannot invade royal privacy they will invent. The Queen's marriage has often broken down in their pages, as has her health; Princess Margaret has bathed in the nude, her swim-suit having been chemically removed; and Prince Charles has sired a child. 'Mylius' rides again. The amount of thought and ingenuity poured out on the British Royal Family by journalists in republican countries is truly phenomenal.

'Natural' was the keynote which viewers used of the wedding of Princess Anne. Nearly half of a group questioned afterwards praised her television appearance with Captain Mark Phillips as 'very natural'. She moved her head naturally in the Abbey despite its high-piled hair and tiara. She whispered and smiled most naturally to her father; she plighted her troth just like any other girl in a village church. 'She is nobody's fairy princess,' wrote one journalist approvingly (though she looked like one). 'She is a determined woman who knows what she wants.'

However, 'naturalness' was by no means the whole story of the wedding. Otherwise there would not have been press representatives converging on London from all over the world, nor the five hundred and fifty million television sets tuned in to Britain. A royal procession from the Palace to Westminster is in a sense utterly familiar, repeating time and time again its own perfection of ceremony without pomp. Yet this time, as at every other time, there was something new to be seen and felt. The 'millions of leaves on the pavement' which pleased John Betjeman had been swept up, but they still whirled across the television screens all day, baring the branches just enough to disclose the noble Duke of York looking down through the trees at the Glass Coach below.

The Princess and Prince Philip were clearly visible against the Glass Coach's blue cushions; her white hands, his white gloves. But, strangely, we also saw the people reflected in its wide glass windows, an open mouth cheering, a hand waving a flag. Who is inside and who is outside? Things are changing into one another. The hooves of the Household Cavalry sound exactly like the clapping of the crowds as the Queen passes. Which is which? This is 'Queen's weather', November sunshine. But the phrase was made for Queen Victoria. Her ornate white statue outside the Palace has long been known to journalists as 'the wedding cake'. Whose wedding? Queen Elizabeth II and King George VI were both married in Westminster Abbey, and so were Richard III and Edmund Crouchback and Henry I who married Scottish Matilda in 1100. This is a time when well worn phrases renew their meaning. *A Family on the Throne*. The crowds want the Family on the balcony. They shout 'We want Anne', 'We want Mark'. Then, as it is already 14 November, they begin singing carols. 'O come all ye faithful . . .'

Some of the biggest changes have been thrust upon this House. One is the loosening of political bonds in the Commonwealth, as with India; or the breaking of those bonds, as with Pakistan, Rhodesia and the Republic of Ireland (though with the last there is a special relationship). Another is the Common Market with all its unknown effects. Does the Queen feel, as some presidents have felt, that in putting her name to the instrument of entry she was signing away something that had been England's? She has said that Britain will carry the Commonwealth with her into the Common Market, while Peter Nicols has suggested that she may find herself opening opera houses for the EEC. Perhaps both.

Smaller changes also have come from outside. No creation of hereditary honours, for instance, since Harold Wilson's advent in 1964. 'Do You Wish To Undermine The Throne, Mr Heath?' asks Angus Maude MP in the *Sunday Express* in 1970, advancing the dubious proposition that a hereditary aristocracy is 'the last prop of the hereditary monarchy'. He is supported by a former Chester Herald, James Frere, who argues that the abolition of presentation parties leaves the Royal Family 'stranded' between the meritocracy and factory workers. But such champions of the past are in a small minority.

Other changes have been made by the Royal Family themselves. Prince Charles was the first royal baby to be born without a ministerial witness and the first royal schoolboy to receive part of his education in the Commonwealth, at Timbertop in

Australia. Voluntary change, says Prince Philip, is the life-blood of the crown. Those ultra-loyalists who urged monarchies to resist change were its bitterest enemies, as the fate of foreign thrones has proved. The British monarchy has lived down two opposite criticisms once thrown at it: that it was 'steely and inhuman' and that it was 'a soap opera'. Today's comparatively low profile means that it can continue to change itself without defacement.

We have seen that the 'new Elizabethans' had asked the impossible of their young Queen. Neither they nor anyone could arrange a 'rendezvous with glory' based entirely on the past. Yet as the reign approaches its Silver Jubilee, it seems that the impossible is being achieved. The Queen and her family have never failed in an increasingly arduous round of duties. Prince Albert once referred to his duties as a 'treadmill'. He might see his descendants as chained to the oars of a quinquereme, despite their obvious enjoyment of the exercise. There they are, always; ready to open, launch, judge, appeal, support, whenever they are asked and there is a free space in the bi-annually compiled schedules. Perfectly regular and reliable, their work is performed with enormous zest and all the skill of trained public servants, but without a pensionable age for the Queen, or a week's complete holiday from the red boxes. As a philosopher once said whimsically: 'I believe in it, because it is impossible.'

Fifty-seven years have passed since this House was founded on 17 July 1917. The nation's wish, *Stet Domus*, has lost none of its conviction. 'Long live the House.'

Select Bibliography

(All published in London unless otherwise stated.)

AIRLIE, Mabell, Countess of: *Thatched with Gold.* (Edited by Jennifer Ellis, 1962)
A King's Story – Memoirs of H.R.H. The Duke of Windsor, K.G. (1951)
ALBERT, HAROLD A.: *The Queen and the Arts* (1963)
ALEXANDRA, H.M. Queen Alexandra of Jugoslavia: *Prince Philip* (1960)
ASQUITH, Lady Cynthia: *Diaries 1915–1918* (1968)
ATTLEE, C.R.: *As It Happened* (1954)
BAGEHOT, Walter: *The English Constitution,* 1st edition (1867)
BALDWIN, A.W.: *My Father – The True Story* (1955)
BARNETT, Correlli: *The Collapse of British Power* (1972)
BATTISCOMBE, Georgina: *Queen Alexandra* (1969)
BEAVERBROOK, Lord: *The Abdication of King Edward the Eighth.* (Edited by A.J.P.Taylor
     1966)
BERE, Brigadier Ivan de la: *The Queen's Orders of Chivalry* (1961)
BIRKENHEAD, Lord: *Walter Monckton* (1969)
BOLITHO, Hector: *George the Sixth* (1937)
BOOTHROYD, Basil: *Philip – An Informal Biography* (1971)
BROAD, Lewis: *The Abdication; Twenty Years After – A Re-appraisal* (1961)
Burke's Guide to the Royal Family (1972)
CAMPBELL, Judith: *Elizabeth and Philip* (1972)
CATHCART, Helen: *Her Majesty* (1962); *The Queen Mother* (1965)
Chips: The Diaries of Sir Henry Channon. (Edited by Robert Rhodes James, 1967)
CHURCHILL, Winston S.: *The World Crisis* (1939)
CHURCHILL, Randolph: *Winston S. Churchill* (Vols. I and II 1966 and 1967)
CLARK, Brigadier Stanley: *Palace Diary* (1958)
COLVILLE, Lady Cynthia: *Crowded Life – An Autobiography* (1963)
COOKE, Colin: *The Life of Richard Stafford Cripps* (1957)
COOPER, Duff: *Old Men Forget* (1953)
COOPER, Lady Diana: *The Light of Common Day* (1959)
CRAWFORD, Marion: *The Little Princesses* (1950)
CROSSMAN, R.H.S.: 'The Royal Tax Avoiders' (*New Statesman* 28 May 1971)
DALTON, Hugh: *The Fateful Years, 1931–1945* (1957); *High Tide and After, 1945–1960*
     (1962)
DAVIDSON, J.C.C.: *Memoirs and Papers 1910–1937.* (Edited by Robert Rhodes James, 1969)
DONOUGHE, Bernard and JONES,G.W.: *Herbert Morrison; Portrait of a Politician* (1973)
DRIBERG, Thomas: *Beaverbrook – A Study in Power and Frustration* (1956)
EDEN, Sir Anthony, Earl of Avon: *Full Circle* (1960), *Facing the Dictators* (1962)

SELECT BIBLIOGRAPHY

ESHER, Viscount: *The Cloud-Capp'd Towers* (1927)

FISHER, Graham and Heather: *Elizabeth Queen & Mother* (1964)

FRERE, James A. Formerly Chester Herald: *The British Monarchy at Home* (1963)

George the Sixth to His Peoples 1936–1951. Select Broadcasts and Speeches (1952)

GILBERT, Martin: *Winston S. Churchill 1914–1916* (Vol. III 1971)

GORE, John: *King George the Fifth – A Personal Memoir* (1941)

HALL, H. Duncan: *The British Commonwealth of Nations – A Study of Its Past and Future Development* (1920)

HANCOCK, W.K.: *Survey of British Commonwealth Affairs – The Problems of Nationality, 1918–1936* (1937); *Smuts – The Sanguine Years 1870–1919* (Vol. I 1962)

HANKEY, Lord: *The Supreme Command, 1914–1918* (Vol. II 1961)

HIBBERT, Christopher: *The Court at Windsor – A Domestic History* (1964)

HOPKINS, H.L.: *The White House Papers of H. L. Hopkins, 1948–9.* (2 Vols.) Re-published as Sherwood, R.E., *Roosevelt and Hopkins; an intimate History* (New York, 1950)

HOUGH, Richard: *Louis & Victoria – The First Mountbattens* (1974)

HYDE, H. Montgomery: *Baldwin – The Unexpected Prime Minister* (1973)

INGLIS, Brian: *Abdication* (1966)

IWI, Edward: 'Mountbatten–Windsor', (*The Law Journal*, 18 March 1960)

JENKINS, Roy: *Asquith* (1964)

JENNINGS, Sir Ivor: *The Queen's Government* (1960)

JOELSON, Annette: *Heirs to the Throne – The Story of the Princes of Wales* (1966)

JONES, Thomas: *Whitehall Diary* (Edited by Keith Middlemas: Vol. I 1916–1925 [1969]; Vol. II 1926–1930 [1969])

JUDD, Denis: *George V* (1973)

KHAN, The Aga: *Memoirs of the Aga Khan* (1954)

KINROSS, Lord: *The Windsor Years – The Life of Edward as Prince of Wales, King and Duke of Windsor* (1967)

LOCKART, J.G.: *Cosmo Gordon Lang* (1949)

LONGFORD, Elizabeth: *Victoria R.I.* (1964). Published as *Born to Succeed* (New York 1965)

MACKENZIE, Compton: *The Windsor Tapestry, Being a Study of the Life, Heritage & Abdication of H.R.H. The Duke of Windsor, K.G.* (1938)

MACMILLAN, Harold: *Riding the Storm, 1956–1959* (1971); *Pointing the Way, 1959–1961* (1972); *The End of the Day, 1961–1963* (1973)

MAGNUS, Philip: *King Edward the Seventh* (1964)

MANSERGH, Nicholas: *Survey of British Commonwealth Affairs.* (Vol. I 1952); *Documents & Speeches on British Commonwealth Affairs, 1931–1952* (Vols. I and II 1953)

MARIE-LOUISE, Princess: *My Life in Six Reigns* (1956)

MARTIN, Kingsley: *The Crown and the Establishment* (1962)

MASSEY, Vincent: *What's Past Is Prologue – Memoirs* (1963)

MENZIES, Sir Robert: *Afternoon Light – Some Memories of Men & Events* (1967)

MIDDLEMAS, Keith: *Edward VII* (1972)

MILLER, J.D.B.: *Survey of Commonwealth Affairs; Problems of Expansion and Attrition, 1953–1969* (1974)

MORRISON, Herbert: *An Autobiography* (1960)

NICOLSON, Harold: *King George the Sixth* (1952); *Monarchy* (1962); *Diaries & Letters* (1966–8)

PAKENHAM, Frank, Earl of Longford: *Peace by Ordeal* (1935)

PETRIE, Sir Charles: *The Modern British Monarchy* (1961)

SELECT BIBLIOGRAPHY

PHILIP, H.R.H. Prince Philip, Duke of Edinburgh:
  Prince Philip Speaks – Selected Speeches, 1956–1959. (Edited by Richard Ollard, 1960)
  Birds from Britannia (1962)
  With James Fisher: *Wildlife Crisis* (1970)
PONSONBY, Sir Frederick: *Recollections of Three Reigns* (Edited by Colin Welch, 1951)
POPE-HENNESSY, James: *Queen Mary, 1867–1953* (1959)
PUDNEY, John: *His Majesty King George the Sixth* (1952)
Report from the Select Committee of the House of Commons on the Civil List, 1971–72. (H.M.S.O.
  1972)
SENCOURT, Robert: *The Reign of Edward The Eighth* (1962)
SHERWOOD, R.E.: See Hopkins, H.L.
SYKES, Christopher: *Nancy – The Life of Lady Astor* (1972)
TAYLOR, A.J.P.: *Beaverbrook* (1972)
TEMPLEWOOD, Viscount: *Nine Troubled Years, 1931–1940 – Memoirs of Sir Samuel Hoare*
  (1954)
TERRAINE, John: *Douglas Haig; The Educated Soldier* (1963)
The History Makers – Leaders and Statesmen of the 20th Century. (Edited by Lord Longford
  and Sir John Wheeler-Bennett, 1973)
TURNER, Clare Forbes: 'The Name Mountbatten–Windsor' (*Genealogists' Magazine*,
  Vol. 17 No. 3, September 1973)
WATSON, Francis: *Dawson of Penn* (1950)
WHEARE, K.C.: *The Statute of Westminster and Dominion Status* (5th Edition, 1953)
WHEELER-BENNETT, John W.: *King George VI – His Life and Reign* (1958)
WILSON, Harold: *The Labour Government, 1964–1970 – A Personal Record* (1971)
WINDSOR, The Duchess of: *The Heart Has Its Reasons – The Memoirs of the Duchess of
  Windsor* (1956)

Genealogical Table

The Royal Line
in relation to the
House of Windsor

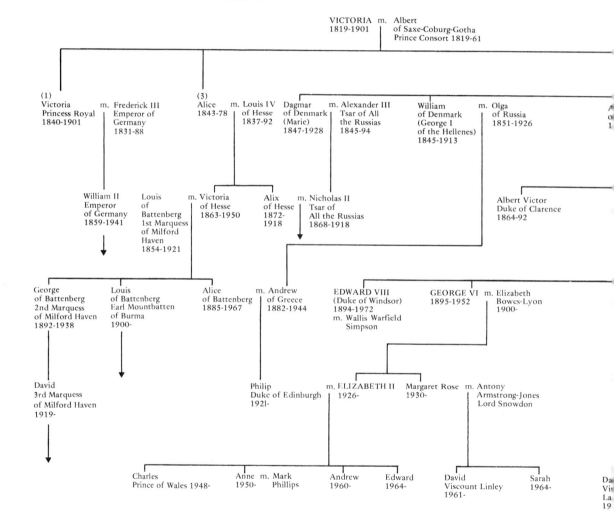

VICTORIA m. Albert
1819-1901 of Saxe-Coburg-Gotha
Prince Consort 1819-61

(1)
Victoria m. Frederick III
Princess Royal Emperor of
1840-1901 Germany
1831-88

(3)
Alice m. Louis IV
1843-78 of Hesse
1837-92

Dagmar m. Alexander III
of Denmark Tsar of All
(Marie) the Russias
1847-1928 1845-94

William m. Olga
of Denmark of Russia
(George I 1851-1926
of the Hellenes)
1845-1913

William II
Emperor
of Germany
1859-1941

Louis
of
Battenberg
1st Marquess
of Milford
Haven
1854-1921

m. Victoria
of Hesse
1863-1950

Alix
of Hesse
1872-
1918

m. Nicholas II
Tsar of
All the Russias
1868-1918

Albert Victor
Duke of Clarence
1864-92

George
of Battenberg
2nd Marquess
of Milford Haven
1892-1938

Louis
of Battenberg
Earl Mountbatten
of Burma
1900-

Alice
of Battenberg
1885-1967

m. Andrew
of Greece
1882-1944

EDWARD VIII
(Duke of Windsor)
1894-1972
m. Wallis Warfield
Simpson

GEORGE VI m. Elizabeth
1895-1952 Bowes-Lyon
1900-

David
3rd Marquess
of Milford Haven
1919-

Philip
Duke of Edinburgh
1921-

m. ELIZABETH II
1926-

Margaret Rose m. Antony
1930- Armstrong-Jones
Lord Snowdon

Charles
Prince of Wales 1948-

Anne m. Mark
1950- Phillips

Andrew
1960-

Edward
1964-

David
Viscount Linley
1961-

Sarah
1964-

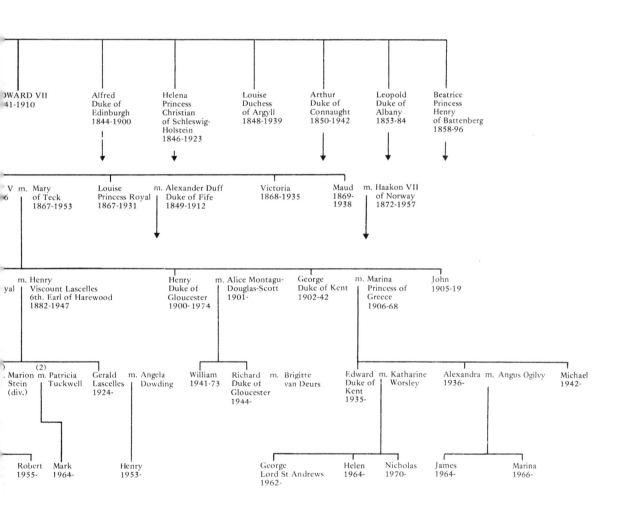

EDWARD VII
1841-1910

Alfred
Duke of
Edinburgh
1844-1900

Helena
Princess
Christian
of Schleswig-
Holstein
1846-1923

Louise
Duchess
of Argyll
1848-1939

Arthur
Duke of
Connaught
1850-1942

Leopold
Duke of
Albany
1853-84

Beatrice
Princess
Henry
of Battenberg
1858-96

V m. Mary
      of Teck
      1867-1953

Louise
Princess Royal
1867-1931

m. Alexander Duff
    Duke of Fife
    1849-1912

Victoria
1868-1935

Maud
1869-
1938

m. Haakon VII
    of Norway
    1872-1957

m. Henry
   Viscount Lascelles
   6th. Earl of Harewood
   1882-1947

Henry
Duke of
Gloucester
1900-1974

m. Alice Montagu-
   Douglas-Scott
   1901-

George
Duke of Kent
1902-42

m. Marina
   Princess of
   Greece
   1906-68

John
1905-19

yal

. Marion   (2)
  Stein m. Patricia
  (div.)   Tuckwell

Gerald
Lascelles
1924-

m. Angela
   Dowding

William
1941-73

Richard
Duke of
Gloucester
1944-

m. Brigitte
   van Deurs

Edward
Duke of
Kent
1935-

m. Katharine
   Worsley

Alexandra
1936-

m. Angus Ogilvy

Michael
1942-

Robert
1955-

Mark
1964-

Henry
1953-

George
Lord St Andrews
1962-

Helen
1964-

Nicholas
1970-

James
1964-

Marina
1966-

Index

INDEX